Service in the Eye of the Nigerian Army

The Way and Manner

By

Lieutenant Colonel Tyozenda Gberikon
Retired

Table of Contents

Copyright

Service in the Eye of the Nigerian Army
Lieutenant Colonel Tyozenda Gberikon Retired

Disclaimer

This book is a first-person narrative. It is primarily about my journey through life and the insights about occurrences around me and beyond. Above all, I witnessed or directly participated in the events narrated herein. However, while drafting this book, I consulted former colleagues on specific areas, especially when there were gaps in my memory or I could not recall details or absolute facts, for clarifications.

In compiling this book, I tried to transmit events that occurred as faithfully as possible. Nonetheless, there were instances where I could not rely on concrete evidence, in which case I resorted to speculations. Moreover, since this was my story, I was at liberty to redact or embellish the facts as suited my fancy. Besides, except in a few instances, I deliberately avoided citing real names in my portrayal of characters. But there were bound to be resemblances. So, if anyone projected themselves onto any of the characters depicted, it was entirely their grouse to bear.

Finally, I did not set out to be nice or nasty. I was swinging. Yet, I shall condone herd mentality or responses from institutionalized lacqueys that populate the service I copiously wrote about. More importantly, I have granted all who may read this book their sentiments, i.e., inflammatory, affirmatory, or contradictory, as a given. The author accepts responsibility for the whole shebang expressed in this book, except delusions, distortions, anxieties, perceptions or prejudices etc., which belong to the reader.

Acknowledgement

All through the many years it took me writing and re-writing this book, I sought assistance and amplifications from colleagues, acquaintances, friends and associates who were not even aware of this project. Those snippets were deployed to enrich the theme of this exertion for which I am eternally grateful to you all.

Dedication

I dedicate this book to the memory of my late beloved parents. First, to my father, Mallam Audu Gberikon Kyado, whose virtues of modesty, contentment, and fair play I shall ever cherish. Also, to my mother, Rebecca Kahemban Kpeese, who loved me endlessly, for her diligence, foresight, and the pains she took to impart all that was good about life and living. To these two, I owe everything because they were there when it all began.

Similarly, I devote this effort to the memory of my siblings, living and dead. Terzungwe, Iorse, Sale, Orvendega, Vihimga, Ijirbee and Ngusuur. In your collective numbers, you showered me with unconditional love and mentoring. More importantly, you provided me with the first audience to throw tantrums at, to scale my capacity for the incendiary, and to hone my skills as a serial opposer. Without your limitless patience and reciprocal chastisement, I would have taken the world for a ride and or, the world would have ridden me roughshod.

Likewise, I devote this effort to my wife, Professor Grace Mwuese Gberikon and my children, as well as the friends, enemies, and detractors etc., that I assembled along the way, over many years at different schools and workplaces. I honestly believe that without your affection, crankiness, and perpetual resentment, I could not have discerned the capacity of humans for meanness and frivolity.

Lastly, I dedicate this book to whoever takes the pains to read it especially those that for whatever reason, may fulminate and froth in the mouth like overworked horses, on account of feigned injuries and dubious credentials as defenders of the status quo.

Lieutenant Colonel Tyozenda Gberikon Retired

Author's Notes

I do not recollect how I came across the first book. However, I was immediately drawn to them, especially those filled with pictures and illustrations. In time, I learned to read them and of the fact that they were written. So, over the years, I avidly read every single material I could lay my hands on. As for writing a book, it felt like a distant prospect, mainly because of an apparent lack of talent nor training. Moreover, I increasingly agonized over the creative concerns of the theme and genre to start with. Perhaps, I could write my life story.

However, a review of my personal history was not remarkable, as the sum of my sojourn in the military was modest. Worse still, I had missed out on real fighting. However, the impulse to tell a story persisted.

In any case, disapproving of one's past was the ultimate act of self-effacement. Even so, it was clear that each person went through the fullness of living in a fashion distinctive to them. Although, the circumstances could be similar, the resultant actions, reactions, and perceptions were bound to be divergent indeed. Thus, every story, despite its triteness, was exceptional and could never be iterated elsewhere.

Nonetheless, I hesitated, not until a chance encounter with a younger colleague prompted me. After a good-natured exchange of pleasantries that morning, he proudly presented advance copies of his book from his publishers and went through the motions of handing me a signed copy. I could not tell what for, but I was instantly seized by melancholic bile over his audacious accomplishment, for whereas I vacillated he had authored a book.

Feeling deflated, I let slip my closet ambitions without the resolve to start, to which his response was rather acerbic. Without even pondering, he blurted that I was indolent. Stung, I rebuked him for use of insubordinate language, but deep inside, I knew he had been truthful, for nothing but laziness held me back.

Driven by this 'distasteful' encounter as one might say, I resolved to write a book to share my story in the Nigerian Army (NA). It was better late than never at all, because I reckoned myself as an embedded and observant participant in an institution that was so beguiling.

For too long, the public missed out on the inner working mechanisms of the NA, because as an institution, it was designed to confound. It was not disputed that, without joining, you never understood what it was like to be a soldier. So, neither its pervasive influence nor the mindset of its operatives was ever accurately deciphered.

Consequently, in the absence of demonstrable evidence, the public strained for salacious gossip about the service. This drift was fed from time to time with dribs of insignificant details by pretenders that were, at best partly facts, exceedingly embellished or utterly falsified. Moreover, because insider accounts were irregular and far apart, the available details were a superfluous combination of hagiography, irreverence, and condescension.

In sum, this book is an expose but not the story of the NA. It was not an attempt to conflate my bloated ego and perceptions in subjective cleverness, but a pen-picture of my odyssey interwoven with my service in the organization. I did not set out to castigate the system, especially as the group hates disclosures, but in a like manner, I did not mollycoddle the service nor its operators.

This book reflects my perceptions. Therefore, any emotions and responses it elicits fulfills the purpose of my exertion. I did not set out on a high horse but of one with a privileged and unobstructed access to the underbelly of the NA for which I invoke artistic liberty.

Lieutenant Colonel Tyozenda Gberikon Retired

Transition by Ordeal

Let me begin at the end. Has it crossed your mind to contemplate a situation by which after many years, service personnel needed to be rehabilitated at the point of discharge? Even more, have you reflected on the eccentric manners of ex-servicemen? For those familiar with the Armed Forces of Nigeria (AFN), at any given time, there were departments, units, and facilities dedicated to the reintegration and resettlement of retiring personnel.

These were outfits set up by various branches of the services to ensure a productive post-service life. So, what was the catch? Whereas it was logical that recruits were inducted to hasten the transition into a structured military society, if at the point of release, it became necessary to rehabilitate and resettle retirees, then it meant that something substantial had given.

It was apparent that after a lengthy service, individuals were drained of their vitality and left at the whims of old age and want. It was a marker that should elicit disquiet and demanded closer scrutiny because a lot was concealed under this facade of an orderly denouement. Even worse, the reality of post-service life was that a greater proportion of ex-servicemen were unemployable except as low-level physical security forces.

Besides, there were occupational traits like meanness and grumpiness that were not easily cast off. At the end, lots of these ex-servicemembers degenerated into cold withdrawal and misery, and yielded to alcoholism, deteriorating mental health, and physical decline.

While there was an option for a tenured term of thirty-five through forty years' service, some personnel, like yours truly, opted for twenty to twenty-five years of regenerative engagement. These were and are still the implicit benchmarks that endlessly agitated the minds of servicemembers.

Hence, it took a determined resolve to confront the dilemma. However, not many had the grit, and most chose to wait out the stretch and every so often, to be officially nudged to make a final call. Although, a greater number also eventually progressed into a pension scheme to the accompaniment of discordant tunes of endless neighing and gnashing of teeth.

It was against this background that on 31 December 2009, I voluntarily retired from the Nigerian Army, a service to which I had dedicated over twenty-one years. This simple personal decision turned into an orchestrated ordeal for me. I discovered rather tardily that; I had fallen from a responsible private person into some public estate. But, oddly, at which point I was divested of my liberty to make decisions about my life, I could not fathom.

Otherwise, how we arrived at a stage where I encountered universal hostility from friends and foes alike on account of disengaging from a service, I had voluntarily joined in the first place. I observed pimps, gigolos, maniacal gold-diggers, commission agents, masquerades, shameless opportunists, court jesters, clowns, scheming speculators, political charlatans, robber barons, magicians, acrobats, assassins, kidnappers, hyenas, jackals, and detritus, all of whom were ill equipped to discern the sagacity of a personal resolve.

While I was at peace with myself, certain individuals were engaged in bombast and spuriousness generating circumstances and insinuations, etc. to unravel the mystery of my retirement from the army. Not appeased by this misplaced travesty, many resorted to conjecture, witchcraft, sorcery, and shamanism to conciliate their compelling need for ripostes.

I endured all the shenanigans and pontifications with ponderous patience and aggregated the umbrage to an egotistical herd mentality. If not, it was uncommon to appropriate an individual's liberty or, engage in invasive posturing on another's behalf. This to me was an overbearing insolence by distasteful meddlers.

The decision to disengage from the army was personal and considered because I reflected on all the dynamics and matrixes. It was taken in my best interest. So, the least I expected, despite any oddball's frustration, was to be respectful of that choice as a given. If by any superficial design, anyone felt uncomfortable, it was entirely on account of pointless superciliousness. However, I recognized it would be nice to put the story in perspective to provide a peek into my sojourn in the NA, as the manner of joining was as dramatic as the grace of exit.

First Picture as an Officer Cadet 1988

Chapter One

In the Beginning

On a late afternoon in the mid-1960s, my heavily pregnant mother felt pressed and went behind a bush not far from the homestead to relieve herself. According to her, what should have been ordinarily an easing evacuation turned into parturition. Initially, she was unbelieving and alarmed as nobody was close at hand to assist, but her nerves held, and she self-delivered me into the household of Mallam Audu Gberikon Kyado. It would be her ninth live birth in twelve pregnancies, after which menopause set in.

My family was of a mixed Christian-Muslim heritage. My father converted to Islam during his long sojourn away from home. He was an accomplished vagrant and for long was away from his native land until a distant cousin forcibly repatriated him. He told me that he left home in 1925 through 1946 and traversed the length and breadth of colonial Nigeria. It was only a chance encounter with a returnee ex-combatant at Apapa Wharf Quayside in 1946 that forced him home the same year. Dad kept his faith during his lifetime amid an overwhelmingly animist and latter-day Christian society.

On the other hand, my mother was of the Christian faith. She was married into the historic family of Sai. Sai village was the first port of call of Christian evangelism among the Tiv people of the middle and lower reaches of Benue Valley of Central Nigeria on 17 April 1911.[1] As a couple both were tolerant and respectful of each other's beliefs and clung to their faiths and none afterward imposed it on their children. I deliberately emphasized my multiple religious upbringings because I took for granted the tolerance of my parents and therefore could not envisage religious intolerance or insularity.

However, the underlying subtleties of our spiritual harmony were irretrievably altered when Nigerians began to fight on behalf of their gods. Frequently, religious charlatans systematized mobs that sallied and howled for the blood of unbelievers. The outcome was gruesome as adherents of foreign cults, whose deities expressly forbade butchery of humans, played sports of killing. More so, the so-called animists or heathens, who were so vehemently denounced by these Eastern creeds, had long abrogated human sacrifice. This spiritual belligerence persisted until Boko Haram, the newest entrant into the macabre dance, put a final seal to the intermittent charlatanerie.

My Mother had two sons from an earlier marriage before she lost her spouse during WWII, on the Burma front. However, being a young widow, she returned home rather than remain behind, to propagate posthumous children for her late husband, which was a widespread practice then. It was at her maiden village in 1947, that an arranged courtship was nurtured with my dad.

My father was an accomplished nomad, a professional gambler, and a neatness freak to the hilt who had evaded all entreaties to get married in his younger days and was coaxed into an arranged marriage with a widow in his middle age. Now and again, I interviewed Momma on how she met my father, she insisted that they never met independently but a mutual acquaintance had introduced them, and that he was exceedingly haughty when he courted her. She remembered with mirth, how he sullenly griped that his relations thought little of him to lead him to a faded old woman.

Yes, the dude was on a cut so high indeed. But graciously, they got married and it was that old woman who bore him children and ensured he had a family. Then Mama's second set of children came in torrents. Sale, Orvendega, Vihimga, Ijirbee, Ngusuur, and finally yours sincerely, Tyozenda. I was the last, and as with all last children, I was my mother's most beloved.

The Tiv Riots

In the closing years of British colonial rule, especially post-independence, Nigeria was almost overwhelmed by tensions and the near collapse of the emergent state. There was strong sensitivity to potential political dominance, inclinations towards corruption, regional loyalty, and tribal jingoism. These portentous tendencies made the country ungovernable, as in all the regions, there were civil disturbances, chaos, and apprehension, of which the Tiv Riots were the most infamous.[1]

It was in the cauldron of the Tiv Riots that I was born. These infamous and brutal mayhem were unremitting for over six years, i.e., from 1960 through 1965. Although the unrest received political mention on the national scene, its final form and impact were localized.

In definitive terms, these riots were a deadly struggle for the control of the recently centralized polity of the Tiv Division. It was an intense disorder orchestrated by self-centered and ruthless local elite composed of colonial clerks, messengers, ex-servicemen, commission agents, produce buyers, pupil-probationer teachers, usurious moneylenders, con artists, clowns, magicians, conjurers, and opportunistic social climbers.[2]

The multiple obstacles the British contended with to create colonial structures and framework of governance among the Tiv people are well chronicled. These challenges arose partly because the Tiv society was an acephalous social order, i.e., an egalitarian society without a sole leader nor chief nor specialized political power mongers.

Consequently, Tivland became the scene of paranoid and exasperating schemes of trialing under shifting jurisdictions. Out of frustration and randomness, the political administration of Tiv Division was coalesced severally and split, under different administrative contraptions. At a point, the division was administered directly from Kaduna, the then regional headquarters but later detached from the Lower Benue and attached to the newly created Muri Province in 1903, and further splintered between Ogoja and the Lower Benue now renamed Nasarawa Province. However, at independence in 1960, the Tiv Division of Benue Province was part of the Northern Region. This constant political and administrative tinkering formed the basis of the continual turbulence between the Tiv and their neighbours in the Benue Valley.[4]

In 1960, the Northern Region was ruled by Ahmadu Rabah, the latter-day Sir Ahmadu Bello, who was the grandson of the great Islamic scholar and cleric, Shehu Usmanu bin Fodiyo. History tells us that bin Fodiyo belonged to the Toronkawa Fulani, one of the most insular ethnic groups in Africa. The sheik was a forceful preacher who advocated reform from the syncretistic practices by Muslims in the Sudan specifically Hausaland. By dint of his remarkable success, his younger brother Abdullahi Gwandu and son, Muhammad Bello, in collaboration with a clutch of murderous Fulani warlords, founded the Sokoto Caliphate over a vast expanse of the hinterlands of West Central Africa.[5]

The said bin Fodiyo may have possibly been an apolitical cleric, but his younger brother, Gwandu, and son Bello, having tasted the bewitching compound brew of political power and preferment, were intoxicated thereof by its potency, and could not let go. Undeniably, while the Sheik was engrossed with his generously stocked library of voluminous books, espousing high philosophy, and ceaselessly churning out theological treatises and the like intellectual gymnastics, Gwandu, Bello, and his cohort of flagbearers were employed in large-scale brigandage, devastation, and pillaging of Hausaland and threatening the ancient Islamic Bornu Empire to its east.[6]

From the 1790s when bin Fodiyo began his itinerant preaching and at his death in 1817, the jihadists had not only defeated all Hausa city-states, Nupe kingdom, and beyond, but they also replaced the Habe Hausa and Nupe dynasties and disrupted the Yoruba Oyo Empire to the south. The ripples of these historical events were especially telling on the animist groups caught in the cauldron of the jihadist rush. These groups inhabited the Bauchi and Jos Plateaus and the Niger-Benue valleys, a locale where a sizable number of natives were forcibly converted to Islam and or enslaved.[7]

In time, hesitant sentiments were voiced as to whether the jihadists intended to create the Sokoto Empire to amass tribute in an area ruled by force, or they were actual religious purists. Whatever the incentive, there were bound to be unintended consequences. In the long run, the power politics of the jihad took on a life of its own and by the closing years of the 19th century, the political domain of Sokoto metropolis and its federating emirates was a fait accompli long before the British arrived on the scene in the early 20th century. The last independent Caliph of Sokoto, Sultan Muhammadu Attahiru 1, was deposed by the British in 1903.[8]

Although the Fulani jihadists equally moved against the Tiv, their impact on the area that became the latter-day Tiv Division, was negligible, especially allowing that the region was neither assailed nor was an emirate founded among them. However, their Benue Valley locale was incessantly raided for slaves.

In the follow-up too, Keffi (1802) and Suleja (1804), cadet branches of the Zazzau Emirate, and Wase Emirate (1817) were founded among Mada, Gbagyi, and in the heart of Tarok country on the lower plateau respectively.[9] In the end, the advent of British colonial rule effectively terminated the Sokoto caliphate and hopefully put paid to any expansionist and forceful tendencies.

In the Tiv Division, the local politicians flourished by stoking castration anxieties over the so-called schemes of political domination and the threat of forceful conversion to Islam.[10] Whether these fears were historical or just a cynical ploy to sequestrate the division as an exclusive fiefdom of a cabal, was a matter of conjecture.

The emblem of these so-called designs was the premier of Northern Nigeria. The much-feared, Sir Ahmadu Bello, started as a local schoolteacher and rose to the political leadership of the Northern People's Congress (NPC). He was the first and only premier of the Northern Region.[10] By his pedigree, he understood the mechanics of power and power politics, some knowledge he deployed and scrupulously exploited.

While it lasted, his opponents recoiled at his political dragnet, and those who interacted with him attested to his compassion and ruthlessness in equal measure. He was also an invasive and meddlesome individual. So, while the other ostensible national politicians secured ethnic enclaves, Sir Ahmadu Bello built bridges, even if they were rickety, across the gulf with Benjamin Nnamdi Azikiwe and other southern minority groups.

He cleverly infiltrated and subverted the ranks of Jeremiah Obafemi Awolowo, the Yoruba arch-tribalist, and poached the treacherous Samuel Ladoke Akintola, the then Premier of Western Region.[11] So great was the premier's political standing that he aroused concern and contempt both at home and abroad.

Although he was from a line of pious and combative Islamic scholars, caliphs, and principal inheritors of the Sokoto caliphate, even if he had propagated extreme religious and fanatical views, the attendant circumstances were untenable to promote such an irredentist agenda.

Moreover, he groomed an array of associates, confidants, and close personal staff, several of whom were Christians. Among these were Sunday Awoniyi, David Dafinone, and even the treacherous Chukwuma Kaduna Nzeogwu, which was a testament to his open-mindedness. Therefore, the premier could not have harbored any schemes to start a latter-day jihad and so it became pertinent to examine the real motives behind the Tiv Riots.[12]

An Ethnicist Confederacy

The masterminds of the riots in the Tiv Division were elements of the United Middle Belt Congress (UMBC). This organization was a nebulous socio-political contraption crafted for a political power grab by any means necessary. Even more, it was a union of strange bedfellows from the far-flung indigenes of Kabba, Benue, and Plateau Provinces with neither historical nor cultural affinity. Apart from latter-day Christian faith common in these localities, they were united more by their undemocratic partisan tendencies and collective hatred for the core Muslim north, with an agenda of internal oppression.[13]

The party was a discordant ethnically driven organization. Predictably, its method was to stir up hatred, tribal sentiments, and propagate fear while it trampled on the very people it claimed to defend. One Joseph Sarwuan Tarka, was the lynchpin of UMBC in the Tiv Division.

Tarka was an ambitious local schoolteacher who made incursions into the politics of the Tiv Division at a time when the British colonial masters allowed nominal participatory politics. His emergence was not a factor of personal pre-eminence nor exceptional gifts, but because he was the son of a village pupil-teacher in an era when Western edification had just begun among the Tiv. He rose to primacy because he was one of the first group of pupils to get a low-level Western education, so it came to pass that in the country of the blind, the one-eyed man became a king.

He was a mere twenty-three-year-old when he won a seat in the Federal House of Representatives to stand for Jemgbar, a Tiv subgroup, at the 1954 general elections.[14]Ironically, he was a very despotic character with saturnine resentment for elders and others more educated than himself. A schemer per excellence, he surrounded himself with fawning mediocre acolytes that constituted no threat to his vaunting leadership. Nonetheless, he possessed primal cunning and native intelligence, the gifts that built enduring political combines.

Yet more, the UMBC was a partisan platform for diverse ethnic groups in central Nigeria covering parts of the present-day Benue, Kogi, Plateau, Nasarawa, Adamawa, and Kwara states. To underline its amorphousness, its confederative structures were loose and devolved to ethnicity within its ranks. So, the key leaders of the party like Solomon Lar held sway among the Tarok, while David Lot and Patrick Dokotri led their Ngas and Berom compatriots. During the UMBC Conference at Lafia in 1957, there was an election to leadership positions. At that point, Tarka was not a top contender even when the congress conceded the presidency to the Tiv, by virtue of being the single most populous group in the region.

The preferred choice of the Tiv delegates was Achirga Abur who got forty-three votes, followed by HO Abaagu with thirty-one, and JS Tarka took twenty-five votes, respectively. However, because the winner could neither speak English nor Hausa, he stood disqualified and Abaagu who was next in the score declined and so the office passed by default to Tarka.[15] It was obvious that something about this Tarka of a character was not agreeable with his compatriots, although the Tiv delegates closed ranks in a dubious tribal solidarity and handed him support to take the prize by default. [16]

Forceful Politicking

Nonetheless, a worrisome concern was the political legacy the UMBC bestowed on the Tiv Division. For instance, one could begin to question why the riots were more ferocious in the division than in the other ethnic components of the party. The answers lay with Tarka and his cohorts who were in politics for preferment and not to uplift their constituents. This fact was reinforced by the political machinations the UMBC deployed in its heydays.

For a start, the party contracted a political alliance with Awolowo's Action Group on 6 May 1957 and forcefully won the 1959 pre-independence Elections.[17] The truth be told, the coalition was a duplicitous marriage of convenience designed to infuriate and confound the national political calculus. In other words, it was akin to running away from the much-loathed Fulani feudalists to embrace opportunistic Yoruba fiends as neither could be linked to any democratic disposition.

During the 1959 pre-independence elections, the UMBC perforce was the predominant political party in the Tiv Division. Yet the party, a dogmatic and despotic group, insisted on being the universal front for all Tiv people, irrespective of individual dissimilarities and predispositions. In simple terms, the UMBC goons considered the division a subjugated fiefdom. Thus, in a twist of irony, an historically egalitarian people who vigorously resisted the loss of freedom was subverted and subjugated by their kind.[18]

After the 1959 Federal Elections, the UMBC plunged the Tiv Division into an orgy of orchestrated mayhem. This was the Nande-Nande (arson) riots of 1960. These incendiaries went on unabated and only subsided temporarily just before Nigeria's independence. Nevertheless, intimidation and threats persisted along with a gradual build-up to the next wave of violence.[19] Hence from November 1960 through 1963, the Tiv Division subsisted as a lawless frontier because instead of mobilizing for membership and support, the UMBC preferred conscription which put the division through further devastations.

Even more, after another round of Federal Elections in 1963 were long gone; the UMBC-led depredations once more racked Tiv Division from 1964 through 1965. This was the notorious Atemtyo, a literal cracking of heads as it were. This coordinated self-immolation persisted until 1965 when the Nigerian Army brutally suppress the riots.21

No words could faithfully capture the primitive and crude viciousness of the UMBC inspired Nande-Nande and Atemtyo in Tiv Division. Some reported incidents included skewering, disembowelment of pregnant women, large scale slaughter of livestock, looting, arson, and wanton destruction of properties.

Ironically, all these massive devastations were not targeted against the much-hated Islamic feudalists but fellow Tiv. It went down to a situation whereby any individual suspected of NPC sentiments was targeted; and being ambivalent did not help either, because with UMBC there was neither room for choice nor neutrality. This was the mark of a forced group.

Our family was a direct victim of UMBC's venomous politics as my name, Tyozenda, bears this out. Dad was a Muslim and therefore a presumed NPC member, in fact he was. It was a constitutional right of association. When the riots broke out, he quickly moved to Wukari, a nearby city, spared the madness that had enveloped Tiv Division. In the meantime, my mother stayed back at a time she was heavily pregnant with me. At that point, the threat of UMBC marauders was so pervading that they were roving danger to all normal socio-economic activities.

Mom recalled a near fatal encounter with an assailant. It was an experience she never got tired of recounting. She told me that on a fateful day in mid-1964, she went to the farm and got too engrossed at tending the patchy earth to notice, when a group of men armed with machetes, spikes, cudgels, and all manner of dangerous weapons suddenly materialized. Of course, on closer examination, they were not strangers but were folks she knew too well.

Soon enough there was a heated council among these murderous hoodlums to decide her fate. While others suggested outright liquidation, some on account of her advanced pregnancy thought otherwise. Mercifully, reason prevailed, and they made to move on. Then abruptly, one depraved character, by the name of Anaan Ugoh, turned around and accused her of holding forth for her husband who had fled so that he could have a head start if he ever returned. He then hit her on the waist with the flat side of his machete.

She collapsed and passed out. When she came to, her assailant had vanished. The blow almost induced premature labour because she had watery discharge but luckily the pregnancy held.

Confronting a Beastly Apparatchik

About 1974, at a local watering hole owned by my stepmother, I overheard someone hailed by that despicable name of Anaan Ugoh. I quickly ran to my mother to confirm and went back to confront him. It was a dramatic moment. The reader could picture a nine-year-old confronting an aging man. He was relishing the potent brew in the company of his friends when I barged in on them. Innocently, I asked among the lot whom Anaan Ugoh was, and the rapscallion owned up, so I challenged him with the story of his assault on my then-pregnant mother.

You could visualize a place that was rowdy just a moment ago stunned into silence by my challenge. A monster was being forced to answer for his infamous past. All he managed was that I could not understand what happened in those dark days. He could not get more presumptuous and preposterous. I perfectly understood that the UMBC had led him and others to conduct themselves like beasts.

For the UMBC mob, the main drive was a power grab for its sake. So, having effectively seized absolute reins of political power, the party ruled impulsively and smothered Tiv Division until the collapse of the First Republic on 15 January 1966. This socio-political rape was not only violent but extortionist as well when the entire Tiv Division was taxed to build a house at Gboko for its leader.

Tarka by disposition was a maximalist totalitarian, such that, he could name a nonentity as a candidate at any electoral contest and of course they won. In this way, he brought one Ibrahim Imam from Borno Province, christened him Wyarwyar Gatie and impos   ed him as a candidate. Imam eventually won an election in the Tiv Division.[22]

Paradoxically, twelve years later, at the start of the Second Republic in 1979, Tarka spurned his one-time ally Awolowo and returned to his former traducers in the NPC by joining the National Party of Nigeria (NPN), a reincarnation of the NPC. By 1979 too, he enacted his final act of nepotism when he got himself and his son elected to the Senate and House of Representatives, respectively.

Although, I did not set out to denounce the UMBC leadership, in fact, it must be, even if belatedly. The intention was to subject the party's legacy or lack of it, to an alternative interpretation and to point out that despite the popular myth, the party and its leadership bestowed a dreadful political antecedent on the Tiv Division. The purpose was to unravel how within fifty-four years of colonial rule, a distinctively egalitarian people were driven to devastation by a ruthless local cabal.

As a forced group, the UMBC was intolerant and enthroned brutal repression, harassment, massive impoverishment through social disruption, targeted killings, and wanton destruction of properties. Perhaps, there was nothing in the democratic disposition of the Tiv people that could have tampered the UMBC to institute a more civilized order in its search for political dominance.

In any case, what role did Tarka as a person play to add to or to stop the violence? He did nothing because it suited his schemes. Not until the First Republic was mercifully terminated in 1966, the UMBC had brazenly trampled on freedom of association and elevated cruelty, depravity, and social dislocation to unprecedented infamy unheard of in the annals of the Tiv people.

Notes

(1). Account of Christianity in Tiv land see: www.nksteducationdepartment.org.

(2). For a comprehensive account of the Tiv Riots 1960 through 1965 see: Tesemchi Makar: The History of Political Change among the Tiv in the 19th and 20th Centuries (Fourth Dimension Publishing Co Ltd, Enugu. 1994).

(3). Tesemchi Makar: The History of Political Change among the Tiv, op cit, p211.

(4). Prof GN Ayittey: Stateless Societies: The Igbo, the Fulani, the Somali, A New Nigeria Feb 2012.

(5). For an account of tinkering with Tiv settlements: Tesemchi Makar: The History of Political Change among the Tiv, op cit, p127.

(6). For a comprehensive accounts of the Jihad and the caliphate see: Murray Last: The Sokoto Caliphate, (London: Longman, 1967).

(7). Murray Last: The Sokoto Caliphate, op cit.

(8). Murray Last: The Sokoto Caliphate, op cit.

(9). Murray Last: The Sokoto Caliphate, op cit.

(10). Encyclopaedia Brittania Inc.

(11). On threat of Islamization: Tesemchi Makar: The History of Political Change among the Tiv, op cit, p223.

(12). For an account on the fear of Ahmadu Rabah see: Kole Omotosho: Just Before Dawn (Spectrum Books, Lagos, 1988).

(13). Poaching of Akintola: Kole Omotosho: Just Before Dawn, op cit.

(14). Ahmadu Rabah denied for the sultanate: Kole Omotosho: Just Before Dawn, op cit.

(15). On UMBC confederacy: Tesemchi Makar: The History of Political Change among the Tiv, op cit, p215.

(16). Tarka wins leadership election: www.guardianngr.com.

(17). On UMBC Lafia Conference elections: Tesemchi Makar: The History of Political Change among the Tiv, op cit, p217.

(18). On UMBC Lafia Conference elections: Tesemchi Makar: The History of Political Change among the Tiv, op cit, p217.

(19). On UMBC-AG Alliance: Tesemchi Makar: The History of Political Change among the Tiv, op cit, p218.

(20). On UMBC coercion: Tesemchi Makar: The History of Political Change among the Tiv, op cit, p223.

(21). Beginning of Tiv Riots: Tesemchi Makar: The History of Political Cange among the Tiv, op cit, p232.

(22). Nigerian Army intervenes in Tiv Riots: Tesemchi Makar: The History of Political Change among the Tiv, op cit, p232.

(23). Ibrahim Imam wins in Tiv Division: Patrick I. Ukase: JS Tarka and Ethnic Minority Agitations and Struggles in Nigeria, 1960-1980: A Eulogy Revisited: Journal of the Historical Society of Nigeria: Vol. 22 (2013), pp. 82-113).

Circa 1982

Chapter Two

Kyado Village

According to legend, Kyado Ma founded his settlement in the late 1850s, after a long trek away from Ber Auna, on the eastern banks of River Katsina-Ala near the present-day Buruku. A warrior-type head of his pack, he chose a spot at the peak of a low-lying hill. It was a strategic frontier outpost, lying just twenty-four kilometres south of the Jukun town of Wukari, a group that has historically maintained caustic relations with their Tiv neighbours. It was the last major Tiv settlement before transiting through a mixed territory of Tiv, Jukun, Ichen, Chamba, Kuteb, and a host of other smaller ethnic groups in the Middle and Upper Benue Valley.

My Dad told me that the present settlement was its second site, as the original location was about five kilometres due west at Upupuu, close to the banks of a stream. The village was relocated to the current spot in the early 20th century after the British imperialists came. Not too long after, the colonialists employed forced labor, mostly of Tiv gangs, to construct a route traversing the village, from the Produce Buying Point on the River Katsina-Ala to Ibi on the Benue River.

That the settlement was relocated was a shrewd decision informed by the changing times. At the outset, the hamlet was populated by his household and the homesteads of his three siblings. However, due to its strategic location, as a halt and provisioning station, it soon attracted long-distance traders, transient residents, strangers, and vagrants. Among its residents were Hausa, Igbo, Jukun, and the Baffoum from Cameroon.

The settlement was a diverse community with the rudimentary elements of cosmopolitanism. Each group was associated with a specific trade, craft, or specialty. The Igbo ran retail shops, the Baffoum were expert mat weavers while the Hausa were butchers, hoarders of grain, and commission agents.

The largest and the most influential cluster was the Hausa-speaking group. This subset has been resident for the last hundred and fifty years. The main families were that of Mallam Ali from Maradin Katsina and the Danjuma family from Zamfara. These two major families together with other Hausa families drawn from far-flung ends of Hausaland like Katagum, Gumel, Bauchi, Gobir, Zaria, and others formed a sizeable part of the settlement.

The Hausa folks were strict Muslims who dutifully observed daily prayers and practiced a strict Islamic code that forbade the consumption of pork and alcohol. It was glaring because when I left home, I met a more relaxed practice among the urban faithful. They married among themselves and occasionally took local brides, but strangely, no Hausa girl ever got married to a Tiv man.

Apart from being engaged in usurious practices, they were intermediaries and collectively had a sharp eye for a commission or killing. Although, not involved in any tedious farming, except planting sugar cane, yet they retailed the all-important farm inputs, that were sold at eternally extortionist prices.

There was a so-called Sarkin Hausawa, chief of the community. Each time he summoned the elders of the village, including my father, I was in disbelief and grief, and pondered how they could allow such a primacy to be set. How could a total stranger summon and superintend over native community leaders? They derisively referred to the locals as arna, unbelievers. It was so pervasive that as a child, I thought the Hausa word for Tiv was arne. This internal colonization would last until 2001 when NA troops destroyed Kyado village as part of reprisal attacks on Zaki Biam.

The other major group was the Igbo who were mostly shopkeepers. They traded in every article on demand. As itinerant traders, they hawked their wares from one local market to the other, all week long. But on Sundays, they would play soccer games in the mornings and in the late afternoons attended town meetings.

Soon, the villagers began to speculate that these meetings were price-fixing assemblies. If they were not, then how come prices of articles always changed uniformly on Mondays among the traders?

These meetings were conducted in low-tone exchanges and rounded up with eating and boisterous drinking.

The Igbo traders always conversed in a funny kind of English. This was pidgin English, I later got to know. This confused me, especially about my teacher, on the one hand, and the traders, on the other, because at school, the basic English greeting was taught as a "good morning" and here, the Igbo traders could be heard hailing themselves "good borning." I sensed; they knew something that our teacher had not told us.

As a group, they were a completely detribalized people, but highly individualistic, profit-oriented, arrogant, and every so often very disrespectful among themselves and to others. They called us ndi akpu nku or akpu for short and like the Hausa, they had affairs with our women but ensured their daughters of marriageable age were shipped home to the "East" to be betrothed among their kin.

The first Igbo man I met was Michael Okoli who returned at the end of the civil war, about February 1970. He made the round greeting the villagers who received him warmly visibly happy he survived the war. The Tiv people, identified as a martial tribe by the British imperialists, took part in the Nigerian civil war at a ratio disproportionate to their population. It was documented that every family contributed at least one combatant to the war effort.[1] But ironically, they were celebrating a survivor of those very people whom they had sent their sons in droves to hunt like wild game.

Of course, during the war, the Tiv had no misgivings about the Igbo and in fact, certain individuals gave refuge to their Igbo compatriots, until it became unsafe to do so. The only isolated case of reported looting was due to an alleged sighting of a Biafran warplane that overflew Gboko, which was discovered to be a false alarm.

Otherwise, the Tiv never harassed the Igbo people, and all recovered their landed property intact at the end of the hostilities. Moreover, the way Michael was welcome back like a long-lost brother was a very forceful testimony that the healing process was desirable to wipe out the blot of that brutal war.

The rest of the residents were artisans. The Jukun were blacksmiths, while their women brewed potent local beer. The Baffoum were adept mat weavers and the itinerant Yergam or Tarok were seasonal migrant farm labourers.

A Grand Oldman

My father told me his old man was a crafty manipulator with a large polygamous family. No one knew the exact number of wives he married in his lifetime, as he was licentious. His serial indiscretions still reverberated in the large family he left behind long after his death over a hundred years ago.

Grandpa was a war chief, wealthy and magnificent. There was a story of his ordeal in the hands of one Captain JC Gordon, the colonial Resident at Ibi. In 1907, the Resident, a young firebrand, arrived at his compound unannounced, unsolicited, and full of impetuosity. The old man was visibly irritated by the presence of this colonizing impostor and his body language was clearly unreceptive. When the Resident sought the most direct route to River Benue, he directed him towards Ali, a prominent settlement, about twenty kilometres west of his, in the opposite direction.

After a circuitous journey, during which hostiles attacked his entourage and killed several carriers, the Resident reached Ali's homestead visibly angry at the Oldman's pranks. On his return trip, he got him arrested and took him along to Ibi and had him illegally detained for over three months for being unhelpful.[2]

Our Homestead

Our family homestead was large and consisted of nine structures, seven of which were round thatched houses, and a rectangular-shaped house called adeda. The ninth structure, the first modern house in the village was rented out as shops to traders. How sardonic it was that the most habitable house was given out.

I found my father very intriguing because he was a calm individual not easily ruffled by most circumstances. He was also non-confrontational and not easily provoked. A measured person, he did not rush precipitately into action under duress. For instance, if you asked for any favors, and it was available, he gave. If you needed school fees and he had the money at hand, he gave. Otherwise, you got nothing.

My dad supported his family modestly, and we were never desperately hungry, especially as there were a thousand places to get fed as communally raised children. Dad never went to the farm and most evenings he rode off on his bicycle to pursue his gambling habit, especially as within our larger extended family it was a long-established tradition. It was so widespread, even among younger people, and not viewed outrageously.

Mama

The burden of taking care of the brood lay with my mother who was a sturdy industrious woman who must have been exceptionally beautiful in her younger days. However, after over twelve pregnancies (she told) and years of manual farm work, accelerated aging took its toll.

Mama was also a prayerful Christian woman. Every morning, she woke up unfailingly, and prayed expansively for everyone and everything in the universe. She prayed on behalf of all her children by name. Surefooted and patient, she was the epitome of sacrifice and determination. When my father played the cold man, she mustered all her resources to save situations.

Still, it was a hard life as a poor family, and expectedly, we lost opportunities. For instance, Sale the eldest, gave up going to school to enable his immediate younger brother, Orvendega, do so. Sale later joined the NA in 1968 at the height of the civil war.

While some people were born with proverbial silver spoons, for my siblings and me, not even a wooden spoon was within sight. However, we appreciated our parents' efforts to nurture us, particularly our mother's, and reciprocated their love and commitment by being handy when needed. In the long run, God in his infinite mercy endowed us all with an average faculty to enjoy going to school. For, it was one thing to love going to school, and another to have the aptitude and by the time we matured to adulthood, illiterate ab initio, my parents were proud on account of having educated an entire litter of children.

Household of A Thousand Wives

The Kyado family was undeniably large with over thirty wives and seventy children while he was still alive. As was typical with such polygamous homes, there was a deadly struggle to gain the attention of the patriarch. All the wives and children competed against each other, but still, many were neglected. However, there was always a lethal cocktail of jealousy, sorcery, and witchcraft in the household. For my father, it was a different kind of struggle because he had lost his mother in his infancy.

My Paternal Grandmother

According to my father, his old man visited Mbajembe, a sub-clan of Tombo Mbalagh. While there, his host delegated his pubescent daughter, Asaayana, as a minder for the duration of his visit. It was a customary practice for the host to nominate one of his wives or daughters to cater to his guests, to ensure they received close attention. The deputized wife or daughter took care of the guest's needs without carnality,

It was a practice that was deliberately misinterpreted by mischievous non-Tiv people. Repeatedly, I have been confronted by ignorant individuals who insisted that it was the custom of my people to give out their wives or daughters to guests. Where they got that awkward misconception may not be known but the belief was rife. It was a lie from the pit of hell and a fallacy that should be renounced. It must be understood that the easiest way to get into real trouble with a Tiv man was to meddle with his womenfolk. But I digress.

The grand old man was charmed by Asaayana who may have gone extra length to be impressive. From a caregiver, he demanded she be handed over as a wife. There were no niceties of courtship, nor was the consent of the young girl sought. It was just two roguish old men guffawing as they decided the fate of a naive girl-child. Her father, Ngyeke, approved and my grandfather, a man of substantial means, paid a token bride price and returned right away with his bride.

There were no impediments of introduction, traditional or white wedding, nor honeymoon to encumber the randy old man. Thus, my paternal grandmother became like the Biblical Abishag, to my aging grandfather. Asaayana died soon after childbirth to bring a miserable story to a tragic end.

For my father, an only child, without a mother to care for him, it must have been a dreadful experience growing up in a large polygamous household. But grandad was committed to him as he reassigned all the love and compassion he had for his youngest wife onto the child.

But this sentiment simply escalated matters. Dad recalled that he was always by his father's side, and this constant companionship elicited a lot of resentment from his other wives and fully grown half-siblings. It was an abhorrence stirred by speculation. The common belief was that gramps had powers of witchcraft, which every son aspired to inherit. Now, being at an advanced age, he might be preparing to hand over his mystic possessions to one of his youngest sons.

It became a routine to be at the receiving end of a heavy knock on the head here and a sharp rebuke there. It must have made life very agonizing for this partially orphaned child. Nonetheless, he endured by his father's side long enough to become a repository of Kyado family history.

Gramps may have given him over a thousand directives, but two stood out namely, in case of his death, he was to leave home at once and join his maternal uncle, Amended Ngyeke., and an order not to partake in the leadership of the market he set up because it was immersed in human sacrifices.

Consequently, when Kyado died in 1925, my father dutifully left at once to live with his mother's people and never came back until 1946. Also, in 1964, when the stool of the Market Chief became vacant upon the demise of the incumbent, he was next in line to step in. But then again, ever mindful of his father's words, he declined to take the stool.

In fact, he went on a second self-exile for a couple of years when the pressure to take the stool became unremitting. This became another source of resentment to his household for avoiding the market chieftaincy. It was baffling to other family members, why of all the Kyado family circle, only one sub-family was specifically barred from dealing in the affairs of the market.

A Comical Encounter

My first encounter with military men was comical indeed. Although I had never seen soldiers before that instant, I was overwhelmed by a sudden premonition that something unpleasant was about to happen. It was an apparition as nothing could explain the event of that day.

The Native Authority police we knew. You could not miss them on their shorts, black shoes, high stockings, and beret bearing the trademark baton. Usually too, it was a lone police officer. One, called Hangeagee, was a tall, huge man with a perpetual severe look on his broad face. These lone police officers could make multiple arrests, in the locality, unarmed except with the token baton as they were the symbol of authority.

Even more, all doubters knew enough to toe the line in his presence and absence. It was common to hear elders reminding aspiring deviants of the long reach of the law. In all its crudeness, as it were, Native Authority police officers were able to quickly uncover the masterminds of most crimes, and arrests were swift.

After an arrest, there were whispers of the fate that had befallen a culprit. The story was that offenders were in custody at the cha-ji-ofis and then onward to koti. At the koti, an unforgiving jooji presided, and he was a man whose duty it was to deliver criminals to purusu. Inside a purusu, the criminals were in the custody of very mean minders called duruba. All these depictions combined to elicit the highest universal reverence for law and order.

Without any intentions to demean, today when I see police officers carrying all manner of sophisticated arms, I get lost. Had the police declared war against the citizens? Unfortunately, at the end of all these displays, more crimes were committed, and insecurity pervaded.

Kyado settlement was a bucolic community in which everyone knew everybody else. Although strangers were warmly received, it was quite easy to detect non-residents. I do not recall the exact month, but one afternoon in early 1970, the community received a unique set of visitors. The village was "invaded" by about eight soldiers in a pickup truck.

In my impressionable mind, nothing could explain the ferocious appearance of those soldiers as they were fully battle-kitted. The camouflage fatigues they wore darkened the space. These aliens wielded slim rifles with curved magazines which I later discovered was the historic AK 47 rifle.

The AK47, a versatile assault rifle, was a mix of American M1 Garand and German Sturmgewehr automatic rifle StG 44, purloined by a Russian corporal, Mikhail Kalashnikov. By dint of imaginative and practical modification, it entered the annals of combat, as a weapon of choice among tyrants, charlatans, terrorists, militants, extremists, bandits, insurgents, armed robbers, assassins, kidnappers, irregular military organizations, and other deliverers of retribution.[3]

A Love Triangle

As earlier noted, apart from a solitary baton-wielding Native Authority police officer, I had never seen a soldier before. It was therefore an overwhelming sight that confronted the hamlet. So, what was their mission that afternoon? It was a great task indeed as the soldiers had come to retrieve a colleague's appropriated wife.

We were a small play group of cousins, and nieces, in short, all of us were kin. For a settlement by a major highway, we were accustomed to the sounds of vehicles. The ceaseless droning had become routine for us not to pay attention anymore. That afternoon, we were an assortment of children, the oldest in the group may not have been more than seven years old. At that point, we were too engrossed in our games to notice the arrival of the soldiers and they suddenly happened upon us.

Our little assembly was interrupted when two boys in a different playgroup ran past ours bawling. We glanced about us instinctively. Lo and behold; a troop of soldiers menacingly dressed, had just disembarked from their vehicle and were advancing directly towards the mango tree under whose canopy we were playing. The spectacle was too terrifying to contemplate. Not needing any further prompting, our response was spontaneous as we dispersed while vocalizing the loudest shrieks and most tremulous wails our small mouths could utter.

Still shrieking, we ran as fast as we could. I toppled over and was up in an instant and went for the nearest open door. It was a storehouse. Still shaky, I hid under a large basket and reassured myself that no harm could come to me but did not summon the courage to peer outside to see the unfolding drama, so I lay still and audited the developing situation.

The soldiers commandingly demanded for one Orga, the culprit and object of their mission. He was a giant from a child's perspective with a strict mien, a tall, muscular, well-built young man at the peak of his youth, who accentuated his machismo by adorning sleeveless vests. He had been indiscreet and eloped with another man's wife. Not just any man but a soldier at the war front.

Orga, an uncle, had gotten married not too long ago, to an attractive lady called Ajim. The marriage could not have lasted for more than six months before the coming of the soldiers. The next sound my ears picked up under the safety of the great basket, was that of a young lady ululating interspersed with groans as the soldiers dragged him away.

The villagers watched as the drama unfolded at a safe distance and wailed vicariously in empathy with him. There was commotion everywhere coupled with the soldiers' shouted commands rapidly delivered and dominated by a word that sounded like "sharrap". It was a cacophony of pleading in the Tiv dialect and curses flying in Hausa and pidgin English. Oh dear, it was such a din outside there.

My intuition proved right, as Orga was having not only a dreadful day, but a raw deal. I waited and waited, cowering under the basket, almost breathless and overwhelmed with fear as the soldiers kept barking out orders.

When all went quiet, and convinced that the soldiers had gone, I emerged from under the great basket and cautiously peered outside and saw the villagers gathered. They were all talking excitedly among themselves at the same time. However, the mood of the crowd did not add up to such a dreadful event just witnessed. As I drew nearer, I watched in bewilderment as the men chuckled with tears in their eyes, while others shook mirthfully. Little girls giggled and women laughed shrilly in a conspiratorial manner. It was a harsh high-pitched malicious laughter suggestive of pleasure at the misfortune of the couple.

From apprehension when the soldiers came into the village and when they finally left, it was a comic relief for all. Soon the village was agog with different versions of the story and what fate had befallen the culprit. The villagers suggested that they would be taken to Gboko, where the nearest military unit was located, while others said it was most likely to be Onugu (Enugu). Nonetheless, all of them agreed that if he eventually returned, he would have been thoroughly maimed.

Not long after, Orga returned on his two feet full of mischievous smiles. The soldiers did not roughen him. Subsequently, he resumed his normal activities after the uproar on his return. For Ajim, being arrested and taunted, may have been too humiliating such that on return, she terminated both marriages to bring an anti-climactic end to a triangular love story.

Looking back, I was too young to discern what transpired then. Otherwise, everyone old enough knew the story. It was a hilarious triangular relationship. Orga had eloped with Ajim in mid-1969 which was perfectly normal. However, the twist in the story was that she was previously married to another man in 1967, and shortly after the husband joined the army and went to the warfront.

For Ajim, the marriage was barely consummated when her husband left. Even worse, no one was sure how he joined the army. Someone suggested that he may have been captured during market day raids; and conscripted into the army, but a majority insisted he joined voluntarily. In any case, whatever method by which he got enlisted into the army, was now unimportant.

The matter at hand was that he was away and left behind a young sensual bride, about seventeen years old, who prudently managed the abrupt departure of her husband when he had barely warmed her side. After over two long years of waiting without any news of her husband, presumably dead by now, Ajim remarried in late 1969, and by January 1970, the war ended.

The elders of the village, alarmed at this indiscretion, called Orga and counseled him. Not only was he chastised but accused of treachery. How could he elope with someone else's wife? What with all the prospective brides abound in surrounding villages? So, he was accused of wishing his cousin dead. Even more, how did he expect to get away with such a scandalous conduct? He was, thereafter, advised to return the lady to her matrimonial home.

In all this conundrum, Ajim was blameless. Although her conduct was adjudged despicable, the community tacitly empathized with her in her precarious balancing act. Alas, Orga got sucked into the vortex of the seductive warmth of a sybaritic young woman. He paid no heed to the elders' homily and on the appointed day, he was reaping bountifully from the seeds of discord he had propagated.

It was not known at which point the news of the incident reached the soldier. Nonetheless, his colleagues came on a deadly mission of recapturing his wife. When they arrived, there was disquiet. When

Orga returned from wherever they had taken him to, he kept defiantly to himself, while the villagers snickered at him. After this day, a new vista opened in my world.

My mother patiently explained the events of the day while looking lovingly into my eyes. She then revealed that I had a brother who was also a soldier. I did not recall, having never met him before. Not too long after and like a burst dam, soldiers in uniforms arrived the village in droves. They all had these loud and swaggering manners about them. Although most of them were from the locality, they appeared so segregated.

The soldiers enjoyed the awe in which they were held by all. Unfortunately, they drank heavily and argued in high-sounding pidgin English. It was equally noticed that they had short fuses and could be provoked easily. Fights broke out often between them and it was common for the soldiers, from time to time, to descend on an unfortunate local and "deal with him." I interviewed my mother who knew all things: "Mama, where are all these soldiers coming from?" She did not disappoint and explained that they were on "liv" (leave pass) at the end of the war and that my eldest brother too, would be home soon. I could hardly hold my excitement, as I wanted to meet my soldier brother.

Notes

(1). For an account of Tiv People as a martial race see: Wikipedia.

(2). Grandfather's interaction with the British see: Tesemchi Makar: The History of Political Change among the Tiv in the 19th and 20th Centuries (Fourth Dimension Publishing Co Ltd, Enugu. 1994). p101-102.

(3). For a history of AK47 rifle see: Ezell, Edward Clinton: The AK47 Story, Evolution of the Kalashnikov Weapons. Stackpole Books. 1986. P 112.

NASMP 2000

Chapter Three

Barrack Boy

In NA jargon, a barrack boy or girl is a child or ward of a servicemember living within the precinct of a military location. In the mid-1960s and the build-up to the Nigerian Civil War, some recruits were married before they joined the service. However, a sizeable number were not, and so many of them went to the front and died without progeny. This was true for both officers and other ranks. So, after the war, the survivors went into a frenzy of marriages.

There were fewer barrack boys and girls in the early 1970s but that would change significantly. After the war, the search for brides was not long as the ex-combatants, officers, and soldiers alike, took spouses among the Igbo and other groups in the vanquished Biafra. To illustrate the urgency of this spousal business, General Yakubu Gowon, the then Head of State, could not wait and took Victoria in the heat of the war and was savagely criticized.[1]

Over the years, it was known that hordes of women and children, even of the enemy, flocked to military camps during pauses in hostilities. Graciously, both belligerents fought the Nigerian civil war without resort to mass rape and depredations characteristic of wars in other parts of Africa. Without a doubt, there was collateral damage and massive casualties, which were occasioned by starvation and forced displacement, not necessarily due to direct combat actions.

It was known that with soldiers, marriages involving Igbo brides were understandably higher. However, even senior officers took Efik and Igbo brides, the most prominent of whom was General Ibrahim Babangida, the latter-day military president. The same gale of war-induced marriages was repeated during the Nigeria-led ECOWAS Monitoring Group (ECOMOG) missions in Liberia and Sierra Leone decades later.

The larger number of the ex-combatants were quite patient and waited to get prospective brides back home in their native lands. However, when the war ended, there were garrison duties. As was customary, it was expedient to alternate leave passes and free passage for the victorious soldiers. The larger number had to bide their time and at the right moment, the survivors started trickling home to the warm embrace of their families.

In the interim, the soldiers resorted to writing letters. These mails notified their families of their survival and requested the families arrange spouses. To drive home the frenzied situation, these absentee suitors enclosed copies of photographs of themselves in combat dresses striking various poses.

By some magic, the soldiers expected the potential brides to accede to their long-distance advances by proxy, just on the strength of their being servicemembers. They were indeed conceited but fortuitously, the vanity worked and shortly afterward, brides were being shipped in droves to the ex-combatants.

Not long after, I picked up whispers of a wife for my brother chosen from a family within our kindred. There was a burst of activities and while the preparations were ongoing, my father got a mail that Sale would be home soon on leave pass. However, not having met him in my full consciousness before, it was difficult to predict how I would react towards him. Finally, he arrived, but I soon drifted away from him, for as a playful five-year-old; I went back to the more urgent business of frolicking with my playfellows. I do not recall when he returned to his unit but in a short while my world changed.

My mother informed me that I would be going away, to live with Sale. The arrangements for the bride were completed, and we were expected to travel shortly. So, with a mix of excitement and unease, I processed the news of this impending trip. Although, thrilled at the prospects of travelling to a distant place, I was equally apprehensive when I realized my mother was not coming along. For as a last child, I was always within her sight and suddenly the bond between us was about to be cut.

In the intervening time, I went round regaling my associates about my upcoming trip. Finally, the appointed day came in March 1971. Dad, Washima the bride, and yours sincerely, left Kyado village by mammy wagon and travelled deep into south-eastern Nigeria. The first phase of the journey took a lifetime before we arrived Ogbete Park in

Enugu, the capital of East Central State. From there we boarded a taxi, a first for me, and got to our destination, Agbani Nkanu, where I started my new career as a barrack boy.

A Railway Town

As of 1971, Agbani was a small railway township along the Enugu-Port Harcourt railroad. Undeniably, the non-stop clattering and whistling of coal-powered locomotives, made the railway station the liveliest part of the town. The station lay about two hundred metres across the main road from the compound we lived. Predictably, the station was an inviting attraction to me especially as I had never seen trains, so I spent time watching them shunted and the engines fired with coal.

The social life and routine in Agbani revolved round the hospital, mission center, local market, and the school. There were little traces of the physical scarification of the just-ended war. The whole kit and caboodle were unremarkable, and things went ahead at an unhurried pace except for the presence of troops on garrison duties.

Agbani was the location of the wartime 130 Battalion, an infantry unit. The town lay about forty kilometres southeast of Enugu, the then-Biafran capital. It was one of the fringe townships garrisoned when the capital city was captured by the Federal troops. In retrospect, Enugu was strategically vulnerable, as it was easily reached from the Northern Sector where the main effort of the opposing Federal side was mobilized.

The location of the Biafran capital was such that, apart from political and emotional affections, it was neither tactically nor strategically vital. The Nsukka sector to the north including key localities like Inyi, Obollo Afor, Obollo Eke, Enugu Ezike, and the University town itself, Orba, Eha-Alumona, Opi, Ukehe, Ngwo and Udi were much more critical as a protective shield for Biafra than Enugu. When the war began and the vulnerability of the capital city became obvious, instead of a logical reassessment of the situation, emotional bluster was resorted to.

By the way, Enugu was captured early in the war, i.e., 4 October 1967, and afterwards, a Biafran field capital was temporarily set up at Agbogugu, then moved to Umuahia and lastly Owerri. From this point going forward, unencumbered by the difficult defensive position of its capital city, the Biafran war efforts became more effective and resourceful.[2]

Barracks by Requisition

At Agbani, the unit had no purpose-built camp. There were no edifices in the manner of residences and administrative complexes. Nonetheless, the unit functioned out of requisitioned quarters. The Battalion Headquarters (HQ) was domiciled at St. John's Primary School near the market. The office complex included the appropriated former residence of the headmaster and a lone-standing classroom block, and the other components of the unit were distributed at several locations all over the town.

For accommodation, the troops were housed in requisitioned buildings. Nearby, St. John's Catholic Church building, which survived the war unscathed, took on the dual role of a church on Sundays and a school during weekdays. At Agbani therefore, there was an irregular barrack life in the unit.

In fact, the policy of appropriating properties and lands was so widespread in the army then. Apart from the old WAFF barracks in Lagos, Enugu, Kaduna, and Kano, new military barracks were not built until after the Civil War. Out of a force of habit, the Nigerian Army and Armed Forces of Nigeria by extension were inclined to commandeer quarters.

Moreover, our stay in Agbani was transitory, as by September 1971, the unit was moved to Agbogugu in the Udi Division. It was here that the semblance of core military activities was seen as Agbani was a civil community. It was at Agbogugu too, that my story within a military barracks proper began.

Meanwhile, I explored Agbani and within three months, I trekked the length and breadth of the town as it was a small settlement. Apart from haunting the train station, I went as far as the Mission Centre across the railway bridge and other places of interest. Nearby, was a tin-box fabricator along the route to the railway station where I watched him turn flat iron sheets into beautifully painted tin boxes. Also, a bakery was another magical spot for me too, as I went there to see the bread-making process.

Living with Soldiers

As a ward to my oldest brother, it was a new experience for me. I have stated repeatedly that, I never met him until when I was about five years old. However, it did not take long for me to grasp the dynamics of my new life. Here I was, a hyperactive five-year-old talkative, dearly beloved last child of my mom, faced with exacting conditions.

It was tough because my brother like all soldiers, was a stiff and grumpy individual. I do not recall ever holding a dialogue, or an advisory chat with him, throughout my first stint from March 1971 through August 1972. He could get irritated easily and was all too physical. For every conceivable reason, he smacked me, and it was difficult to understand why he was ever so harsh to his new wife and me.

It must be said that by 1971, when I came to live among soldiers; there was lots of abuse of spouses, children, and wards. The community of soldiers and their families was saturated with buffeting that was easily observed, even as a child. It took no effort to notice the intensity with which soldiers and spouses smacked their children and wards. These lot were highly creative at pummeling indeed. They unleashed barrages or cocktails of whacks and prolonged flogging, which I thought was bewildering as to imagine whether the child or ward was an error in the first place. It was so pervasive that it became odd if a particularly garrulous couple did not stage one of their sporadic public spectacles.

It was also important, to ponder the fact that, having undergone active combat for eighteen grim months on average, the army did not grasp the emotional consequences of the war on its combatants. Soon, the indicators of Post-Traumatic Stress Disorder (PTSD), manifested so conspicuously, that daily there were reports of soldiers involved in affray and assault of civilians. The troops morphed into a nuisance that made them individually and collectively erratic and disruptive on occasion.

The Scars You Cannot See

The army job was fraught with complications, as its main articles of trade i.e., the management of violence and war were complex. Whereas there could be a definite start point, the terminal point was undefined. By design, every activity and exercise, was a drill. In marching, as in going to war or any form of combat, there were routines and firm procedures that were adhered to. If all went well, things worked according to plan.

Otherwise, one could as well come out of it in a disorderly manner. It never really mattered, if troops engaged or disengaged in a tidy manner or were dislodged by forced rear-guard action. What counted was that a semblance of a process was adhered to before, during, and after operations.

Therefore, after the war it was expected that therapeutic measures would be put in place to ensure the ex-combatants were clinically managed against anxiety, nightmares, and depression. Overall, the health of the troops needed to be evaluated before being reunited with their families or reintegrated into the larger society. Even worse, the Nigerian Army then knew little or nothing about the impact of combat actions on the surviving troops.

After the Nigerian Civil War (6 July 1967-15 January 1970), the Nigerian Army did not de-induct i.e., to recalibrate its ex-combatants away from a belligerent stance. The surrender of Biafra was imminent but when it came, it was rather abrupt. At that point, countless combatants were still hunkered down and skirmishing in murderous trenches when the hostilities ceased. Again, since the Nigerian civil war stopped on all fronts without any further pressure on the service, there was a lot of paper over of crucial post-war therapies, the most prominent of which was the negligent management of PTSD.

According to research findings, PTSD developed in individuals who experienced shocking, scary, or dangerous events. Selectively though, certain categories of individuals or groups were identified as being at risk; particularly combat-hardened military personnel, victims of violent crimes, and natural disasters and occasionally emergency workers. It was also a condition that could be triggered by occurrences that involved death, severe injury, or such threats to others. Such incidents induced intense fear, horror, or the feeling of powerlessness which led most people to anxiety reactions after the shock.[2]

Further studies also revealed that the gestation period of the malaise could be as short as a few months or might take years, long after the event. In general terms, its symptoms presented as an inability to engage in ordinary daily tasks like going to work, school, or socializing with people, or in extreme cases, even family members.[3]

This phenomenon was observed in other armies too, as it was discovered that when soldiers disengaged from the fronts, they exhibited dangerous and injurious behaviours. The antics displayed constituted risks, not only to themselves but to innocent persons and the society at large as they inserted themselves in visibly perilous situations.[4]

In the immediate aftermath of the war, everywhere ex-combatants clustered, they picked up fights among themselves and against others. Perhaps, these were attempts to recreate the chaotic feel of combat zones since brawling was identified as a typical symptom of embryonic PTSD. Unfortunately, their conditions were improperly diagnosed and in time degenerated into a situation by which soldiers systematically assaulted their spouses, children, wards, and the civilian public.[5]

The malady persisted in the ranks of the NA from 1970 into the early 1980s until death, insanity, and renewed enlistment into the service significantly diluted the disorder. It was one of the probable causes of the caustic liaison between "bloody" civilians and soldiers. Overwhelmingly, it was a situation driven by mental disorders that needed clinical support but regrettably, none came the way of the ailing ex-combatants. Funnily or tragically, as the condition persisted, the soldiers contrived dubious camaraderie executed by mob actions, or bouts of free-for-alls without questions, and many got involved in reprisal actions over perceived infractions.

All along, the underlying triggers were edgy and visibly intoxicated soldiers being nasty or on illegal duties. So, when the public complained about assaults by service personnel, they were not mindful to factor in PTSD occasioned by the recent exposure of the ex-combatants to the just-decided war. The situation was that bad. Sure enough, there may have been isolated cases of soldiers' cruelty in the pre-war period, but this escalated after the war.

Again, at the end of the hostilities, there were between eighty to two hundred and fifty thousand ex-combatants that were lately involved in the war.[6] Regrettably, there was neither counselling nor therapy nor demobilization by which time the ex-combatants embedded themselves to the woe of the larger society.

The fallout was that the level of domestic violence perpetrated was on an institutional scale. Soldiers pummeled their wives; who in turn savagely whipped their children or wards in reprisals. Like I said, for every conceivable reason, I expected a heavy knock on the head or slapped furiously or whipped. The beating became so central in my relationship with my guardian that I became uneasy and sore in his presence. The severity of the physical buffeting got me downhill into progressive timidity and I emaciated rapidly.

A nightmare I endured was bedwetting. For bed, I slept on a mat in the tiny living room. However, at over five years old, I was still bedwetting. It was a personal shame that persisted for a long time as every night's sleep turned into an early morning dose of scourging. As certainly as I knew I would bed wet, assuredly I knew I would get a hiding early in the mornings.

Well, I did not feel ill at ease to talk about my affliction because I overcame it. It was not until very much later that I discovered that I was prone to urinary incontinence, and it took ages for me to be able to control a situation that thoroughly embarrassed me.

Pupil Teachers and Babel Schools

At about six years of age, a child should be in school, but it was not to be for children of my generation. As late as the 1970s, western education was still a novelty among my Tiv people. Apart from Native Authority schools that were few and far apart in the Tiv Division, the bulk of the schools were Christian missionary owned. The Roman Catholic Mission (RCM) and Nongo u Kristu u ken Sudan hen Tiv (NKST), set up primary and later secondary schools. In my hometown though, the NKST church owned a Christian Reformed Institute (CRI), also called Babel (Bible) School that was predictably, staffed by pupil-teachers as a preparatory school. The pupils took classes under a thatched shed attached to the church.

It still baffles me that it never occurred to anyone to enroll me at the school. Well, part of the problem was the requirements to register. Unlike these days that one-year-old babies go to school, in those days, a pupil's hand astride the head grabbed the earlobe at the opposite end of their head to be eligible for enrolment. It was indeed such an odd but ingenious criterion that was logical because I believe, there was a nexus between age, aptitude, and skills acquisition. Simply told, I was unqualified.

Another intervening factor was labour. A typical Tiv household was engaged in manual farm work and the labour was gotten from the joint services of wives and children. Inconveniently too, regular school hours coincided with the period all hands were needed on the farms. As a result, enrolment at schools was incredibly low and further aggravated by the fees demanded.

By early 1970, I was eager to go to school, so I regularly hung outside the classroom as pupils were instructed. During breaks and manual labour periods, I joined and took part. Awkwardly, it was a long wait before I finally enrolled at a school far away from my hometown.

Learning by Singing

By April 1971, I began my elementary school at St John's Primary School Agbani. It was a miracle that I was able to learn at all during my first year at school. For when I was moved from a rustic Tiv village to Agbani in the heart of Igbo country, I spoke only the Tiv language, no English much less Igbo. My guardian led me to the headmaster's office, and after a short exchange, I was handed over and assigned a class which was the open hall of St. John's Catholic Church. Inside its bowel was a din as pupils in groups of twenty to thirty chattered excitedly, and it was into one such group of young pupils, I was ushered. It was obvious that in my new cluster, none was more than five years of age.

From the excitement of the pupils, I presumed that it was the commencement of a new school year. Nervous amid my new group, I felt like a cornered bunny with anxiety all over me. Then suddenly, a school bell rang, and hell broke loose when all the pupils shouted at the top of their voices and charged towards the church exits, it was dismissal time. On my first day at school, there were no lessons.

The next morning, as I headed to school, my minder handed me a black slate and a piece of white chalk. Those constituted my first set of writing tools and I set off and went to my allotted group and section in the church and sat down. However, I noted that none of the pupils were seated, as each dropped their slates and went out again. Swimming against the tide, I collected myself and went out and joined the others. We swept and picked pieces of paper strewn all over and tidied the schoolyard.

The school bell rang again but this time, all the pupils clustered at the main entrance of the church and covered up orderly. Men and women stood in front, possibly the teachers, and the headmaster led the morning devotion at the assembly. I did not understand a word of what was said. After a session of raucous singing, chants, and recitations the assembly broke up and we walked in a single file into our classrooms.

The seating arrangement was simple; there were rows of benches facing the teacher's desk and a blackboard suspended on a tripod contraption. I snugly settled down. The teacher, a lady, stood in front of the group and started her lesson. She spoke in Igbo, the then introductory language of instruction in Eastern Nigeria. I did not understand a word as she rambled on, punctuated by responses from the other pupils. Left to me, she could as well have been speaking Greek or any other such arcane language. She spoke, gesticulated, and made inscriptions on the board. There was no diffusion because I saw and heard her but could not understand.

All I did was to steel myself and pay attention in vain. She went to the board, inscribed some more stripes, and stood aside for a while and I saw my fellows scribbled on their miniature boards too. I just sat doing nothing. The lady started making the rounds and came to a halt directly in my front. She noticed I was not writing and launched into a harangue that lasted the world.

From the tone of her monologue, I supposed that she must have been asking questions. This encounter became a redeeming moment for me because the teacher had just made a great discovery that one of her pupils was unteachable. After this moment, she deployed all her didactic ingenuity as well as her expansive patience to find ways to help me. If she had not accepted the reality of my predicament, I would not have gotten educated.

During the lessons, we counted and recited, through the medium of singing. Without knowing what it was I sang about, I mumbled through the rhymes. The counting went thus:

One-Ofu

Two-Abua

Three-Ito

Four-Ino

Five-Ise

Ten-Iri

Twenty-Ogu etc.

During the second part of the instructional session, pupils approached the teacher seated at her desk and presented their boards for assessment. She appended an X for wrong and a tick for correct. For as many times as I presented my board, that number of times I scored an X. These marked boards, the pupils took home to their parents or minders for perusal. For all I remember, I kept arriving home with an X-marked board from my earliest days as a pupil at school. Then one day out of exasperation, my teacher ticked a good for me. By that singular act, she spurred me into self-belief, and I eventually got educated.

To capture my confounded state during my first year at school, I do not recall any of my classmates, their names nor even the name of the good lady who gifted me education. I could have returned to my hometown to start all over again, but the foundation was important. Eventually, my time at Agbani ended as the unit moved to Agbogugu in August 1971.

All Things Makeshift and Ugly

Agbogugu was a smaller settlement compared to Agbani. The village had a grove-like market and, a few homesteads rectilinearly situated along Nenwe road. The main landmark was St Vincent's Cathedral, an Anglican Mission Centre. The cathedral ran a group of schools which included St Vincent's Secondary School and a Primary School. Collectively, the complex made up one-half of Agbogugu as of August 1971.

The barracks was situated west of the settlement on a low plateau which flattened out at an elevation of about six hundred metres above the sea level. It was a vast ground split naturally into two equal halves, the southern Mammy Market end, and the Northern Downhill Barracks.

It was a standard practice during the war that redundant and degraded units were coalesced. In fact, 130 Battalion was such a unit. These units shared a common process of formation as troops were cobbled from odds and ends. Typically, units either depleted, split, or had fallen understrength due to combat action. The gravity of this fragmentations was substantial and at the end of the fighting, loose detachments, stragglers, and the like were fused with units found closest to them.

At Agbogugu too, it was the same makeshift situation, as it was at Agbani. But again, the army had fewer barracks back then. Apart from army camps inherited by Queen's Own Nigeria Regiment from Royal West African Frontier Force (RWAFF), in Lagos (An, Myhoung, Abalti, Tego, Arakan and Ikeja barracks); Kaduna (81 aka Ribadu Cantonment and Dalet Barracks), Kano (Bukavu) and the Enugu barracks, there were no newly constructed barracks until the 1970s.

The trend by which units ran out of provisional and requisitioned properties became a long-standing policy of the service. It was a time-worn approach by which the authorities requisitioned or leased a piece of land or property, then built temporary structures where troops camped. Routinely, soldiers were individually allotted plots in a layout and design by which a mud house or an adobe structure was hastily erected. If the command was benevolent, building materials like cement and roofing sheets were issued at a fee, to hasten the process of constructing those squalid and unsightly contraptions.

The legal drawbacks to these provisional arrangements were that the finer details of the land and property transactions were not mutually agreed upon and the terms of tenancy were most often indeterminate. As a result, the service suffered as it did not embark on long-term programs as no new barracks were constructed. On the other hand, the owners also lost income or returns on their lands and properties.

Worse still, as an organization, the NA was an undesirable tenant as it habitually never paid rent promptly, i.e., if it ever paid at all. It took ages to process rental fees due to the web of official bureaucracy. To compound its reputation as bad tenants, they were not easily evicted from such lands or properties. As a result, countless lessors did not get paid and died awaiting their claims. Even when they got paid, cases of short payment were reported because apart from certain individuals, nobody could tell what sums were factored in.

Furthermore, the lacuna created by the unclear terms of tenancy and pointless delays in payments were seized upon by speculators, dubious lawyers, dishonest community leaders, and other undeserving conspirators, with the active connivance of the responsible people, regularly embezzled the proceeds, especially in cases of communally held lands.[7] Hence, no new barracks were delivered even as the civil war had significantly distended the strength of the NA.

This kind of fluid approach ushered in the era of ramshackle personnel-built contraptions in the name of barracks. But for the spectacle, here lay a sprawl of rows and rows of hastily and shoddily constructed mud structures. They were a garish sight indeed and effectually shanty towns. These encampments shorn of all trappings of niceties and finesse were practical thingamajigs in which the victorious army and their families would live and die for the glory of the fatherland.

The administrative complex was located mid-section of the barracks, consisting of two long blocks of offices, a Motor Transport Yard, a Parade, and Sports Grounds. The Northern End was the newer part of the barracks. However, here too, the structures were temporarily built with plywood and composed of rows of two-room blocks arranged by sub-units i.e., companies. The spatial zoning of the layout showed a quantum of clear thinking. Nonetheless, the troops were hurriedly moved before the completion of these makeshift structures.

The soldiers and their families had to improvise with ceiling boards and whatever articles found on site to partition their rooms. Later, contractors completed the works, and the occupants were surcharged about Seven Pounds (£7.00) each, an extortion that existed in one form or the other, at various levels throughout the army.[8]

The barracks at Agbogugu was a large and isolated community but its population and relative economic wherewithal became a stimulant to the surrounding area. It was the focal point of socio-economic activities as locals and soldiers alike patronized it. Such markets were an indispensable part of any military camp.

To Kill a Market

From the first mammy market I encountered at Agbogugu and later at other barracks, they were ancillary premises occasioned by the presence of military cantonments. Although controlled, the markets, have remained a veritable source of pepper soup, ladies of easy virtue, and alcohol in its entire spectrum. Other activities included pool betting, and sales of suya, dog meat, cannabis, and other narcotics. They were also safe havens for fugitives and a first point of call for many new entrants into cities.

Mammy markets were socio-economically central to the activities of military locations and variants could be either residential or non-residential. These markets likewise served as sanctuaries against forced temperance, and pseudo-religious narrow-mindedness that inundated our political space lately. Over the years, the military authorities made futile attempts to curtail these markets, but they still had wider appeal and greater pull than the members-only Officers' Messes and Other Ranks Clubs.

During my time at Agbogugu, I finally crystallized and became fully conscious of myself and my surroundings. The insular character of the barracks set me on the path to improving my communication skills. By now I spoke a smattering of pidgin English and Hausa which were and still are the most common languages used in Nigeria's military circles. It was here too that core military activities like tattoos, manual labour aka fatigue, drills, and other related routines could be observed.

Further north, on the way to Four Corner, was a big stream to which we went swimming, laundering, and drawing water for domestic use. Besides, the unit command deserved praise because it deployed water tankers to ferry water to the barracks. But then again, the effort could not effectively cover the demand of all barracks residents. So, going down to the stream to fetch water became a daily routine.

A Touch of Parsimony

In those days, when I lived among soldiers, there was always a unit kitchen. The 130 Battalion kitchen was located just behind our block. It was the most fascinating facility on offer, from a child's perspective. Up to that point, the army still fed its troops from a common pot.

In the main, I found it strange that men were cooking because before now, I had associated cooking with women only. But daily, on wood-fueled open fires, the chief cook, one Corporal Sunday, supervised a retinue of sweaty soldiers that prepared breakfast, lunch, and dinner to which the troops and their families went to feed communally. Apart from tea and bread, and corn gruel (akamu) served with bean cake (akara), which were wholesome meals, the garri (eba), jollof rice, yam, and beans were cooked into unpalatable concoctions of which much ended up trashed.

But then a substantial number of the troops did not partake in the fair except for their children and wards. This perpetually hungry class of barrack associates, with religious passion, patronized the kitchen in droves, especially for the daily bread. Unfortunately, the cooking never improved and due to wastefulness and alleged rising costs, the kitchen system was scrapped in the service.

Was it not a wonder that the Nigerian Army, with inadequate resources and just coming out of a materially draining war was more humanely disposed to communally feed its troops? Regrettably, when a new crop of leadership inherited the system, greed and lack of compassion were invested. So, instead of improving on the cooking standards of the kitchen system and cutting the discernibly wasteful aspects, the authorities in one swoop abrogated the unit kitchen and, in its place, instituted the dubious and easily manipulated Ration Cash Allowance (RCA).

Uniformity and Accountability

On all occasions, the troops were fully kitted. If soldiers went out for games or drills, they were uniformly equipped. There was no jumble, or an assortment of uniforms worn nowadays by troops. The key to this functional system was the Quartermaster Department (QM Dept).

The QM Dept was the logistic heart of a unit. The department supplied food, uniforms, and accommodation to the troops. It also held in stock such consumables necessary for the efficient running of a unit. If the branch was efficient, it reflected on the general turnout of personnel and other related minor elements in a unit.

As of 1972, the QM Dept of130 Battalion was very functional. The system worked because soldiers presented worn-out items at the store and got high-grade replacements. Also, from the stores materialized white branded army towels routinely distributed to the troops. Even children got a replacement if they took worn items to the QM store because the operational principle was utility and accountability not hoarding.

It was the same with other military items like boot rags, polish, brushes, brown canvases, worsted stockings, green vests, PT shorts and uniforms. For instance, beat-up uniforms were instantaneously replaced, with readymade uniforms and not drapes of materials. It was unlike the widespread practice during my years in service, officers and soldiers neither bought uniforms nor other military kits.

Minimalist Indirect Rule

Living in a barrack, it did not take long before I had a glimpse of the mechanics of military hierarchy. Apart from the concentration camp-like spatial arrangement of subunits and control over personnel, there was a marked chain of command as power radiated from the top down. The administrative approach by nature was minimalist and indirect as power diffused from the commanding officer (CO), through company officers (OCs), senior non-commissioned officers (SNCOs) to block non-commissioned officers (NCOs) and women leaders called Magajiyas. The unit adjutant coordinated the varied departments and personnel. In general, the CO and commissioned officers were a rare sight and not easily seen in the unit.

It was more common to come across the Regimental Sergeant Major (RSM) and Regimental Provosts (RPs). These were the enforcers and the face of the authority. The team dictated the rhythm of the unit. Thus, a hierarchy of graduated authority, at all levels, was established.

School at Agbogugu

There was no primary school, not even the ubiquitous Army Children School (ACS) at the unit location. Consequently, the entire school-age children enrolled at the school closest to the unit, which was St Vincent's Primary School Agbogugu. Unlike at Agbani where my guardian led me to my new school, I went along with one Nathaniel, who may have been twelve years or thereabout.

By some prior arrangement, all were speedily enrolled because the school authorities knew of the new military unit in the neighbourhood. The school was about four kilometres away from the barracks, a distance we trekked daily. We all coped well and soon started exploring the surrounding areas too.

Adjoining the school was a large poultry farm and St Vincent's Secondary School that shared common playgrounds with the primary school. It was here that I first saw the physical scarification of the war because Agbogugu was the first alternate capital of Biafra when Enugu fell to Federal troops in 1967, before its final relocation to Umuahia.

The village lay about forty-five kilometres southeast of Enugu along Four Corner-Nenwe Road. The lie of the ground was suitable, and the joint cathedral and school complexes were excellent infrastructure for a field capital in transit. From the relics spotted all around, it was obvious that Agbogugu had been a scene of heavy fighting as copious quantities of expended ammo shells of different calibres were strewn all over the place.

The poultry farm buildings had pockmarks, and the road to the school grounds was littered with empty shells and even more within the school complex. Innocently, we frolicked all over the place, but providentially no unexploded ordnances ever detonated. It was a credit to the belligerents that none resorted to the indiscriminate use of deadly landmines

Along the road was a hulk of a Biafran Red Devil, an ingenious piece of equipment fabricated by the operatives of the legendary Biafran Research and Production (RAP) Unit. On closer scrutiny, it was a farm tractor swathed in thick metal sheet on which high calibre machine guns (MG) were mounted. Apart from mobility, it offered limited cover from fire but was vulnerable at close quarter. It was sad that a victorious Nigeria thought little of the creative genius of RAP.

At the stream, it could be seen that Biafran Army Engineers had demolished the concrete span of the bridge. In its place, their NA counterparts had superimposed a Bailey bridge on the surviving piers. There was so much evidence of the past war abound.

My time at Agbogugu was over as by mid-1972,and this coincided the visit of my other sibling, Orvendega, my guardian's immediate younger brother. From the striking resemblance between them I knew we were related otherwise; I had never met him before now too. I was away at school when he arrived. When I got home, we met. But I could see he was melancholic because I was a little withered and adorned in rags.

Lessons in Undressing

A lot of people might not be aware that children decked in rags were and are still a common sight in army barracks. The troops that fought in the civil war, collectively known as NA and 63NA soldiers, did not bother about their wardrobes. Since soldiers wore uniforms all the time, the result was a deficit of civil dresses. The troops ensured they owned all the numbered dresses, i.e., uniforms associated with specific functions including numbers one through six dresses but were bereft of mufti.

Although over time, later generations of recruits marginally altered this trend as I wrote, on the aggregate, servicemen owned more military uniforms than civil outfits. In this way, soldiers appeared drab out of uniform and their children and wards were universally clad in rags. There were hardly any barrack children who wore complete dresses. If the shirt, always without buttons held, the bottom was sure to be tattered, and vice versa. Even worse, most had no uniforms and went to school in those same rags. Folks who have been in uniform-attired professions appreciate the invasive influence of the uniform.

It was obvious that Orvendega was not comfortable with the rags, more so, I looked scrawny. However, I was thoroughly amused by the scenario because it was not strange to us barrack children. All said, I was not even an accomplished raggist. We had unanimously reserved that honour for a boy named Bulus. He was the greatest when it came to arranging his multi-layered folds of rags. Whether he discussed his misgivings with Sale I could not tell.

Not long after Orvendega left, I was told of my imminent return to Kyado by August 1972. The battalion was to be moved to Keffi or whatever. Once again, I was reunited with my mother. She held onto me and examined every inch of my rickety structure contorting her face. She never uttered a word, but her countenance and body language expressed suppressed anger and deep pain. From late 1972 through August 1974, I stayed in the village until I re-joined my serviceman brother again to resume the second and final phase of my life as a barrack boy.

Notes

(1). Despite the ongoing Biafran War on 19 April 1969, then-Nigerian Head of State, Major-General Yakubu Gowon, married Ms. Victoria Zakari at the Christ Church Cathedral, Lagos.

(2). For insight on PTSD read literature from: The National Institute of Mental Health (NIMH) is part of NIH, a part of the U.S. Department of Health and Human Services.

(3-6). https://www.ptsd.va.gov/(7). My guardian told me this.

Chapter Four

Kyado 1972

I was home once again, but the village was not any different from what it had been when I left over a year earlier. Naturally, I became a centre of attraction to my mates. By now, I spoke a smattering of pidgin English, Igbo, and Hausa languages and took time regaling my fellows about the strange places I had been to, stories I told repeatedly with portions embellished. It was amazing when I engaged traders switching from pidgin English to Igbo language.

The only downside to my newfound fame was my dresses. Friends had expected me to change dresses more often, but it never happened. So, I kept exchanging one rag for another, until my father replenished my depleted collection of rags with second-hand clothes.

When I returned, my elder brother, Vihimga, enrolled me at Roman Catholic Mission (RCM) School, Akaa, which was about seven kilometres south of Kyado, along Zaki Biam road. As of 1972, there was still no elementary school in Kyado village, and the existing Babel school remained officially unrecognized. An alternative was the NKST Primary School, Pevikyaa about eight kilometres due north of the village.

RCM Primary School Akaa 1972

In 1972, RCM Primary School Akaa ran out of a pair of 2-classroom blocks, one lined behind the other. In between the buildings, thatched sheds were erected. The school had a large expansive compound with well-designated muster and playgrounds. I was taken to the headmaster's office and after a brief chat during which I was repeatedly looked at and ignored; I was eventually accepted and assigned to Primary Two.

I do not recollect whether any school fee was paid but before I was led out of the office, the headmaster reached a locker and brought out four exercise books namely 2A for Composition, 2B for Arithmetic, 2D for Writing, and 2E for Drawing along with a pencil, an eraser and a ruler which were handed to me. The truth was that under the Local Education Authority, schools were better supplied. Obviously, there was no motivation for the headmaster to appropriate the instructional materials in his care. The beauty of it all was that you could replace used exercise books at the same headmaster's office from time to time.

A shack in the name of a classroom harboured primary two pupils. The class composed of thirty-five boys, and a solitary girl. The structure had no outer walls, and its floor was uncompacted. In place of desks and chairs, were seats fashioned out of logs suspended on forked stands arranged in rows facing a blackboard which itself hung from a tripod. Writing from these seats became a challenge as pupils placed books on their laps and wrote in hunched positions which may have been the cause of my appalling handwriting.

As early as 0600hrs each morning, we left home in little groups and headed to school. Along the route, more children coalesced from adjoining footpaths and soon a steady stream of pupils flowed towards the school. Each day we followed a routine as pupils worked on a portion earlier assigned to them, in an area of the school, either to sweep or brush.

Afterward, we marched to drumbeats and flutes and formed up for morning assembly. The headmaster always issued exhortations and led the morning devotion. Subsequently, all dispersed into the classrooms and the day's business started.

At Akaa too, I had a second run-in with a language obstacle. From my first entanglement with the Igbo language at Agbani, back home, I had a challenge with hardcore Tiv language, my native tongue. At just five, I was uprooted and returned after a year, so by now, I was more comfortable with pidgin English than Tiv language. The first few months at my new school were therefore as bewildering as my earlier experience, and as a result, I failed my first examinations.

Meanwhile, the school authorities adopted a very harrowing method of broadcasting exam results. With hindsight, I presume it was meant to humiliate and inspire at the same time. So, the whole school assembled, and the teachers called the results one class after the other. If your name was not called out from the roster, it meant you had failed.

I never heard mine, so I presumed I had failed for that term but subsequently passed all my exams.

To the best of my knowledge, most pupils came to school on an empty stomach. There were neither lunch boxes nor snack packs of today. However, once in a long while, you got a penny from your mother, dad or wherever, which was employed to the greatest utility at the school vendors.

Tucked away to the south end of the school under a great mango tree was the open market run by food vendors. About everything in the local cuisine was on the menu. Pupils converged at the vendors during breaks. However, not until the food captain dutifully tasted a morsel from each of the pots and certified them wholesome, did pupils patronize.

Occasionally, some pupils had money, but a sizeable number had nothing, so during break times, most played rag footballs on the green patches abound. Still, more milled around and surveyed the arena closely. As soon as someone bought food, a multitude converged on the hard-pressed fellow begging for a bite or crumb.

While my elder brother was still around, to stave off this invasion, he would buy food for me and have me crouch in front of him to eat. All this time, he stood over me with a cane. Naturally, the urchins dared not come close. Funnily, I was most uncomfortable but at least I enjoyed my fair without unnecessary distractions.

Very worrisome too, was the state of the pupils' hygiene and health. Lots of the children came to school unkempt and covered in rashes, scabies, and even the nauseous guinea worm infections. Although, the teachers tried to impose a level of personal hygiene by physical checks in the mornings, which they complemented with generous whacks and irregular patterns, carved on bushy hairs.

Child Labour

Back then, it was a norm for pupils to work on teachers' farms. All the teachers were residents within the school premises and engaged in gardening or farming. It could be a small rice plot, cassava, or groundnuts, but yam farms were predominant.

There were lazy days on the school calendar. After weeks of intense tutorials, one of those lazy days crept in. Typically, the headmaster proclaimed a manual labour day. Wherein, all arrived the next day armed with hoes and cutlasses. While some pupils brushed and weeded the school grounds, others were dispatched to teachers' farms.

On the other hand, the teachers could also order pupils to a farm plot after school hours. This was frequently done, and I felt then and as now that, it was too demanding on minors between the ages of six and ten years to be made to work so hard after a long day at school.

One afternoon in early 1974, our class was sent, to work on our teacher's farm, incidentally she was the headmaster's wife. It was a cassava plot, so while weeding and chatting animatedly with my fellows, I comically declaimed that I had used my money to buy hard labour, in reference to the school fees we paid and the resultant unrequited labour. Lo, and behold, madam was making the round in the farm and was right by my side and overheard me. She became visibly angry and known for her dexterity with the cane, she thrashed me lengthily.

Otherwise, the curriculum at the school was engaging and well-rounded with subjects like Singing, Handcraft, Hygiene, Arithmetic, English and Tiv languages and Social Studies. There were extra-curricular activities that kept us engaged and we enjoyed being at school.

Basic Airborne Course 1994

Chapter Five

Keffi 1974

Yet again, I would go to live with my soldier sibling from mid-1974. This time it was at Keffi, a historic town in north-central Nigeria. I do not know the terms of settlement under which a decision was made because as a minor I was not consulted. If I were, the outcome would have been definitely different. But I was not and had to accept the decision as it came.

All I recalled was that my mother called me to her side and then got a calabash bow filled with water and performed a ritual. At that time, I did not instantaneously appreciate the significance of the ceremony. First, she filled her mouth with water and sprayed it out while muttering in a low tone. She repeated the same motions thrice after which she used the remaining water to wash my feet.

Then I was too young to understand, yet my mom had just enacted an ancient Tiv rite. Since she was a steadfast Christian, I did not expect her to invoke what was a profoundly pagan ritual. It was long after, that I got to understand the significance of that solemn act in 1974. The spraying part meant she was releasing herself from an avowal.

When I interviewed her years later, she told me that when I returned after my first stint as a ward to my brother; she was horrified by my haggardly state and swore she would not allow me back in his care again. It took convincing before she acceded and therefore, she needed to ritually vitiate her decree otherwise something untoward happened to me on its account.

Washing my feet was an act of consecration against misfortunes. The enactment was akin to conjuring protective spirits, i.e., casting and binding all evil forces that lurked everywhere, planned, or incidental, against yours sincerely. It was also to ensure good luck in all my efforts and bountiful favours from all I came across. It was obvious that her maternal petition was granted, and it became the basis for my survival in the face of many torments and machinations I encountered at various stages of my life.

Inherited Ruins

On the eve of the 1973 National Population Census, 130 Battalion was moved once again, this time from Agbogugu to Jerme near Keffi. The barracks at Jerme was not any different from the caricature in Agbogugu. It was the same old story of a vast land leased with a layout hastily drafted and few edifices put up without conveniences and amenities. The new location had hosted 46 Battalion previously and graciously, the disbanded unit left behind shells of adobe structures which the incoming unit inherited.[1]

Curiously, troops moved into the location first and later returned to fetch their families. For a second time, I saw a situation where soldiers constructed their living quarters. Remarkably, at Jerme barrack, it was larger and more tasteless than the former location at Agbogugu. It was pertinent to point out that, the relocation of troops on such a large scale was not an incidental event, but a policy decision that called for adequate pre-planning.

Fair enough, at the end of the civil war, it was excusable to conduct such hasty removals due to the exigencies of restructuring and paucity of funds. But by 1973, it was an act of official arbitrariness and sheer insolence to move troops and their families only to deposit them in the middle of a remote location with little or no infrastructure or amenities.

Hence, common services like schools and hospitals were in Keffi town about eight kilometres away from the unit location. To stretch the gracelessness, contractors were engaged to supply timber and roofing sheets for which the authorities illegally surcharged soldiers, Fifteen Naira, which was paid in two instalments.[2]

As of 1974, there was an Army Children's School at the unit. However, the school was meant for younger pupils so older children and wards enrolled at schools in Keffi town and outlying villages. A sizeable number of pupils registered at St Williams, Baptist, Ahmadu Maikwato, Abdu Zanga, and Islamiyah in Keffi town, while others went to Marke and Sabon Gida primary schools in the direction of Akwanga town. So, every morning, we trekked eight kilometres to Keffi and for those at St Williams, an added three kilometres.

At this unit too, it was ominous that the administrative and logistical glitches that would bedevil the post-civil war Nigerian Army were beginning to present. The inherited colonial troops known as NA and 63NA were still active after the Civil War. By now, infractions and laxity against military discipline manifested in the unit and across the service.[3] The drift was gradual, but it was noticed that there were increased cases of drunkenness, Away Without Official Leave (AWOL), indebtedness, shabbiness, and desertion among the troops.

Desertion was particularly high and funnily, the deserters would be exploited by the negative ingenuity of army pay personnel. It was glaring that systemic decay had set in and became a trend that continued relentlessly and by the 1990s, the Nigerian Army was in near shambles.

Also in 1974, a special enlistment of Grade Two teachers into the Education Section was conducted. It was an exercise limited in scope and it appeared there were neither emphasis on the age nor carriage of the recruits, as they were never any younger than the older troops.[4]

A Curst Blessing

Back in the 1970s, the salaries of public servants were quite derisory. In the army then, officers and soldiers managed to survive on incredibly low take-home packets that could barely cater for their needs. Therefore, military personnel resorted to borrowing to augment the ridiculous salaries. From the flood of creditors that besieged the unit HQ on paydays; it was clear that a greater percentage of the troops were perpetually in someone's debt.

Consequently, in 1974, the Nigerian government contemplated a review of salaries through a welfare package known as the Udoji Award, or formally the Jerome Udoji Commission (Nigerian Public Service Reforms 1974). The review was a compassionate public gesture by the government of the day to shore up the poor wages in public service.[5]

Regrettably, the machinations of traders and speculators ruined the policy. The awards were pounced upon by mercantilist intrigues and overwhelmed by an induced inflationary spiral unprecedented in the annals of the country. It was a distasteful tendency that would recur against all palliative policies in Nigeria.

St Williams Keffi

I was enrolled at St Williams Primary School Keffi, and spent August 1974 through July 1975, studiously attending classes but once again, barely clad. Most pupils wore no shoes, not even slippers (flip-flops). An incident in 1975, although hilariously distressing, I remember. For over six months at a new school, I went without the prescribed school uniform and periodically suffered the indignity of being scourged for this infraction during morning assemblies.

Then one day my guardian sent me to a tailor, so he could make a school uniform for me. It took five weeks for the tailor to sew the garment and I wore it to school. When I sauntered into the classroom that morning there was an uproar. I did not expect that on account of wearing a new uniform, I would excite a commotion.

The whole class erupted in mock cheers as fellows came forward to congratulate me on my new apparel. I endured the comic relief since I had spent half of the school year coming to class clad in rags. With a benefit of hindsight, I could not fault my guardian because there was no pressing need for him to do so. It was an unrealistic demand to make of a soldier with a scanty wardrobe to do otherwise.

So, daily in the mornings and afternoons, we trekked the long distances. Possibly, because we were so young, we endured and even enjoyed it. However, I got a reprieve in early 1975, because my guardian travelled home on annual leave pass, and was left in the care of his friend resident in the town. It was a relief, i.e., from walking the long distance to school, I took a short leisurely hike of about three kilometres.

Living in Keffi town now and having abundant free time on hand, I explored the nooks and crannies of the historic town. Always a posse, we scoured Antau, a stream in the town and made a point of repeatedly scaling the knoll near the Emir's palace, the summit at which Captain Maloney, killed by Dan Magajin Yamusa, was buried in 1904.[6]

Unlike the barracks, the townsfolk suffered extreme water shortages. The barracks for all its inadequacies was strategically sited close to a stream by a waterworks that served Keffi town. The dammed section of the stream was large and retained water all year round. It was at this river that the barrack residents got water.

A memorable event of that year was the visit of General Yakubu Gowon. The then Nigeria's Head of State literarily dropped out of the sky when he emerged from one of two helicopters that landed at the unit parade ground. From the apparition of two helicopters landing in the unit location, was the startling appearance of the leader himself. There he stood amid the swelling number of troops and their families, bereft of any stifling security detail.

It was surreal, considering the remoteness of the unit and the unannounced visit. No one, not even the Commanding Officer, was forewarned. It was a spontaneous carnival which the troops and their families relished. The visit lasted about forty-five minutes and he left. This flying visit generated excitement among the troops. However, on 29 July 1975, Gowon's regime was overthrown in a military coup by Brigadier Murtala Mohammed, who led a new regime that lasted a short and turbulent six months.

As a kid, General Gowon appeared to me as a beloved and humanized leader. I first saw him in 1970, when he embarked on an extended drive along the dusty road running through my village at the end of the civil war. I felt intensely for him, and although I never quite understood the underlying reasons for his removal, my empathy lay with him.

Mid-1975, my minder switched his service branch from the Infantry to the Military Police, as the section was expanded. To draft qualified personnel as provost officers, all army units were trawled. By this time, I had picked a hushed buzz that the new inductees were to be assembled at First Brigade Minna for training and deployment. An affirmation of this rumour also meant that once again I returned to my hometown.

I was back to the village at the close of the school year. It was a bumpy but thrilling trip. As of 1975, an asphalted road traversed the village, and the pace of life was faster, but the general outline of the settlement remained unchanged.

Kyado 1975

When I returned that year, I was due for enrolment into the sixth grade. There was a choice, to continue at my former school, but instead I was registered at NKST Pevikyaa which lay about seven kilometres north of Kyado. Once more, I trekked a long distance to school.

My new school was NKST Church-owned. It was a Christian mission set up by the Dutch Reformed Church Mission (DRCM) of South Africa. In Tiv Division, the number of Native Authority, later

Local Education Authority (LEA) primary schools, were few and far apart. The first primary school in the division was set up by DRCM at Sai in 1911. In comparison, the other sections of colonial Nigeria had had over eighty years of Western education. It was a trend replicated by the Roman Catholic Mission (RCM), which also set up more primary schools.[7] Once Tiv people began to embrace Western edification, setting up schools was easy for the missionaries and colonial authorities.

In succession, communities freely donated large tracts of land to build schools. Even more, a clutch of communities went a step further to set up community-owned elementary and at the right time high schools. The willingness to cede large tracts of land was a gesture that Christian missions thoroughly abused by encroachment.

The school in Pevikyaa was situated on ample land and made up of three buildings with each aligned in such a way that there was an open space to the frontage of the school. There were two football fields, one to the front and the other to the back of the school. The staff quarters formed a crescent around the school and all teachers were residents on the school grounds. The headteacher also lived on the school compound. Back then, this was how sincerely the primary school system was set up.

In this new place too, it was routine school business as I started in the sixth grade, and things got along well. Later that year, my brother handed me an old Phoenix bicycle. But even before this helpful gesture, my father owned a very high-framed Rudge bicycle and its use depended on his mood. So, comfortably, in my last eighteen months in elementary school, I had a bicycle to overcome the long distance.

Hitching a Horse to a Cart

During the 1976/1977 school calendar, there were two noteworthy historical events. First, the Federal Government of Nigeria introduced the Universal Primary Education (UPE) in 1976. Although regional administrations had experimented with the model in one form or the other, the 1976 scheme had a national outlook.

It was accurately discerned that apart from educational imbalances between the regions, enrolment in primary schools was significantly lower in parts, or all over the country. It was such a stimulating policy, as it tried to address the discrepancies and deficiencies nationwide. It was essentially a freebie scheme during which the enrolment age, was lowered from eight to six years.[8]

From the massive intake and sheer number of eligible pupils, it was quite insightful and successful. However, inadequate preparations preceding the official launch resulted in a poorly executed scheme which showed the planners had put the cart before the horse.

From the glitches observed, it was obvious that the scheme got launched before the enormity of the constraints against its execution were considered.[9] For instance, no new classroom blocks were constructed. There was also no evidence that more teachers were recruited nor trained in advance, for such a massive surge in enrolment that was predicted. Instead, what we saw were thatched sheds hurriedly erected about all primary schools in the locality.

Consequently, when the school year began, it was a bedlam as pupils, reckoned in hundreds of thousands locally, and millions nationwide, overwhelmed the existing schools. The UPE pupils were a spectacle to behold as they were an assortment of unkempt, malnourished, poorly clad, and noticeably underage children, even for the lowered six-year bar. They wore no uniforms, and the parade of rags was beyond description. Intriguingly, the 1976 UPE scheme was slain by its remarkable success. The policy could not manage its outstanding achievement and due to several factors, the remarkable feat of its inaugural year could not be repeated.

There were problems everywhere, particularly with a shortfall of qualified teachers. The volume of enrolment far outstripped the extant teachers. For instance, in most schools, the ratio of teacher to pupils was in the region of 1:100. Such a proportion was not sustainable for effective instruction. To address the gap, the authorities resorted to hiring low-level primary school leavers and high school graduates as auxiliary teachers.[10]

Customarily, to qualify as teachers, individuals had teachers' certifications obtained at dedicated teachers' training colleges or institutes. However, since it took ages (at least five years) to produce qualified teachers, an interim abridged teacher training scheme was set up, by which the unqualified enrolled at teachers' colleges for a two-year remedial programme to receive pedagogical upgrading.[11]

Although the Teacher's Grade Two Certificate may have been a low-level qualification, it was a professional educator certification. The holders were proficient and imparted solid foundational education. Unwittingly though, this sowed the seeds of the coming degeneration of public primary schools in Nigeria.

Lamentably, due to countless challenges and setbacks in implementing the UPE scheme, especially against a backdrop of repeated policy somersaults, the decay of the primary education system set in. Afterwards, public primary schools declined while private schools proliferated. A new system of privately-owned schools run by charlatans, extortionists, swindlers, mercantilists, speculators, magicians and contortionists, etc., demanded and received extortionate fees and an unspecified number of levies.[12]

As things stood, it was amazing how much energy and resources were deployed by parents to send children or wards to some high-end private schools to obtain questionable pseudo-elitist education. In this new dispensation, parents and guardians spent fortunes to educate a child at a low-level elementary school. It was there for all to see that once every quarter of the year, sweaty parents and guardians rallied and sallied to couple tuition fees.

Now, the interrogative. Was it necessary for a toddler's day care or a primary school pupil's tuition fees per term to exceed the parents' income? Why did folks put themselves under so much pressure to get their children or wards educated? I knew that my parents exerted themselves to send me to school, but I would not have supported them if they were deprived and disconcerted to do so, since educating a child was just an aspect of parenting and should not morph into an emotionally and financially draining obsession.

Moreover, I believed the local public schools which most folks in my generation attended, were affordable(almost for free) and quite satisfactory, to the extent that they instituted an edifying foundation that sustained. Also, I strongly felt that a child with the aptitude to learn would do well at the right moment of self-crystallization. Funnily, I watched parents agonize over non-performance of their children or wards, at those expensive schools.

Furthermore, the emergent private schools were fraught with problems, of which the most acute was location. It would appear school proprietors and supervising authorities were unbothered about the location of schools. Negligently, the criterion for an ideal and conducive learning environment were unspecified. So, anywhere, and everywhere schools could be found including spaces near crowded and noisy markets, business districts, busy roads, and other disagreeable spots which impeded pupils' ability to concentrate and learn optimally. Even worse, the amenities at these schools were abysmally substandard. For some high-end schools though, there might be a couple of flashy classroom blocks, majority were cardboards, wood shacks, discarded zinc sheets, stacks of storied buildings, and other indescribable architectural thingies without considerations for traditional playgrounds or open spaces that were essential wherever children were assembled in numbers.

Furthermore, to cut costs, private schools hardly ever employ qualified professional teachers. This was accentuated by the shifting educational policies that scrapped the Teachers' Grade Two Certificates in favour of a grandiose National Certificate of Education. Whereas, Grade Two modules trained teachers at elementary and dedicated colleges, the new pretentious NCE was all-comers' affair.

To compound the situation was the curriculum conundrum. There was no standardized curriculum of study but a bewildering array which included a caricature of the American, an aping of the British, Swiss counterfeit, or poor French imitation. Overall, the impact was an absence of a common Nigerian national syllabus other than a preponderance of half-baked and poorly purloined copies of other well-established educational systems. Unfortunately, this folly spread through high schools, and latterly the university system.

It was such that, today in Nigeria, there were Chinese, Lebanese, Indian, Turkish, Afghan, Iraqi, Cambodian, Tibetan, Mongolian, Korean, and Russian curricula of study, among others. All these worked at cross purposes to the Nigerian national curricula and engendered policy dissonance. Thus, despite the increased cost of education, the contemporary Nigerian child was not in any way better educated than the standard of those who attended public schools three generations ago.

In retrospect, the new-fangled UPE policy with a lowered enrolment age failed because it did not provide for school feeding. It was clear that by 1976, most pupils came to school on an empty stomach. The policymakers did not consider this mundane aspect. Even still, it was not clear if this was an honest omission or lack of compassion, characteristic of public policy in Nigeria.

It was obvious that hunger contributed to the decline of the scheme regardless of its success in the first year. It denuded the eagerness with which the scheme was accepted because the children preferred to remain at home or on the farms with full bellies. More so, there was the wherewithal to cater for at least one mid-day meal which might have sustained the success of the UPE scheme.

End of the Seventh Grade

The second historic event of that school year was the scrapping of the seventh grade in primary schools in the old Northern Region. Before now, unlike elementary schools in the former Western and Eastern regions which ran for six grades, in the old political North, it was seven grades. However, in 1977, there was a joint graduation of primary six and seven pupils and a termination of the latter.

However, if the policy was meant to reduce the disparities in basic education; it created a gridlock of its own. For instance, in most states, the number of prospective entrants into high schools far outstripped available spaces. This led to a forced decision to co-opt private schools into the selection process. Before now, private schools were not in the pool of national common entrances but traditionally conducted their dedicated entrance exams.

By mid-1977, as we prepared to leave elementary school, we took the National Common Entrance Examinations into high schools while other pupils opted for additional entrance tests to private schools. However, due to the shortage of vacancies earlier mentioned, private schools tapped into the excess pool of candidates destined for public schools. Thus, at the venue of interviews, candidates were distributed arbitrarily to interviewing panels that were drawn from public and private schools. By August 1977, I was admitted into Doy Secondary School Harga (DSSH).

Notes

(1). There were traces of the former unit at the location.

(2). My brother told me this fact.

(3). As a barrack boy, I saw shabbily dressed soldiers, drunkenness and neighbours that simply disappeared and never returned.

(4). In 1974, new entrants arrived 130 Bn, they were the butt of jokes because of their carriage and poor military orientation which we noticed even as wards.

(5). For a full account of the Udoji Award see: Udoji Jerome: Under Three Masters: Memoirs of an African Administrator: Spectrum Books, Ibadan, 1995.

(6). To gain an insight on Captain Maloney: Kole Omotosho: Just Before Dawn (Spectrum Books, Lagos, 1988).

(7). For a concise account of schools in Tiv Division see: Tesemchi Makar: The History of Political Change among the Tiv in the 19th and 20th Centuries (Fourth Dimension Publishing Co Ltd, Enugu. 1994). p188.

(8). For an insight into 1976 UPE Scheme see: Adewole, Musiliu, Adeolu and Fadayomi, Theophilus, 1976 Universal Primary Education and Schooling Attainment in Nigeria (November 2015

(9). For accounts of increased enrolment see: Universal Primary Education in Nigeria: Its Problems and Implications: African Studies Review, Vol 26 Issues, March 1983. Pp.91-106.

(10). For challenges of UPE see: Hyattractions: Discuss the Achievements and Problems of Universal Primary Education in Nigeria (December 23, 2017).

(11). African Studies Review, Vol 26 Issues, March 1983. op cit, Pp.91-106.

(12). For accounts of proliferation of private schools see: Path of Science. 2024. Vol 10. No 1.: Echujegahi Anthony Angwaomaodoko: An Analytical Study of the Proliferation of Private Schools in Nigeria.

Sierra Leone 2002

Chapter Six

At a Bush School

Although I was admitted to Doy Secondary School Harga (DSSH), it was not my choice of a high school. For then, all knew it was preferable to go to a government owned institution, if for nothing, for the fact that they were better organized. At that point, as much as my wishes were not met and my lot fell with a privately owned high school, I had to prepare for resumption.

I got my admission letter by post with a list of items to be brought along on resumption. These bits and pieces comprised an iron box, a bucket, two pairs of uniform (white shirts over blue shorts), white trousers and shirt for outing, white canvas shoe, a cutlass, and a small hoe, among others.

The school was founded in 1974 by Daniel Orkuma Yaaya, a barely literate missionary-trained carpenter-cum-entrepreneur. It was located at Harga, a village along Katsina-Ala-Takum Road, which lay within a ring of mountains, with an inselberg soaring over the settlement. On clear days, it was possible to catch glimpses of the peaks of the Cameroon Mountains on Nigeria's eastern border.

Apart from DSSH, the settlement also hosted a missionary outpost of the NKST church. Here, the American Reformed Churches led by Calvin College of Grand Rapids, Michigan, set up a quasi-seminary called Benue Bible Institute (BBI). Indeed, BBI with its serene, well-manicured lawns were a reproduction of an American village right there in the bush.

The resumption date for new intakes was 2 September 1977. However, my father, who accompanied me to report on my first day at high school, ever guarded, insisted I resumed a day earlier and so by Thursday 1st September I reported at DSSH. When we got to the school, there was a lone teacher on ground, who took us in for the night.

Early the next morning, my father returned home, and I went to the halls of residence where my little box and its contents were inspected, and I was assigned to Benue Hostel. By this time, some mates had also resumed and more during the weekend. Incidentally, this marked the first time I was away from home on my own.

Learning with Hard Labour

When I reported to DSSH, we were the fourth intake at the school. The level of physical infrastructure was moderately satisfactory. There were two classroom blocks, an administrative block newly built as well as residences for the students and teachers. The school itself was located on a very expansive stretch of land.

By the succeeding week, school activities were in full swing, and almost all the students had resumed. From our strength, the class was split into two streams i.e., A and B, respectively. I was assigned to Form One A and guardians whom we called masters.

DSSH was a co-educational boarding school. All the staff and students were resident within a two-kilometre radius of the school grounds. The boys' dormitories were to the north of the school while the girls' lay southerly and were superintended over by a boarding master and a matron, in that order.

The dormitories consisted of a long single structure partitioned into four compartments named after prominent local rivers namely Benue, Niger, Katsina-Ala, and later Loko Houses. For bed space, double bunk beds were provided and within those four partitions was engendered a great spirit of rivalry and of identity that suffused the school.

The student leadership at the school was organized along an old-fashioned model. It composed of a Head Boy and Girl supported by prefects with portfolios like Food, Health, Discipline, Labour, and Sports among others. The hierarchy was rounded off with a complement of House Captains and Class Monitors etc., which proved adequate to monitor and control all students' activities.

The student population I guess was slightly greater than two hundred in strength. Although, no perimeter wall delineated the school, but in a short time, it was clear that each one of us had to confine themselves to that patch of ground hosting the school and within which a routine and community developed full of constrictions.

By the time I reported at DSSH, I was four months shy of my thirteenth birthday. Apart from my previous experience with a pecking order in the primary school, being of much younger age, I had not encountered such a confined and structured social order. It was obvious that I had to deploy all my ingenuity to navigate the mordant turbulence of interactions and of association between the junior, always younger and the older senior students.

It was a given that, our seniors at the school were not only physically bigger, but older in every sense of the word. Unmistakably too, they were collectively determined to impart the fact of their superiority to remove every iota of doubt. It was at this boarding school that I began to observe the capricious disposition of individuals.

As we tried to live by the code of absolute seniority, it was not only tedious but garnished with a generous dose of corporal chastisement. Away from home and relatives, it was time to tell apart all the manifold shades of humanity. Soon enough, I discovered people enjoyed inflicting physical and emotional pains on others.

Consequently, the relational maxim of the community that evolved was about the rights of a superior. Every senior student could scourge you at will, at any time and for whatever reasons. They could also task you on errand to carry out an assortment of odd tasks which included washing, fetching water and about any chore of fancy.

The seniors I encountered were a blend of the compassionate, considerate, helpful and inspiring type that could be approachable and friendly. But by the same token, there were bullies and out-and-out mean lot that delighted in causing inconvenience and inflicting pains on their juniors.

The smallish thugs especially those in Forms Two and Three tormented us to no end. What I resented most about this group was the tendency to frequently smack others in the face instead of using a cane to administer corporal punishment, if it was necessary at all. As much as possible, I tried to keep out of their way with little success.

Popularity: Pricey and Excruciating

Less than one month at school, I became an extremely popular character in a manner bordering on the positively notorious. I could not recall how all the hype began, but suddenly I turned out to be the most admired and hated Form One boy in town. Every time I arrived amid my fellows; I was hailed with a thousand names.

None seemed to be able to greet or acclaim me with a normal modulated voice; it was always a shout, and it came at a price. I could now understand that being so well-liked and hated in equal measure was not only an albatross, but it allowed me to observe at first hand the elastic capacity of individuals for pettiness, jealousy and impertinence. In the meantime, my seniors were very watchful indeed and sure enough it made them quite uncomfortable.

Perhaps, it was on account of my being an accomplished mimic who drew guffaws. Otherwise, I was just an energetic kid always at the receiving end of my constant altercations with my seniors, especially the smallish thugs. Much as I tried, I could not shed off this toga and it was to replicate itself during my years of service in the NA.

A Week of Injustice

At DSSH, activities for each week were driven by a Duty Prefect of the Week. All the proceedings and routines assigned were published in the school bulletin and pasted on a notice board. From the bulletin, each student identified their chores for the week which included the portion of the school to be swept, toilet-washing and weeding out grasses and shrubs.

At full swing, students were awakened at 0530 hours from Mondays through Fridays by the school timekeeper. All dutifully attended to their assigned portion and afterwards went on to fetch water for their masters and wash themselves. Sometimes too, any senior could accost and set one at a random task. To beat time and avoid arriving late to the morning assembly, we resorted to fetching water late in the evenings to circumvent the overcrowding in the mornings.

It was also at DSSH too that I observed partisan conduct. Some seniors were very protective of their juniors and went to a great length to shield them from punishment and manual labour. Yes, manual labour! There was a lot of it, some of it in form of punishment especially as the school was still a work in progress. While some of us were doing a lot of weeding and brushing of grasses, other students were engaged in some dubious assignment for their masters.

I recall an incident that occurred in 1978. Late in my form one days, I was assigned a toilet-washing chore during a previous week. However, my name reappeared again for the same task the succeeding week and I went to the Labour Prefect to complain but he ignored me. Even so, I was determined to oppose the inequity. Besides, I was not the only form one student, and it was only fair that others also undertook their share of common services. Since, it was meant for all, it should be shared out to all.

During the first day of the week, I deliberately refused to wash the toilets. The duty prefect on his part, instead of listening to my entreaties, was more concerned with compelling me to do it by massive battering. I stood my ground. I had resolved that no amount of flogging would deter me. It was at this point that I came to appreciate that partiality, nepotism, or cronyism, was an abiding principle of human conduct. One had to stand up to injustice, otherwise, one would be trampled upon like a piece of rag. This was a trend that I found especially true in my adult life as a soldier.

The smallish seniors were very irksome as I earlier told. What baffled me even more was that older senior students too were equally mean. These types were dreaded and appeared to delight in their brutish reputations. My response to these bullies at school was a mixed bag of obedience and defiance. At my age, I was already expressive and made it a point to verbally engage my tormentors. If I could steal away from them, even by openly taking flight, I did. In this way I could survive and await another encounter.

Unquestionably, bullying by fellow students was ongoing, but the school authorities never bothered to confront the malaise which raged at DSSH and other schools in general. It was an atavistic impulse to control and intimidate others which became the causal kernel that germinated into the murderous cultism that was ravaging Nigeria's school system at present.

University of Rome Alumni

When I started at DSSH, the substantive principal was absent those early days. He was always on transit. Although, he occasionally drove into the school and again disappeared. Eventually, he left never to come back. We later understood he was transferred. I do not remember what his academic qualifications were, but he was replaced by another, a B.Ed English Education graduate. The academic qualifications of the balance of teachers were ambiguous.

When a school magazine was being compiled in 1979, most claimed to have attended a certain University of Rome. Besides, one started as a French teacher, a language he neither spoke nor understood, and transformed into the History master. In between, the school hosted a few itinerant teachers, who always never stayed for long. Finally, the faculty was seasonally complimented by student teachers from Advanced Teachers' College, Katsina-Ala.

A sizable number of the teachers were of Igbo stock. They were direct employees of the proprietor. It remained a mystery how he managed it because there was no way, the Benue State Teaching Service Board would employ non-indigenes with its mindset about state of origin. However, irrespective of where they were coming from and their doubtful low-level qualifications, they were still competent enough to enlarge us with rigorous knowledge.

Liberal Arts or Sciences

The subjects taught at DSSH were liberal arts. Unfortunately, we were never taught core science subjects like Physics, Chemistry and Biology, the closest subject to science being General Science. The beginning was important to institute a balanced foothold which had profound influence on future choice of vocation. Unfortunately, at DSSH, liberal arts subjects were dominant. This was a great drawback that adversely affected students though it was not evident then.

Fighting a Friend

It was obvious that I was not comfortable at DSSH. Try as I could, I never got around to liking neither the school nor the locality. This soon began to reflect on my performance and demeanour. In time, I was having brush-ins and my first major altercation was with the French/History master, whom I considered a friend.

From time to time, I went to do minor household chores like tidying up for him. This I did during my days in Form One. So, I still considered him a friend at the point we fell apart. However, this person was handicapped, as he was extremely poor at practical teaching. This fact was apparent to all the students, for which he was given all sorts of nicknames associated with his inability.

He had a peculiar style of writing noisily on the board. This and his other teaching mannerisms, I observed, mastered, and faithfully reenacted to the delight of my classmates during free periods. Unfortunately, a Judas in the fold snitched on me that I was in the habit of impersonating him before the class. It was treachery, which was ubiquitous and there were consequences.

One afternoon, the whip-bearing teacher arrived the class almost breathless. He was allowed to carry a cane because the school system endorsed corporal punishment. Obviously, there was trouble in the air and this short exchange ensued.

"Where is Gberikon?" He shouted. "I am here sir" I quickly replied. He then rambled about my being not only a rascally boy but disrespectful, and many other uncomplimentary babbles. I was amazed because I could not connect the current scene with any incident, nothing even remotely. No doubt, just like every young person, I was full of mischief and escapades but that afternoon I could not put a finger to whatsoever thing.

The more he spoke, the more visibly enraged he became as my mates, waited excitedly for a twist or an end to the unfolding drama. However, my "friend" did not contrive to complicate matters and chose a short end to the rambunctious conversation. He grabbed me by my shorts and thrashed me with all the strength he could muster until he exhausted himself and let go. All through the whipping I did not wince.

I concluded that he lacked the elementary manners to tell me my transgression. He mentioned nothing except disparaging remarks and allowed his bloated sense of officiousness to drive him to trample on me without the rudimentary courtesy of an allegation. More so, if I had imagined that the deal was a "one off" affair, I was mistaken. My teacher and friend had become my anathema. The next time he was scheduled for a lesson, he arrived with an intimidating visage.

All through the lesson, I wore an amused smile on my face. Then, even as a small boy, I was perceptive enough to identify injustice and evil. I also understood the unnerving power of a smile especially when directed at someone who had treaded upon you. This graceless brute endured my torment for just a little longer and exploded demanding to know why I was beaming at him. As far as I was concerned, it was a rhetorical question as I fixed my gaze on him, determined not to allow him to hit me again under whatever pretext.

Sure enough, he hurled himself at me, but I was prepared and sidestepped. Next, he stood between me and the class exit, while ordering my mates to grab me so that he could continue his assault against my person. Without hesitation, I took an aim at the door with the intention of charging through him, but he ducked, and I was safely outside.

He then went to the next class and commissioned some senior students to accost me and drag me to the Staff Room. I did not take flight but calmly told his potential accomplices to let me be and assured them that I would take myself to wherever on my own, that I just did not wish to be injured by this grumpy unqualified teacher. So, to fulfil all righteousness, they accompanied me. When I entered the staff room, it was then I saw a pile of sticks he had prepared for me, and I thought of the grimness of the man.

It was clear that he had cast aspersion on me to justify his mean-mindedness. But I was attentive, as I observed a couple of teachers manoeuvring to box me in. I did not wait for them I charged through one of them, a student teacher with a big hog belly. Once outside, I went to a safe shelter where I sat down and composed a letter of petition to the principal to plead my case against the gremlin.

This incident took place over forty-seven years ago, and I do not recollect details of the petition, but the substance of the letter was that I could not tell what it was that I had done to the teacher and that he had repeatedly battered me and disrupted my rhythm as a student.

So, I requested that I be allowed to go home to fetch my father to come over and sort the problem. It was a reversal of roles. While it was usual for students to be sent home on account of unruly behaviour by the school authorities, I pleaded that I be asked home to invite my father. When I recollect that decision when I was still a teenager, I found it an attribute to self-preservation.

Far from it, I was not cowardly and could cope with all the pressures of superior-subordinate relations quite well. I did not need my father to fortify me at a boarding school. Even still, I had no illusion that my dad would support me to do wrong. But more importantly, I was not identified with truancy, transgression, or any disruptive behaviour because for effects, I even displayed flashes of brilliance.

Sadly, I was handicapped due to my stuttering speech because at the crucial time, I could not argue my case lucidly. Else, I had felt sufficiently sore to plead against my teacher, at which point the hounding ceased. This was in my estimation an appropriate response of which I remain immensely proud of even today. If I had not cried out when I did, that brute of a teacher would have rendered me functionally illiterate.

When I took the letter to the principal in his office, he graciously accepted it and read it helpfully or so I thought then. He looked up and asked me what transpired, and I recounted the calamity of my encounter with my assailant and told him that apart from fear of bodily injuries, he was a present distraction and that he should let me be. I displayed my skinny body with lacerated whip marks that he had inflicted on me. Finally, the principal granted me leave and I left the school to Katsina Ala, about thirty kilometres southwest of Harga.

First, I transited through my late older brother, Vihimga, who was a student at the Advanced Teachers' College, Katsina Ala. By the time I got to him, it was late in the evening, and he received me with the trepidation of an elder sibling. He thereafter listened to the story of my encounters at the school and probed me further just to ensure that I had not fabricated any tales while he examined my scarred body. In the main, he chided me and hoped that I was being studious and not disobedient. He frowned against disturbing our father over trivialities and complained of lack of time on his part especially as he was in his final year at the college. After the exchange, he accepted to accompany me to the school.

A Dubious Suspension

The next morning, we set off to Harga on his bike. Back then, the present decrepit Takum-Katsina Ala road was still a dirt road. On a bike, the trip took about an hour and a half. By the time we arrived, classes were in session. He rode directly to the principal's office and halted. I remained where he parked his bike and allowed him to process his way through the office red tape to an audience with the principal. After what appeared like eternity, I was ushered in before the principal and my older brother without my assailant.

It was likely that the principal and my attacker had exchanged notes, which put me on the defensive. The offences I stood accused of, included mimicry in a manner disrespectful to a teacher, provocation to wit amusingly smiling at him and refusing to submit myself to corporal punishment.

Primarily, when I called attention to the needless beating and hounding, I was convinced the teacher had exceeded his limit. I felt it because as he exhausted himself delivering blows at me, he was demented with rage. I was neither prepared to antagonize nor contradict anyone. I also knew I could not skip his lessons. All I just wanted, was to get this fellow off my back so I could concentrate on my school business.

The principal then summarily delivered his verdict. I would be suspended from the school for two weeks and at the expiration of which I must be lashed in front of the school assembly. I was incredibly sad about the verdict especially the suspension component. Before now, I thought suspension from school was a retribution reserved for truants and non-conformist students and not a supplicant. We accepted this diktat and I left for home on two weeks suspension.

Now as then, I thought it was heavy-handed. Perhaps, the principal may have privately reproved the teacher, but he was not going to commit class suicide by openly acknowledging his overreach. No matter how twisted the ruling, it still felt like I had achieved my intention, as I had my tormentor where I wanted. He could remain my teacher but not by assaulting me on impulse.

It would have been easier for me to conceal this part of my story. But then, I was not motivated to do so especially when I was a victim of a combined assault and bullying by fellow students and an element in the teaching staff. Back then, as there are cults now, there were bullies in schools. The intensity of the combined activities of these bullies, both students and teachers, were very unsettling, the proof of which was the ever-growing cases of runaway students, absenteeism, and truancy among younger students.

I must also point out that I appreciated the disconcerting possibility of being maltreated and tormented in any assembled group, especially of young people. In time, I discovered that there were bullies at all the schools I attended, including the military academy, at workplaces and even neighborhoods in different forms and manifestations.

For some curious reasons, I also observed that across a wide spectrum, individuals or even groups, were always drawn to meanness and exasperation to the inferior other. Luckily for me, I had in quick time identified my detractor especially as he had some official status. Otherwise, among my fellow students, as tyrannical as they were, I could oppose them. Like any other student at a boarding school, I had devised contrivances to circumvent the predatory and bruising senior students without resorting to deviancy or unruliness.

It was then recognizable that issues of non-participation in school activities and even poor performances at workplaces were not a factor of rebelliousness or lack of capacity but had a lot to do with distractions engendered by distasteful characters within the fold.

On a Clean Slate

When the two-week suspension elapsed, I resumed and was whipped in front of the assembled school. Back then, the military government had introduced a policy of deploying soldiers to high schools to improve discipline among students. These soldiers universally called zombies by the students, were tasked with the grisly duty of administering corporal punishment. So, for twelve times the soldier struck and that number of times, I never as much as flinched. I took a hiding without outward display of pain to validate my strong resolve to be liberated from the torment of a hysterical aggressor.

All these took place in the latter part of my second year at DSSH but by now I liked the school less and less. At the end of the school year, I complained to my older brother, Orvendega, that I wanted a change of school. Graciously, he understood my unease because my academic performance had become markedly poor. When the new school year began, he arranged and got me transferred to King's Comprehensive College (KCC) at Mkar near Gboko.

KCC

In October 1980, I resumed at KCC. It was also a private school. Now at a new school, a different environment, and a fresh set of friends, I got a renewed opportunity to start on a clean slate and did not disappoint as I went on to become one of the best-performing students at the school during my time.

By way of comparison, KCC was not markedly different from DSSH except in key areas of infrastructure and faculty. It was a well-built boarding school with provisions for housing teachers, students, and other allied staff of the school. But like DSSH, it offered no science subjects as what was on offer was a touch of arts with a preponderance of commercial subjects.

In the early 1970s, the military government seized missionary and private schools by executive fiat. Outside this offhanded seizure, they neither put up more infrastructure nor produced an innovative strategy. The schools remained fundamentally the same, save for governmental control of key areas, like the amount of school fees payable and the appointment of teaching staff.

However, the school proprietors kept a degree of control, especially in the feeding of students. At this new school too, there were many inadequacies, of which the most acute were potable water and electricity. Fortunately for the students, abutting the school was a stream that flowed, sometimes in trickles, all year round. It was at this stream, students refreshed, did laundry, and summary sanitation.

City and Guilds and Miscellaneous

When I transferred to KCC in 1980, I met a modest faculty. As a result of its recent history as a commercial college, there were mostly City and Guilds certified teachers in Shorthand and Typewriting. There were also graduates, but not trained educationists and NCE holders too. From time to time, inductees of the National Youth Service Corps (NYSC), augmented the teaching staff , as well as Student Teachers. This patchwork of staff was satisfactory enough to further deepen the foundations I had gotten at a rustic school.

Between Six and Half a Dozen

KCC was more endowed in the sense of having better physical infrastructure. There were beautiful buildings, plentiful playgrounds, and more amenities. However, despite its rural setting, DSSH was at parity in terms of the quality of teaching and better in the welfare of students. These marginal differences were highlighted by two incidents in 1980 and 1981.

In November 1980, I witnessed my first student protest at KCC. I had no inkling of what had taken place or who had planned the peaceful demonstration. I only woke up in the morning to a school with students refusing to attend classes. The reasons for the protest were lack of electricity, potable water, and a mélange of grievances.

There was so much apprehension during the demonstration, especially, when a truck full of baton-wielding policemen drove by. However, wise counsel prevailed as the conduct of the students was peaceful and the police officers drove away. The result of the students' action was the immediate restoration of electricity to the school although water problems persisted until I graduated.

Another notable event was the suspension of a section of Fourth-year students. As earlier stated, potable water was a severe problem and to resolve this challenge, junior students from forms one through three, fetched water for use at the school kitchen. The two topmost classes, i.e., forms four and five, were exempted from this daily chore. However, when we resumed during the first term in our fourth year, we were assigned water-fetching duties again. It was unprecedented as we had expected to be released from the task. Our class was in six streams, i.e. A to F. It was like a testing of wills by our seniors and started with the first three arms, A to C, which were assigned to fetch water. Naturally, they refused, because it was not the tradition then. We were all appalled as to why our immediate seniors deliberately undermined our status. Before we could even figure out the puzzle, that section of our class was suspended for two weeks, an arbitrary decision indeed.

The next day the remaining half of the class was assigned the same task with a threat of suspension hanging over our heads. It was fiercely debated among our mates that we should act in solidarity with our suspended fellows. However, by now our ranks had been broken and many of our mates complied.

The lame excuse offered was that our class was the largest in the school and since we had advanced to the next most senior class, exempting us from the routine would cause a shortfall in the water supplied. The whole affair ended in distaste. In which case, we expected to fetch water even in our final year. Uncannily, it was an experience that I would meet repeatedly, in the military, in a more primitive form. It was a human trait in which superiors looked to humiliate and chasten their subordinates.

Hard Road to Travel

The new school smoothened out my rough edges, but it was not without its excitement. At KCC just like DSSH and other secondary schools around, the problems, and the pressures of managing intra-juvenile interaction within structured and confined surroundings were the same, apart from local colour. I had brushes, both good and nasty, and my share of escapades as a boarding school student, like breaking the bounds and other adolescent mischief.

Although I never called attention to myself, my hyperactivity soon drew positive reviews as well as negative insinuations. Nonetheless, being modestly brilliant and of sharp reflexes became my redeeming qualities. Much as I had many detractors, then and even now, those attributes were very helpful as I schemed and steered through such adverse interpersonal encounters at close quarters. At last, I enjoyed three years of uninterrupted academic pursuit shorn of unease and hounding.

Finally, we were on the home run. Already, the greater part of the job was done with, and we were set to leave high school. We had to visualize our dreams and project our lives after school. It was a very hopeful prospect indeed. However, just before that, we had to contend with the final qualifying exams. It was an assessment so innocuous, yet so central in defining the prospects and further academic progress, or lack of it, for all of us. This exam marked the culmination of all the knowledge we had gotten over those five long years. It was therefore pivotal as to guarantee continual progress or premature termination of scholarly pursuit.

The final exams were held at the school auditorium, the Great Hall. It was a very expansive building with enough space to accommodate all candidates. The seating arrangement ensured candidates evenly spread out to avoid cheating. One Mr. Kofi Nana Badu, a lively but strict Ghanaian, was the main invigilator and during the exams proper, the supervision was quite vigorous. Exams malpractices in any form were forbidden and all the rules adhered to. It was a sad commentary on our educational system that we now had miracle centres where parents pay so their children or wards could pass exams. Conveniently, I cleared School Certificate/General Certificate of Education Ordinary Level (SC/GCE O/L) and scored credits in all the subjects I had attempted at a single sitting.

Acting Commander 81 Division Provost Group 2007

Lagos 2007

Chapter Seven

The Great Expectations

After high school, I was naturally hopeful about the future. Understandably, it was a time to grow, move on, and look forward to the next phase of life where providence would lead me. The prospects were unlimited but there were challenges too, particularly about the choice of profession. It was tricky to decide because I belonged to the first generation in my family to get a low-level Western education and had to seek where my interests and strengths lay.

School of Basic Studies

During my last days at high school, I applied for the Joint Matriculation Examinations Board (JAMB) and School of Basic Studies (SBS) at Ahmadu Bello University but never received any feedback, so I assumed I was not accepted. Subsequently, my elder brother had to press my case to get me placement into SBS Makurdi, as a supplementary candidate.

Although I was overqualified, but since I did not apply at the outset for admission, I endured the indignity of being pushed for a placement. Eventually, I was admitted and commenced classes in September but spent only a couple of months before I left to the University of Ife.

However, as soon as the session started, the academic staff declared a strike during which all school activities were suspended. Such strikes I would encounter more frequently at the university. In the interim, students had to vacate the school grounds as all instructional activities ceased.

SBS: An Assessment

During my short stay at SBS, I explored the activities at the school. The SBS module was basically designed for the Interim Joint Matriculation Board (IJMB) Test, after which successful candidates were eligible for direct entry into the second year at most Nigerian universities. The school inherited the old site of the former Murtala College of Arts,

Science and Technology (MUCAST). Remarkably, the hostels and classrooms on campus were in a rundown state and it was amid these ruins that I had my first taste of a higher institution.

Hovels for Free

There were hostel blocks, but the drawback was that the structures were in ruins. The beauty of it was that bed spaces were taken for free. Each student found his corner amid the rubble. Those who resumed earlier took the more habitable lairs for themselves, and late arrivals had to make a nest at the worst hostel block appropriately nicknamed Earthquake. It was by sheer providence that the buildings never caved-in on the students.

Quantity Not Quality

The students were served meals thrice daily gratis at a large cafeteria run by sweaty cooks. The dining hall was sparsely furnished with rickety furniture and so students hung by the windows to grab their meals. The quality or wholesomeness of the meals was not a major concern. At least, the school authorities gave free meals by which the students subsisted.

Vibrancy

The academic activities at SBS were vibrant as students were admitted either to a Straight Course or a Remedial class. The IJMB module was heavily stacked and demanded full concentration to obtain the requisite scores. Otherwise, it was not a standalone module that could be deployed to any useful purposes. So, for years, the school was a catalyst for aspiring students who progressed to high offices and great careers.

End of Strike

The strike that sent us home was remarkably brief. The issues raised were resolved, and the school reopened to full academic activity. However, for me, it marked the end of my layover. I had to leave because on an afternoon in early November 1982, a friend and junior at KCC, came to the campus and handed me a JAMB admission slip to read Dramatic Arts at the University of Ife. It was almost two months into resumption, as I forgot my forwarding address was to my former high school.

All said, though the school grounds were appalling, it was compensated for by the rigorous academic activity that took place within its confines. As to the ramshackle physical state of the structures, it was a harbinger of the coming widespread decay of national infrastructure that included failed roads, poorly maintained public buildings, facilities, and installations.

Unending Lawns and Flowers

At the main entrance into the University of Ife was a towering gate. As one passed the gate, the first-time visitor's attention was engaged by a divided highway hemmed by perfectly manicured lawns with a profusion of blooming flowers of all varieties, as far as the eyes could see. From the gate, the road descended steeply down the valley for about two hundred metres, then banked left over a culvert and rose steeply uphill.

It was a charming spectacle, enhanced by flowers in the median and beyond the shoulders of the road. Yet, the real excitement was the point at which the peak of the hill was surmounted, as it cinematically unveiled a majestic panorama of magnificence that exploded in the distance. This was and still is the manner the university unfolded its high design and architectural masterpieces.

In the skyline stood imposing structures arranged most aesthetically. In fact, as of 1982, no public edifices were anything near the splendour of the meticulously planned University of Ife campus. The layout and functionality of the university were on a scale so grand, it was impossible not to be impressed. When I got into the campus, fellows directed me, a Jambite, to the Student Union Director of Welfare, who received me and gave me a place to lay my head for that night.

Nothing by Half

The university was set up by the government of Western Nigeria in 1962. However, its temporary take-off site was at Ibadan, and was moved by 1964 to its permanent site. By this time, there were solid physical structures and infrastructure. An Israeli company, Solel Boneh, built the university and it delivered a stunningly excellent job of a beautifully integrated modern university campus.

Idlers and Blabbermouths

The next morning, I went to the administrative offices at the Senate Building to confirm my admission status. At those offices were a group of garrulous staff who kept me waiting for over an hour to complete a five-minute task. From there I headed to the faculty office, to a secretary who clattered interminably at an old typewriter. It took him ages to complete his chores. Afterward, he engaged in idle gossip with his colleagues who came and went.

Along with another new student, we waited for him patiently to attend to us at his pleasure. From this point forward, I recognized it was the unproductive work ethic of university staff and by extension public service in Nigeria. The task was simple, it was no more than handing me course registration forms, but that took only two hours.

Afterwards, I walked over to the Institute of African Studies that housed the Department of Dramatic Arts. Here too, the secretary replicated the delay, as I waited for over an hour to receive a departmental handbook that served as a guide during registration. At the end, I spent an entire day to accomplish an hour's task.

An Excuse for Pageantry

When I got my notification of admission, it was a little late but luckily, the university had not yet matriculated. The matriculation ceremony was scheduled a week into my resumption, on a Saturday. Ordinarily, I thought it would be a low-level induction ceremony, but it was a grand occasion. It was an introduction to the epicurean Yoruba culture at its cradle. So, apart from Jambites dandified for the occasion, the campus was inundated by individuals, families, and groups bedecked in colourful attires.

The festive atmosphere was enveloped in gaiety as visitors and guests were hectored by dexterous musicians. These forceful musicians, armed with talking drums and an array of musical instruments and trappings, thumped out pulsating dance-inducing rhythms. Predictably, following a short rite characterized by recitations and an attestation, the new students pledged to submit themselves to scholarship.

After the official rites, Oduduwa Hall, the venue and environs of the matriculation ceremony were transformed into a vast picnic ground besieged by photographers, where a lot of merriment was complemented by much drinking and eating. The Yoruba penchant for festivity was understandable, but I found the excuse of a matriculation quite capricious for the extravagant pageants that overwhelmed the campus.**Courses and Electives**

There were core courses and electives for each department and students could choose across the faculty. For instance, at the Faculty of Arts, electives were picked mostly from complementary departments like English, Literature, Philosophy, History, Religion, and Psychology, all weighted and reckoned towards the final assessment. It was projected that by the terminal date of a course, the individual would have been refined with well-rounded knowledge to a universal standard.

Unfree Education

There were no tuition fees except for a one-off Twenty Naira refundable caution fee and four Naira student union fees paid annually at the start of every academic calendar. However, there was a hotchpotch of token student-imposed surcharges by departmental associations ranging from One Naira to Two Naira Fifty Kobo at most. Apart from those symbolic charges, there were no levies or contributions under any pretext.

Moreover, the university authorities had no powers to impose levies. So, it was bewildering when latter-day administrators mouthed elitist inanities about the impossibility of free education. Ironically, collective amnesia had deluded those gullible obscurantists to believe otherwise.

Even if what existed did not pass for free education, a semblance of what was possible had always been there and Nigerians who studied at the universities from the earliest times until the mid-1980s were beneficiaries. Even then, there were still students who could not sustain themselves due to their indigent conditions. This mindset led to a pointless subversion of the Nigerian university system over the years.

Thus, successive governments reeling under the accumulated effects of profligacy and financial vandalism were done in by dwindling resources. The paucity of funds then engendered a contest between the demands of public obligations against the ferocious avarice of public servants including civil, military, and political pillagers.

Along the line too, governments began a gradual emasculation of the funding of education inveigled by the IMF-World Bank cartel. Further propelled by infamy, the responsible abdicated and shifted the bulk of supporting public universities onto the shoulders of parents and guardians. Far worse, governments bewitched by dubious scholars and econometricians, churned out vast amounts of apocryphal statistics that extolled comparative advantages, economies of scale, and other travesties in support of extortionist schemes to inundate already impoverished Nigerians.

Consequently, with the collusion of governments of the day, the beast of internally generated revenue was unleashed on hapless parents and guardians. This was in turn seized upon by predatory administrators that instituted bloated tuition fees and endless levies. Finally, university education in Nigeria became unfree to assuage the ravenousness of careerist freebooters.

Moreover, in those days, state governments awarded bursaries or stipends in support of students. The Benue state government, for instance, paid an annual scholarship allowance of Eight Hundred and Fifty Naira, which was one of the highest in the country then. To be eligible for a grant was a streamlined process. It was automatic upon gaining admission at any higher institution of learning. The allowances were every so often paid, in full or instalments, by a scholarship board not yet swamped in graft jointly executed by state officials and dishonest student representatives.

Academics

The system of instruction at the university was by lectures and tutorials. For each course, there was a lead lecturer complemented by tutorial masters who conducted interactive groups. By this arrangement, a lecture centrally broadcast was reinforced further at the less crowded tutorial sessions. These were conducted by way of discussions, assignments, and tests to constantly assess the students.

Faculty at the University

During my time, the academic and support staff at the university were quite adequate. Across board, there was a faculty of professors, doctorates, and higher-degree scholars. Likewise, its composition reflected a blend of the ancient and modern. The faculty was garnished from time to time by international scholars and visiting professors and lecturers. Therefore, by any factor, the teaching staff at the university was satisfactory.

Lecture Halls and Classrooms

In general terms, the colleges were domiciled in large multi-story complexes. In each set of buildings were embedded lecture theatres and a couple of 40-seater classrooms integrated into its spatial zoning. The Faculty of Arts had two of the largest and oldest auditoria which by 1982 were already showing signs of wear and tear.

Furthermore, there were newer auditoria at the faculties of Agriculture, Law, Pharmacy, and Medicine. Now and then, courses were oversubscribed, which called for larger venues to host outsized classes. Thus, extra-large classes were held at the stands of the Sports Centre.

Noblemen and Barbarians

The university was residential. The main halls of residence were Obafemi Awolowo and Adekunle Fajuyi for men, and Moremi Hall for women and mixed-use residences namely Murtala Mohammed (Postgraduate) and Sports Halls. Others were the emergency contraptions of Angola and Mozambique constructed lately.

Apart from these halls, there were uncompleted hostel projects strewn all over the campus. As of 1982, the bed spaces on offer were grossly inadequate compared to the number of potential residents. To overcome this shortfall, the accommodation policy of the university prioritized first and final-year students. But this did not abate the fact of overcrowding that characterized the hostels.

The available spaces were populated with double-bunked beds. However, there were situations when those tiny cubicles originally designed for two students hosted over a dozen, and worse at night, sleeping students covered the passages and floors. Equally, a sizeable number of students lived off-campus. but still, the costs of rent and of commuting daily to the campus were a burden. As a result, the students resorted to squatting.

Each hall of residence had its identifying character. Fajuyi Hall was a gentleman's hostel, while Awolowo Hall was noticeably a crude hotbed of raucous manners, campus politics, and mobilization. How these definitive peculiarities evolved was unknown, but each made its iconic impression, as it was quite easy to link a student's deportment with their halls of residence.

On the other hand, Angola Hall was for male Jambites while Mozambique Hall, nicknamed Motherless Babies Home, was occupied by younger female students. At the other end, was Moremi Hall, aka Babyless Mothers Home, in reference to its more elderly female residents.

Society on Campus

The university community was a cosmopolitan cluster. Within its confines could be found a mix of nerds, oddballs, and all brands of weirdoes. Apart from its multi-ethnic composition, the university was home to international scholars as there were strong cultural influences of the British and American university systems.

However, regardless of the multiple tendencies, these were overshadowed by Yoruba culture in the backdrop. The campus was not insular because it sustained a seamless interaction with the main Ile-Ife town. Apart from many staff, other ancillary service providers flocked to the campus daily as they engaged in multiple economic activities.

Campus Entertainment

The hub of entertainment on the campus was Oduduwa Hall, where a variety of entertaining activities were programmed. It was a massive structure consisting of a partially roofed half and an open-air arena. Apart from film shows, beauty pageants and comedy show etc., live performances were also regularly held at this venue.

The social circuit on campus was wired in a way that most acts at the National Theatre Lagos were followed by stopovers at the campus always. In this way, we had visiting American bands and musicians like Raphael Cameron, Evelyn King, Lakeside, and the Jamaican Reggae group, Third World, that performed at one time or the other.

Caricatures and Counterfeits

There were a handful of student fraternities, the most prominent of which were Rotaract, Jaycees, and the pseudo-elitist Alpha Club. Each of these was a caricature of existing groups in the larger society. At one extreme of the sororities was Palm Wine Drinkards Club, which claimed the campus as its world headquarters.

With a high-sounding name, the alleged world head office was a shack in a bamboo grove behind the Institute of African Studies, run by a middle-aged lady officiously addressed by the equally grandiloquent title of World Accountant. This accountant was technically in charge of the sales of palm wine. The regalia adorning Drinkards were an exceptionally flamboyant group that from time to time engaged in imbibition and gyration accompanied by rhythmic drumming to the complement of melodious singing and ribaldry.

Cultism

During my time as a student, we heard so many stories about secret cults, but they had neither a commanding presence on the campus nor the overall student body. There were rarely any outrageous activities. Although, often mentioned was the Pyrates Confraternity (which Nobel Laureate Wole Soyinka allegedly co-founded), Eiye, and others again there was none of the violence and mayhem of latter-day campus cults. Unless otherwise you got involved, the presence of cultism remained in a shadowy background.

Breeding Demagogues

The students at University of Ife took pride in being at the vanguard of the struggle for the emancipation of Nigerian students. It was a nationwide task that was undertaken to unshackle the articulate students from the clutches of oppressors epitomized by the university authorities and governments of the day. Structurally, student politics was divided into the local autonomous Student Union and the federated National Association of Nigerian Students (NANS).

Student politics on campus was animated. While it was markedly non-partisan, it must not be assumed that there were no underlying sentiments pivotal to the election of union leadership. The student union agenda was implemented through a series of boisterous protests and lecture boycotts that were excited by anything within the campus or from without in solidarity with the endless calls by NANS.

Several student union leaders were, what we termed, professional students, i.e., a set of students whose graduation dates were indeterminate. They could easily decamp from one institution to the other to continue with their activism. But for their persistence, many of them evolved into politicians of note at both local and national levels.

The high point of campus politics was the election season. The electoral period began with elections into the Students Representative

Council (SRC), at the departmental and faculty constituencies. A sizeable number of candidates contested, and handbills were distributed and or pasted all over the campus accompanied by vigorous canvassing for votes. However, all these proceeded in a subdued atmosphere.

It was the next phase of stumping on the campaign trail that absorbed the energy of all the students, i.e., the elections of the central Student Union leadership. These were the offices of the President, Vice president, Secretary General, Directors of Sports, Socials, and Welfare, as well as Public Relations Officer, Financial Secretary, and a host of deputies. At this point, the whole campus was turned into one giant live organism writhing to music and lively speeches.

During this segment, roving campaign bands sallied with candidates at its head. Each contestant sold themselves as the most credible. The high point of these spectacles was the Manifesto Night which was typically held at the Sports Centre. The night was a highly anticipated event in the political calendar of campus politics. It was an event that drew a large crowd of students and all who attended arrived promptly. At this venue, the stage was set for a call and response speechifying between the electorates and contestants. The crowd was always vibrant, boisterous, and responsive as candidates made their orchestrated entries.

Indeed, demagoguery and charlatanism were an essential ingredient of this very often farcical night. It was a night during which the merits of a candidate were measured not by their lucidity but by reactionary antics. The students listened or did not, and lent their applause, not to the intelligibility or logic of the presentation, but to the aggregate citations of Karl Marx, Adam Smith, John Locke, Aristotle, Socrates, and other ancient sages in high-sounding gibberish.

At every quotation, the arena was thrown into raucous baying and tumult, which took time to subside. While some contestants made sense, others were upended by stage fright and for some reason, other candidates were not granted an audience at all. However, the overall atmosphere was lively and stimulating.

The union elections of the 1982/83 session were very remarkable. Student unionism at the university had suffered a setback from the fallout of the 1981 killing of students during a protest.[1] The union was under the leadership of one Femi. He was a wiry middle-aged man, whose visage to me did not fit in as an undergraduate student. In the aftermath of the tragedy, student union activities were provisionally proscribed but soon reverted. Subsequently, Femi lived the rest of his student days as a tragic and often lonely figure since he was blamed for the death of the students.

During that election, the frontrunner for the union presidency was one Georgie, who rode the crest of goodwill with the crown within his grasp. Then suddenly, out of the blue, a Chris who must be recognized for his feat as a political con artist, sprung up a week before the election and took the wind out of the former's sail. From a leading contender, Georgie trailed and eventually lost the elections.

During that election, one Funmi got elected as the Vice President, the first lady to reach that distinction in student unionism in any Nigerian university. Not too long after, Chris and his executive council were accused of profligacy and sundry misdemeanours. In one instance, a brand-new Student Union bus was driven to a private party in Lagos and wrecked. As it was natural with all politicians, they had discovered our collective patrimony and lavished it on themselves.

Eat to Live or Live to Eat

In my time, students were fed at three refectories on campus. These were located at Fajuyi and Awolowo Halls and one at a central location. Given the variety and decent quality of the meals, it was clearly above the Fifty Kobo we paid for. Apart from diners, there were food vendors at the local Bukateria and at elitist joints like Merry Times, Forks and Fingers at the Student Union Building, etc. Even so, students had cause to complain about the cost and quality. But again, there were still students who could not afford the meals at the cafeterias and resorted to cooking in the hostels.

In a sudden policy somersault in 1985, implemented by the military junta of Major General Mohammed Buhari, a purported "subsidy" on meals was removed and services at the cafeterias ceased. The university administration then hurriedly built a new food court which was rented to private caterers to sell at commercial rates. Also, the authorities attempted to demolish the local Bukateria which was run by a host of Mama-Puts, but this was fiercely resisted by the students.

This marked my first encounter with the political economy term called subsidy. Along these lines, each time a government policy led to the withdrawal of a subsidy, it was marked by widespread hardship and resentment by the public. Consequently, the whole Nigerian student body mobilized and protested nationwide to no avail.

Theory or Hands-On

Having gone through the academic curriculum at the university, it was obvious that my department had some of the leading lights in the Nigerian theatre scene. These were Professor Wole Soyinka, who made irregular appearances, and Drs Kole Omotosho, Segun Akinbola, and Femi Euba, who were later joined by Professor Femi Osofisan and Dr Ahmed Yerima. By its antecedents, it was the best drama school in Nigeria.

Nevertheless, it was obvious that when it came to production, the department preferred to work with its resident theatre company. These were staff, a sizable number of whom came over from Ibadan and specialized in Yoruba drama. The curriculum of the Ife Drama School was therefore of little help in moulding actors out of its undergraduate students. It was the Certificate Course students, who spent more time on practical productions that became adept at acting.

Moreover, the Yoruba repertoire was a handicap to non-Yoruba students. In any case, there were no group or class productions, so everyone had to seek their strength in Directing, Management, Production, and others in Film, Radio, and Television.

Even worse, the academic activities were unduly disrupted by incessant student union actions. It was a situation in which both the faculty and students were unable to check the excesses of the student leaders. The university stood out notoriously as the most strike-prone university in the country. It was an experience that would last until the very end. Ironically, the situation had been inverted; with the students being belaboured by the never-ending teaching staff-led disruptions of academic calendars. The chickens had finally come to roost.

The Closing Days at Ife

By late May 1986, as we prepared for our final graduating exams, the campus once again erupted for whatever reason I could not recall. The final exams scheduled for the first week of June were disrupted, but mercifully, the melee lasted only for a couple of weeks and when the school resumed, the lost time was managed by scheduling two or more papers per day in most cases. At last, by the fourth week of June, the exams were concluded, and we became presumed graduates. For all the exams I attempted during those four years of study, I recorded a 100% pass.

Note

(1). For an insight of 1981 killing of students at Ile-Ife see: Fajokun, Kayode O. Revisiting the Cause of Death in a School-Police Violent Face-Off: African Journal Online 2012.

Burma Battalion 1989

Chapter Eight

An Encounter Grisly and Broken

After my final exams, I left Ile-Ife for Lagos enroute to my hometown to await my results and call up for the National Youth Service Corps (NYSC) scheme. It was supposed to be a joyous moment for me because, at just slightly above twenty-one years, I was a university graduate. This to me was an extraordinary achievement, given where I was coming from, i.e., sired by "illiterate" parents. However, my feel-good mood was overturned abruptly by a horrific encounter with four soldiers.

Newly out of school, I chose to pass some time with my former guardian who was still a soldier. I often spent holidays with him in Lagos before now. But this time around, it was only natural that I retreated to Lagos as I rounded up at the university. The intention was to spend a fleeting time and head back to the village.

My brief retreat was meant to last only a couple of days because you could not have an extended stay with military personnel because of the never-ending lack. My brother tried to sustain us both, but I knew it was a struggle for him. So, it was only reasonable to leave him to manage himself without the added burden of my demanding presence. The plan was to travel back home, and it was on account of this that I went to Alaba market to arrange for my passage.

Food Alcohol Dance and Women

Tiv traders ran a yam market at Alaba in the Okokomaiko district of Lagos. The market was formerly near the stench filled Iddo Railway Terminus, at a spot where sewage was dumped into the Lagos lagoon. When I first visited the market in 1981, my stomach churned for days on end. Along the line, it was moved temporarily to Tin Can Island and finally to its permanent site at Alaba in 1984.

The market functioned in multiple roles for the Tiv diaspora in Lagos. It was not just a food market, but a dispatch and delivery point, a transport depot, and most importantly, a rendezvous for socializing. It was a watering hole.

Those familiar with Tiv people will attest to the fact that they took their drinking business seriously. Also, being a highly musical race, they were inclined to revel, even when far from home. When they congregated, there was a lot of drinking, energetic music, dancing, and all the subterranean things that went with group excitement.

Again, not too long ago, transportation from Lagos to Gboko and other parts of Tivland was by open cargo trucks aka gongoro. These trucks brought yam tubers, fruits, and varieties of farm produce from Tivland to Lagos. On the return trips, the vehicles were laden with cargo and passengers.

Therefore, I went to the market that evening to confirm the availability of a truck for a trip the next morning. It turned out to be a day I would never forget. It was 29 June 1986; the day Argentina beat West Germany to lift the FIFA World Cup trophy in Mexico. At one of the bars, the owner had placed a TV outdoors to receive a live broadcast of the final match. Although the reception was grainy because of the terrestrial analogue broadcast, it still delivered live proceedings from far away Mexico. Even more, I had enough time on hand to kill and a rare opportunity to watch a historic match live.

Accordingly, I went behind the crowd surrounding the TV and found myself a seat near a boisterous group of young men in the company of ladies, whose virtue, I could not vouch for. Even worse, I realized rather late that I was seated next to a hornet's nest. It did not take long to detect by their gruffly and rough manners that they were soldiers. In a commensal setup, one individual was buying the drinks and food, while others were freeloading and engaged in unconcealed sycophancy.

I tried to ignore the pack and focus on the excitement of the match but a girl in the group would not let me be. Please give me flowers, by 1986, I was a highly desirable smooth-faced young man. A young lady, whom I had never met before, was so besotted with me that it felt uncomfortable.

She tried to initiate an exchange, but I was very brusque, just to keep her at bay. I foresaw danger lurking in her seductive baiting, but she would not let me be, as women were very persistent when they wanted a man.

The crowd next to the television was sizable but the surrounding area was poorly lit. The girl propped me by the leg and gave me a cold bottle of beer under the cover of darkness. I felt uneasy but on a balance of scale, the beer was going to cheer me up, so I drank wishing for more. Hardly done with the beer, she again groped for my hand and handed me a juicy chicken lap, which I devoured at once.

All the while, one of the soldiers noticed these antics. Soon the soldiers were whispering in hushed tones and looking in my direction. At this point, I stood up and went to a corner to ease myself. It was halfway into relieving my alcohol-induced incontinence that one of them confronted me. Soldiers, always vain and pompous, demanded an explanation for my uninvited sharing of the fair at their table.

"My friend, what is the meaning of this nonsense" He interrogated me angrily. "Am sorry, I don't know what you are talking about" I retorted. "So, you think we are as foolish as you" He suggested.as I pandered to his arrogance and visage of a losing bitter ender.

"If only you would tell me what you mean instead of speaking in parables, please excuse me"

I made to walk away but he barred my way. "What is he saying" one of his companions shouted from the distance. "Don't mind the bagger, him dey speak grammar" My interceptor interjected as excitement surged in me. "You bloody civilian, you have the guts to be toasting our girlfriend and even eating out of our table" He finally divulged.

I ignored him and tried to walk away a second time, but he still blocked me. When I exerted myself to get free, the next thing, I noticed he was down spread-eagled in the mud. The representative from the sumptuous table was very feeble indeed.

It was then that the other three joined him, and the pounding began. By the time they were done, my right arm had broken from deflecting blows to my head. The thumping eventually stopped and when the soldiers were asked the reason for so much beating, they were too ashamed to reveal the cause.

I found my way back to the barracks and informed my brother. Later, my assailants were arrested and detained. These low-ranking soldiers that assaulted me could only be forgiven; else they were not able to take care of themselves much less pay my medical bills.

When I joined the army two years later, people aware of the incident presumed that it was on account of that affair. The decision to become a soldier was not in way connected to this incident. Not being a vengeful individual, I could not fathom the frivolousness of such insinuation. For me, the pursuit of reprisal could not be the motivation to choose a grunt job. Meanwhile, I needed to get my swollen hand treated either by traditional bone setters or orthodox treatment.

National Orthopaedic Relics

To get medical care for the broken arm, my first point of call was National Orthopaedic Hospital Igbobi, Lagos. Apart from routine registration at the Outpatient Department (OPD), I spent a full day at the hospital without receiving any attention. In the interim, I saw broken people all over the place with varieties of injuries beyond description. While a sizeable number lay silently, others writhed in agony. So, I double-checked and reassured myself that my injury was not too serious in comparison.

Although the broken arm appeared outwardly innocuous, it was a complex fracture because the two bones of the forearm, namely the ulna and radius had broken and displaced. It would be a tricky orthopaedic procedure to perform. At last, when an effusive junior doctor attended to me, he prescribed surgery. Unfortunately, the bits and screws needed for the operation were out of stock, even at the medical dealerships adjoining the hospital. On the third day, a senior doctor immobilized the fractured forearm in a cast.

With an itchy hand in cast, I went trawling through the National Orthopaedic Hospitals system from Enugu to Kano to no avail. Meanwhile, natural healing was underway except the bones were not well set. After the long travails and travels in search of those bits and pieces, I had the plaster removed. It was alarming to see a poorly healed forearm that dangled freely.

Out of desperation, I resorted to traditional bone setters with their crude procedures. The defectively healed arm was broken all over again for resetting. I was fortunate that being in my prime ensured that the fracture healed even though the bones were poorly set. Ultimately, I was called-up for NYSC and deployed to Oyo state.

The Dispersal

The NYSC scheme was the brainchild of General Yakubu Gowon's administration. Its pioneer chairperson, Professor Adebayo Adedeji helped set up the organization. The programme was modelled on the American Peace Corps and designed to be a year of sojourn away from home. Even more, it was intended as a transition between the excitement of leaving school and the reality of attaining adulthood.[1]

Furthermore, it was meant to apprise the youth of the diversity and scale of Nigeria. To a degree, the scheme tampered the widespread insularity that was reinforced by cultural and ethnic exclusivity. On a balance of scale, despite the deliberate attempts to sabotage the scheme by cynics, it remained the most enduring signature achievement of that regime.

The NYSC Orientation Camp opened on 7 September 1986 at the defunct Teachers' Training College (TTC), Iyana-Offa along Iwo Road, Ibadan. It was a late joint camp of inductees deployed to Lagos, Ogun, Ondo, and Oyo states and full of excitement. Everyone was properly kitted up and proud to adorn the unique uniform of corps members.

The camp lasted three weeks and there were activities like drills, obstacle scaling, and monkey bridges. What I enjoyed most were the times I volunteered at the kitchen preparing meals. The camp ended three weeks later, and marked a dispersal, the end of a phase of my life, i.e., being in a large group of young people.

Place of Primary Assignment

For my Place of Primary Assignment, I was deployed to Modakeke High School as a teacher. Modakeke is an enclave within Ile-Ife town. Nonetheless, both communities had a difficult rapport. It was a relation wrecked by revisionism and partisan depositions as to the origin and settlement by both people. Otherwise, Ile-Ife and Modakeke were seamlessly co-located.

If you recall, I reported to the orientation camp with a defectively healed arm. This injury became a source of constant pain which almost disrupted my service year as I repeatedly sought medical remedy at the National Orthopaedic Hospital Dala, Kano. It was the most functional of the three Orthopaedic hospitals and yet after over two months, out of which the last was spent on hospital admission, no respite came my way. With time, the pains abated and expediently I forgot about the partially deformed arm and life never ceased.

However, my determination to ensure it was properly treated, almost marred my service year because at a point my allowances were withheld. Despite the travails, my service year came to a blissful end and by that date, I was three months short of being twenty-three years old. It also dawned on me that, for the first time, I was truly an adult and presumed independent.

Economic Tinkering

After my service year, I was thrown into the labour market by September 1987. By then, Nigeria was in the throes of political and economic convulsion occasioned by the endless tinkering under the watch of General Ibrahim Babangida, the impostor military president. Although inept and unqualified at these tasks, he was attended by a coterie of mercenary mercantilist guns. In time, a combination of wrongful prescriptions and outright sham plunged Nigeria into a virtual breakdown of law and order.

General Babangida had attained political power by treachery. As the then Chief of the Army Staff, he conspired to unseat a conceited Major General Muhammadu Buhari on 27 August 1985. The ramrod Buhari, so vainglorious and fixated on imposing iron discipline, forgot to humanize his leadership and was easily toppled by his more calculating colleagues led by Babangida whose eight-year rule was premised on economic and pseudo-political restructuring.

Chasing a Wild Goose

The principal focus of the Babangida junta was the transition of power from military to civil rule. To this vague end, the government crafted one of the longest and most nebulous political calendars in Nigeria's history. Nonetheless, the transition plans were applauded because they came along with innovations like mass political mobilization, Option A4, zero-party elections, and a two-party system.

For a start, the administration set up a National Electoral Commission (NEC) and decreed into existence two political parties namely the Social Democratic Party (SDP) and the National Republican Convention (NRC). However, the programme came to a dead-end after a series of false starts and the dubious annulment of the Presidential Elections of June 12, 1993.[2]

Subsequently, the administration was caught in the maze of deceit and treachery it had woven. Thus, concerted pressure from within and outside the military forced the president to abdicate. The cost of the transition plan was colossal and stopped when an interim national government was instituted in the aftermath of his abdication.

Structural Adjustment Programme

By the time I started the hunt for a job in 1987, the Nigerian economy was in the throes of reforms. The new-fangled economic mantra was the Structural Adjustment Programme (SAP), which was a standard one-size-fits-all economic modification policy promoted by the IMF-World Bank cartel.[3]

In general terms, it was a cocktail of policies designed for the wobbly economies of impoverished countries. The kernel of its remedies was based on external debt management, currency manipulation, and the removal of subsidies. The policy also prescribed only a supportive role in a shambolic economic environment of highly reduced government ownership and control of enterprises

Further strangulations included features like privatization, commercialization, trade liberalization, and interest rate deregulation. It was an overkill and expectedly the measures spurned an inflationary spiral and economic recession. The impacts of the pernicious experimentation were depletion of external reserves and worsened balance of payments position as unemployment, layoffs, and retrenchment escalated. The government had force-fed her citizens with bitter pills, and when they reacted violently, the regime in turn used a heavy hand to restore order. It was a tough time to be an applicant.[4]

Ambling on the Streets

I took to the streets in search of those elusive jobs that every graduate hoped for. In the middle 1980s, the expanding Nigerian educational sector churned out fresh graduates from the Polytechnics, Advanced Teachers' Colleges, Colleges of Education and Universities in hundreds of thousands, if not millions. Meanwhile, in private companies and the public sector, personnel and operations were being rationalized, downsized, or outrightly shut down. It was a precarious situation of great tension that was very demanding on young people as the streets were filled with unease.

The Nigerian youth, a generation or two earlier, did not endure the concomitant rate of unemployment as it was a given for graduates to be offered jobs. For a sizable number, there was even a luxury of options. In the changing times, the value of paper qualifications had become ridiculously cheap indeed.

Once again, I headed back to Lagos to scour for a job. The jobs were just not there, and the number of applicants far outstripped available vacancies, if any existed. Even when there were openings, they were not designed to hire new entrants as offers were tied to years of work experience.

Meanwhile, to transit from Ojo to Lagos Island, took not only supreme efforts but a circuitous route over water and land. Usually, I boarded a bus at Ojo and disembarked at Mile 2 Jetty onward to Marina by boat through Apapa Wharf. On the Marina, all further movements were on foot. It was a forced daily regimen, as I went from one company, ministry, government agency, or department to the other. It was a futile quest, with no cheering news in sight. One of those days, I bumped into a schoolmate who was walking in the opposite direction. Sure, as hell, he was also a vagrant along that crowded stretch of Lagos Marina.

On occasions, I got a compassionate reception at some offices but, I was unceremoniously ignored and hostilely driven away, especially by security guards who through no fault of theirs were suspicious of me on account of my hunger-induced scruffiness. After ambling for three luckless months on the streets of Lagos, I retraced my steps and returned to Makurdi in December 1987.

Although, the prospect of securing a job in Makurdi, the Benue state capital was much more hopeless, it was less tedious due primarily to its proximity to my hometown. It was during this period that I saw at close range, the inexplicable resentment from company staff and career civil servants, who for whatever reason could not stand the sight of young wannabes looking to join the senior ranks of an organization.

At one point, I went to a high school that was poorly staffed and offered to teach for free to kill boredom, but funnily I was yet refused.

Although it was a difficult situation, I never faltered but worked at my older brother's copy shop in Katsina-Ala Township. The rising graduate unemployment altered the historic dynamics of demand and supply in the Nigerian labour market. However, the new dynamics were the full-blown symptoms of failed educational planning and misplaced emphasis.

This counterproductive trend developed from the low-level education available in the colonial environment. Historically, the incentive for getting educated was to qualify for a clerical job or such other menial tasks allowed in colonial service. Although, artisanal skills were ranked side by side with clerical jobs, clerks who worked at closer quarters to colonial administrators had more prestige than the grunt jobs of plumbers, mechanics, masons, carpenters, and a host of others.

The fallout was an emphasis on uppity paper qualifications that took precedence over artisanal skill acquisition. So, graduates disparaged menial jobs that provided transitory relief in place of the endless wait for the illusive white-collar jobs. The calamity of unemployment persisted as I orbited under this limbo until I joined the Nigerian Army in 1988.

Notes

(1). For an insight into the NYSC scheme in Nigeria see: Obadare, Ebenezer: Statism, Youth and the Civic Imagination: A Critical Study of the National Youth Service Corps (NYSC) Programme in Nigeria: Centre for Social Development Global Service Institute. CSD Report 05-18.

(2). For an account of Babangida's transition programme see: Ojo, Emmanuel O : The military and democratic transition in Nigeria: An in-depth analysis of General Babangida's transition program (1985-1993) Journal of Political & Military Sociology 28(1): June 2000. pp1-20.

(3). See report on SAP: National Centre for Economic Management and Administration: Structural Adjustment Programme in Nigeria: Causes, Processes and Outcomes: Revised Technical Proposal.(4). For an insight on Anti-SAP riots see: Eboh, Marie Pauline: Anti-SAP Upheaval in Nigeria: Philosophy and Social Action, 16(3) 1990.

Basic Airborne 7/1994

Chapter Nine

The Making of an Officer

When I returned from my futile job-hunting expedition to Lagos, I tried my hands on a myriad of activities like managing a stationery store and copy shop with little success. However, all these would change in February 1988. A public service announcement drew my attention to the sales of application forms for the Nigerian Defence Academy (NDA). Not until that moment, I did not contemplate the possibility of joining a military service. But I recall that a long time ago, I jokingly told friends that I hoped to join the army after my university studies.

Even then, in 1982, a cousin offered me an already filled-out NDA application form, but I declined on account of its being defaced before submission. This was a long-forgotten gesture but with the new reality, I was keen about the next phase of my life which was to become an officer of the army.

Although, I had lived among soldiers as a barrack boy, and there may have been many attractions about the job, but I never contemplated joining. So, this was the outlook and all through my teenage years, the prospect of army job never crossed my mind. So, I took time to deliberate its subtleties, teased myself and played mind games.

Of course, the first thing that came to my mind was isolating the motive that would make me join the army. This simple reflection generated mixed responses which spawned a medley of answers even as an individual that regressed on a scale, from the annoyingly pretentious through messianic charlatanism and pathetic opportunism. So many superficialities also cropped up, incorporating such glibness as service to the nation and officer careerism.

All these were superfluous to the underlying drive of lust for power, as well as the potential for primitive accumulation it portended. It would be a sacrifice, as the prospect of severe injury and quick death were all too real. Otherwise, the fictitious claims of service and professionalism were a travesty that must be seen as such.

Furthermore, the army was a grunt job without tact. By design, virtually all armies, were feudal in character and structure. Far worse, post-colonial armies of Africa were a cut high as deputation armies. Whereas regular armies were organized and equipped to preserve sovereignties, proxy armies originated as militias of enclosures and occupation, and historically too, they evolved into conspiratorial instruments of domination.

These forces, especially those bequeathed lately at the dissolution of the European colonial enterprise in Africa, were often used as claws of reactionary state power mongers. Therefore, a common shared attribute of these armies included fights within their ranks and often against the populace.

Besides, the military subsisted on a system of discipline by which its members obeyed orders unquestioningly and acquiesced to superiors of all shades. A rank system and hierarchy of command reinforced this literal tyranny. Therefore, armies were organizations driven by institutionalized arbitrariness and narrow-mindedness. By any factors therefore, as a free spirit, I could not voluntarily join such a blatantly deleterious group.

But again, these were the days of military rule in Nigeria, and it was a known fact that Nigerians loved power and would go to any length to become powerful by themselves or by association. It was obvious that Nigeria's prolonged military rule had subconsciously set the country on the path of militarization.

It was a commonplace manifestation to see individuals and different organizations decked in uniforms and military-like kits. Even more, state security operatives, for instance, the Nigeria Police dropped the baton and picked up Mark 4 rifles, only to be replaced by AK 47 assault rifles. The same trend was replicated by the Nigeria Prisons, Immigration, Customs, Civil Defence, private guards, and a host of ancillary groups that became legally and illegally armed. Each of these armed services and groups claimed parallel capricious lines of authority on behalf of themselves, families, friends, in-laws, co-religionists, tribal members etc., to oppress those without a corresponding facility.

Furthermore, the Nigerian military superintended over by the Nigerian Army, sat atop a vulturine neo-imperialist potpourri called Nigeria. While in power, careerist civil servants manipulated military figureheads, though in many instances they could be powerful by themselves. Whereas military rule could be minimalist in form, it was matchless in its invasiveness and autocratic tendencies.

Given the above models, a fluid system evolved whereby avaricious military elements, in cahoots with civilian collaborators, masqueraded as governors, diplomats, architects, political scientists, athletes, aristocrats, mercantilists, witchdoctors, acrobats, conjurers, contortionists, money-doublers, debt and rent collectors, judges, land grabbers-cum-arbitrators and even offered such exotic services like thuggery for hire. From the odds registered, it was reasonable for anyone to look to join a service to secure themselves and by extension their families against fellow Nigerians.

Another inducement was the high rate of unemployment prevalent then. Over time, I tried running a small retail and service business but still desired a paid job. On one hand, it was obvious that I was not cut out for a civil service job and explored the possibility of going back to the university to get a higher degree. On the other, officer cadets got stipends while in training and the prospects of a job were a given. But then again, to join I had to doubly bend back sort of.

There were manifold requirements as well. For instance, to qualify for enlistment, potential entrants were expected to be within a certain age bracket, apart from a sound bodily and mental state. As for the age criterion, since my birth was not registered officially, I had the leverage to decide this at the courts, either truthfully or dishonestly, which I did. Otherwise, I was in a top physical and sound mental state, even though I had a broken right arm that was poorly set.

Furthermore, the academic qualification for entry was five GCE credits at the ordinary level. In which case, I was overqualified having graduated from a university in 1986 and completed NYSC by 1987. It was a shrewd decision, for I figured out that, if I became an officer cadet, I would become "powerful" and live above average Nigerian laws and if driven by adequate greed, I could acquire illicit wealth.

In other words, despite potential risks, all considerations of service to the nation and professionalism were subordinate to the incentive of barefaced self-interest. It was true for me at the point of entry, as it was for others regardless of decoys and intensifications. So, as a first step, I had to warehouse my first degree and scheme as a school leaver and stoop in the hope that I would conquer. It was a hard resolve that overstrained the profundity of my patience, strength, and determination in the next twenty-two years after I took the plunge.

NDA Form

The decision to join the army was only a first step. The next step of equal importance was obtaining the application form, which was available at the Cabinet Office for the sum of Five Naira only. Nonetheless, my economy then was understandably in sympathetic throes with the ailing national economy with no dime in my name. I could have easily gotten money from my elder brother, but I was disinclined to explain the debatable decision to join the army as a regular cadet.

Luckily, it did not take me long trawling. One of my high schoolmates graciously gave me the money with which I bought the form. Afterwards, I sat for the entrance examinations into the Nigerian Defence Academy (NDA) at Tilley Gyado College, Makurdi. Then, I left for Lagos once again where I would remain until a fellow candidate at the entrance exams came to inform me that I was shortlisted for a selection board. The board took place in Kaduna in July and by September 1988, I was selected as an Officer Cadet of the Fortieth Regular Combatant Course of the Nigerian Defence Academy.

It was quite sudden for those without an insight into my new preoccupation. On a more general note, it was expected that if I had chosen to join the army, I would opt for a Short Service Commission (SSC). This was the typical entry point for university graduates with the training period abbreviated to six months. However, I chose regular combatant commission which meant I would undergo five years of grueling training at the Academy.

Irregular Posses and Militias

The Armed Forces of Nigeria (AFN) consist of the Nigerian Army (NA), the Nigerian Navy (NN) and the Nigerian Air Force (NAF). It was in the NA, the biggest of the three that I served, and it is my discernment about the service that I wrote in this book. However, I shall begin with an outline history of the three services.

Pre-colonial Africa

An outline history of contemporary standing armies in Sub-Saharan Africa was inextricably interwoven with her liaison with the outlying civilizations of Europe, the Middle East, and the Asiatic. A great deal has been documented about Africa but two significant historical events, specifically the dual evils of the transatlantic (and its Arab version) slave trade and its colonial residue altered the pattern of the relationship. It is therefore essential to situate the context of both historical events.

Sub-Saharan Africa may not have had steady contact with medieval Europe and Arabs to the North and the Middle East and Asia to the East, does not imply she was insulated from the rest of humanity. African states and societies took part in international trade and diplomacy since ancient times. As a result, there were widespread international trading networks, especially at the pinnacle of ancient Ghana, Mali, Songhai, Kongo, Zimbabwe empires, and a host of other autonomous societies south of the Sahara.[1]

The riches of these empires and sovereignties were quite enormous as reckoned by the volume of trade in gold, spices, and exotic products. Similarly, they were engaged in manifold exchanges of articles like salt, glassware, and perfumes, complemented by cultural and religious infiltrations. To a degree too, these states relied on levying of customs duties, taxes, and tariffs on foreign trade to build national wealth and finance public expenditure.[2]

Historically, Africa to the North, long before the Arab Muslim conquest of the 7th and 8th centuries, was defined by a host of cultural influences. In fact, it was a melting pot. Historically too, Ancient Egypt ruled the region, at a time when Europeans still subsisted as Stone Age cave dwellers. In time, Carthaginians, Phoenicians, and Greeks, instituted lasting impact on the northern coast as trade expanded and seafaring improved.[3]

To a degree, an amalgam of factors like topography, unsavoury climate, mosquito infestations, and sundry diseases ensured that sub-Saharan Africa remained uncharted. Meanwhile, the scant knowledge of the continent's hinterland contributed to her inaccessibility and limited contact with the outside world. Whereas there was continuous contact between the Iberian Peninsula, the Mediterranean littorals, and

North Africa, these were tempered by the impedimenta of the Mediterranean Sea, the medieval upsurge of Moorish power, and the great Sahara Desert astride North Africa.[4]

Arab Hegemony and Acculturation

The Arabs were the first outlanders to maintain an unbroken contact with Africa south of the Sahara. With a land bridge in the Middle East, by the 7th Century AD, they first conquered the remnants of Greek and Roman Egypt and later overwhelmed Nubian and Berber lands of the middle Sahara from the Atlantic coast to the Red Sea and extended their influence onto coastal East Africa. Over time, particularly with the aid of camels and dhows, the Arabs penetrated the Sahara and maintained commercial links with the Sahelian empires of Ghana, Mali, and Songhai to the south and the Swahili coast of Africa.[5]

The Arab merchants typically clustered as they crossed the blistering Sahara with caravans laden with valuable merchandise in either direction during the passage. From the onset, the uncharted lands were not only unforgiving but inundated by hostile tribes. It was also a desolate landscape vulnerable to robbery and banditry that led to the loss of lives and merchandise. So, to ensure shared safety for their caravans, the merchants contracted Amazigh guides and moved in fortified cavalcades. This was the ideal option against isolated individual crossings as caravans were outfitted as de facto quasi-military expeditions.

Apart from protection parties, the merchants also engaged drivers, carriers, and minders to tend to the camels and expediencies of the caravans. Besides, for those whose services were so engaged, it became a one-way passage, as they often against their wishes became permanent residents in the Arab world. Meanwhile, others were forced into chattel slavery, the precursor to the East African, trans-Saharan and the four-hundred-year trans-Atlantic slave trade.[6]

The trans-Saharan trade in humans was understandably very profitable and more attractive. The merchandise was gotten through captives of endless tribal wars and slave raids instigated by Arab and later European merchants. As a result, conflicts and raids became constant plagues to these societies.[7]

Historically too, in their dealings, these merchants commonly undervalued and swindled Africans of their wares. As it happened, Africans from the start of this intercourse were subjected to condescension and racism, first by the Arabs and later by Europeans. With this kind of despondency, the Arab villains and European plunderers could not expect to be accorded protected persons status and granted free passage in the territories they so ceaselessly tormented. Although the Arabs never acquired vast colonies except for the Zanzibar archipelago and enclaves like Mombasa, they instituted enduring cultural changes in the form of Islam in sub-Saharan Africa.[8]

Gamblers and Outlaws

Similarly, just like the contact with the Arabs before them, European interaction with Sub-Saharan Africa was marginal. In time, they became acquainted with the Gulf of Guinea on the Atlantic and its outlying hinterland. This was chiefly due to the activities of Iberian sailors adrift in the early decades of the 15th century. As seafaring improved, visits became more regular, and trade in goods evolved.

In the long run, the mercantilist pursuits of Europeans also led to a high demand for labour in faraway Americas. First, the vast so-called New World was violently seized from its native owners and the new lands were put to massive agricultural use which spurred a high demand for labour on the plantations. Regrettably, the native population, virtually decimated by diseases transmitted by European invaders and genocidal wars, could not suffice.

Consequently, as the demand for cheap labour to work on the plantations grew, Europeans set their sights on Africa and thereafter a massive trade in slaves developed. In this way, enslaved people stolen from Africa became the most valuable 'commodity' in the new trade. Subsequently, for the next four hundred years, the west coast of Africa became the main source of human merchandise for Christian and God-fearing European plunderers.[10]

At the dawn of the 19th century, the Industrial Revolution significantly altered the systems of production as machines begun to replace humans in key areas of production and manufacture. This transformative technology accelerated the prospects of an abundance of material provisions and led to a review of the demographic ravages of the slave trade.

Moreover, the joint efforts of adventurers and gamblers like Mungo Park (1771-1806), Captain Hugh Clapperton (1788-1827), Richard Francis Burton (1821-1890), John Hanning Speke (1827-1864), David Livingstone (1813-1873), Henry Morton Stanley (1841-1901), Richard Lander (1804-1834), Dr Heinrich Barth (1821-1865) and other alleged explorers, Africa's hinterland was steadily penetrated. Graciously, many of these sentinels of destruction died during those dubious expeditions.[11]

The emergent focus was on the search for markets for products and sources of raw materials that could be found in the far-flung expanses of Africa. As a result, Britain the mother slaving nation, also a leading industrial power, craftily declared slave trade and traffic in slaves outlawed.[12]

However, not all European slave trading nations and their African runners enthusiastically embraced the new dynamics. So, the trade persisted clandestinely. On its heels, the British stationed naval squadrons along the coast of the Gulf of Guinea to intercept slave-laden ships. Apart from provocation and insolence, the squadrons escalated skirmishes against local coastal communities. As a result, in 1851, the West Africa Squadron bombarded Lagos, the so-called chief slave market of West Africa, into submission. This foothold, was the little beginnings of the British Colony of Lagos proclaimed in 1861, which evolved into what became known as Nigeria.[13]

Historically though, adventurers, traders, and Christian missionaries preceded the proclamation of colonies. These traders were granted dubious charters by European powers. Later, hastily formed Christian missionary societies besieged Africa with religion, unequal trade, new consumption patterns, and cultural imperialism that upturned societies and stole lands.

With the active support of their home governments, traders and missionaries were engaged in a harvest of ill-defined treaties granting monopolies, ceding territories, and acquiescent protection by such powers represented by its makers delineating the so-called spheres of economic interest.[14]

The humiliation of these falsifications and brigandage were awarded false seals of approval through the General Act of Berlin that was crafted after the Berlin Conference of 1884-1885. Consequently, Africa was arbitrarily dismembered among European imperialists. Although the French contested the outcome, the conference recognized a British claim to a protectorate over a vast territory later named Nigeria. The French contention also led to a long-drawn race to effectively occupy the self-styled spheres of economic interest.[15]

The area in question was endowed with a long coast and a belt of about sixty miles in depth of dense mangrove forests and swamps. It was also crisscrossed by the branches of the Niger Delta which were interlocked one with another by innumerable creeks, into an unbroken inland waterway. Nonetheless, Britain's power and influence extended little beyond the banks of the rivers.

Besides, the inability of the charter companies to stamp authority and fend off other European rivals, especially French aggression on the western frontiers, compelled the British Government to assume direct control over those treaty areas. Nevertheless, the impudence with which the British colonial enterprise was driven gave neither quarter for cooperation nor consent. It was only natural that from the start, African sovereignties ferociously resisted colonial posturing. In the face of mounting altercations, it was clear that power and authority could only be projected by the force of arms. Herein lay the foundations of ragtag armies, irregular posses, and militias that became veritable tools of colonial enclosure, subjugation, and occupation.

In addition, the resolve to subdue recalcitrant local irredentists was unambiguous as the British set up a framework of a predacious colonial economy. Men were needed to work on the construction of railways, roads, and residences for colonial officers as well as to survey the colonies. All these were unrequited, poorly paid or forced labour that was violently repudiated unless otherwise enforced.

Thus, the nucleus of the forces that set up a new colonial order started life as protection parties for trading convoys of the Royal Niger Company against hostile hordes. This band of irregulars also took part in colonial wars of occupation and subjugation. They also formed the bulk of the troops that were used in the British-Ijebu war in 1892, the 1894 expedition against Nana Olomu, the 1895 bombardment of Oyo, the 1897 Benin Expedition, and the 1916 suppression of Egba uprising.

The Nigerian Army

Historically, the oldest element that evolved into the NA was formed on 1 June 1863. It was a force of eighty men hastily assembled by then Lieutenant John Glover, later an Administrator of Lagos. He needed a protection party to travel overland to Lagos following a shipwreck at Jebba.[16]

The force was christened Glover's Hausas since it was populated by runaway Hausa slaves, gadabouts, and camp boys. Even more, Hausa elements were a critical driving force in support of the British conquest of Nigeria. The conquered peoples found it detestable that the forces were staffed by slave factotum and other tribes. This provoked open hostility to British claims since it was not yet enforced.

Over time, the band came to be known by different nomenclatures including Hausa Militia or Hausa Constabulary and later the Lagos Constabulary from 1865 through 1873. It was a paramilitary force with dual military and policing roles especially in Lagos in the latter part of the 19th century.

Furthermore, Frederick Lugard of the Royal Niger Company was also involved in the founding of the NA. Historical sources indicate that in 1898, apart from founding the Royal Niger Company Constabulary, which was merged into the new force, he planned to recruit a force locally with a tentative staff of British officers. However, a drive for the consolidation of occupied territories meant the plan for such a force was overridden by the policies of the War Office.

Since the new policy plank on local troops emphasized a concentration of forces, the plan was suspended. Even more, the newly constituted Colonial Office centralized forces in the colonies to achieve better coordination, economy of force, and efficiency in firming up colonial rule in West Africa. To achieve this plan, a committee superintended by William Palmer, aka Lord Selborne explored the possibility of creating localized forces.

The work of the committee led to the formal separation of police (irregular) from military (regular) roles and the merging of all colonial forces. The final product was the West African Frontier Force (WAFF) composed of Lagos Constabulary, Gold Coast Constabulary, and Sierra Leone Frontier Police. The balance of forces was coupled from Niger

Coast Constabulary, West African Field Force, and the Royal Niger Company Constabulary.[17]

The distinguishing feature of WAFF was its British officers and African troops. At the opportune time, these forces were deployed to pacify the rulers of Hausa states and the Bornu Empire. More significantly, the presence of British elements became the precursor of the inequitable officer-soldier relations that was instituted in the NA.

When colonial hegemony was enforced, sovereignties or centres of powers were dismantled piecemeal with new collaborators appointed that governed according to British notions. Even still, to reinforce effective occupation, British Residents and military bands were stationed throughout the colony to exercise nefarious checks on any tendencies to relapse to hostilities.

Although in southern Nigeria there were fewer large states by the late 19th century to effectively resist encroachment, there was on the lower reaches of the Benin River, a flamboyant Itsekiri chief and palm oil merchant, Nana Olomu, who defended his independence and defied protectorate shenanigans. The chief and his Itsekiri agents openly transacted against the double-dealing British oil robbers who tried to bypass his network to trade directly in the interior.[18]

Meanwhile, composite forces were deployed to mount punitive expeditions against Nana. The Itsekiri Chief was attacked by naval and land forces and routed in 1894 following fierce fighting. At this point, a pattern had appeared, it could be seen that the earlier bombardment of Lagos and the expedition against Nana, Akassa, and King Jaja of Opobo underscored the gunboat origins of the Nigerian Navy.

The Nigerian Navy

Along the stretch of the Gulf of Guinea and the contiguous hinterland which later became known as Nigeria, there were many rivers some of which were seasonally navigable. The most prominent of these were the Niger, Benue, Cross and Imo rivers. The region was also home to the Niger Delta with rivers that interconnected to one another by innumerable creeks into a seamless inland waterway.

As the British occupation took hold alongside a renewed spirit of greed and plunder, pseudo-military flotillas were deployed to explore the navigable upper reaches of River Niger as far as Baro. On the River Benue too, there were seasonal boat services upland to Makurdi and occasionally Yola on the upper Benue when water volumes permitted. Customarily, these steamboats moved passengers, provisions, and mails and on the turnaround, ferried produce, and precious stones from the hinterland, given the then perilous state of roads and trails.[19]

It was clear that the colonial government was not disposed to creating a proper naval force since the Royal Navy undertook maritime protection duties of the territorial waters of Nigeria and the adjoining colonies. In its place, a Marine Department, a quasi-military organization was set up and tasked with keeping watch over the security of ports, and coastal approaches, as well as providing harbour services to Royal Navy ships on patrol of West African waters.[20]
Along these lines too, the marine division became the inheritor and custodian of gunboats that were invested in the bombardment and subjugation of the Niger Delta coastal societies and creeks inland onto the Imo River. These relics were never discarded but endured as nominal naval platforms easily accessed against unforeseen security situations.[21]

Similarly, the department was bequeathed an assortment of steamboats, barges, tugboats, boathouses, and light crafts used on inland waterways. It was also assigned the duties of dredging channels, ferrying services, and touring launches that plied the countless creeks and waterways.

However, in the closing days of colonial rule and Nigeria's self-rule from the early 1950s, there was a groundswell for the formation of a naval force modelled on the Royal Navy. In time, political engagements led to the disbandment of the Marine Department in 1956. However, the officers and men of the defunct unit were re-engaged, and more recruits were coalesced to form the nucleus of a Nigerian Naval Force (NNF) in April 1956 which was operationalized on 1 June 1956 with the inherited flotsam.[22]

Ultimately, a Nigerian Navy Ordinance was enacted by the House of Representatives and assented to by the Governor-General of Nigeria, making the Naval Defence Force (NDF), a legal entity on 1 May 1958, with a dubious statutory operational limit of only three nautical miles of territorial waters. Ultimately, the Navy Act of 1964 set up the NN followed by an extension of the country's territorial waters.

The Nigerian Air Force

The science of practical flying and the use of planes for military purposes was a 20th-century development. The airplane was a novel, complex, and expensive technology not yet mastered. Although, limited numbers of planes were deployed on surveillance and sorties during the First World War, these were proof of concept trials that only fully crystalized during the Second World War.[23]

Meanwhile, the scale of devastations and rebuilding efforts significantly gobbled the resources of a ruined post-war Britain to make it untenable to plan the creation of air forces in the colonies. However, the strategic value of Nigeria's airspace was recognized especially during the Second World War when Kano and Lagos airports were used as Forward Operational Bases (FOB). Other usages included Refueling Points, Logistics Dumps and Transit Ports. Thus, the Nigeria Air Force (NAF) was the only branch of the Armed Forces of Nigeria without a colonial heritage of enclosure, conquest, and occupation.[24]

In general terms, the need for an air force arose from Nigeria's growing participation in peace-keeping operations in the Congo and Tanganyika. During those missions, Nigeria outsourced the airlift of her contingents into and out of the theatres of operations to other nations. It was a drawback that portended risk to national security and a decision was taken to set up an air force.

In pursuit of this vision, the groundwork to set up NAF began in the wake of parliamentary approval. From 1962, Nigeria signed bilateral agreements with several countries to train her manpower in different aspects of aviation. Finally, the pioneer officers of the force were poached from NA in June 1962. The first batch consisted of ten cadets trained by the Ethiopian Air Force. Yet another batch of sixteen were trained by the Royal Canadian Air Force in February 1963, while a balance of six were accepted by the Indian Air Force for training by 1963.[25]

In addition, Nigeria entered into a partnership with West German Air Force as a technical partner which was run by Dornier with a base at Kaduna and was tasked with conducting localized training of NAF personnel. When the NAF Act was signed in April 1964 into law, the force was officially instated.[26]

It was therefore an untested NAF that was thrust into the fray of the Nigerian civil war. Its inventory and capability were doubtful as it was equipped with only a few planes. But as the war progressed, fighter planes like MiG 15 and 17 were acquired and flown by mercenary pilots from Egypt and Russia. When the war ended in 1970, NAF was significantly expanded, re-organized and upgraded

Therefore, from the outline history of modern military forces in Nigeria, it was conclusive that the NA and NN were inextricably linked to the imposition of foreign rule, institution of colonial economy, and protection of atavistic mercantilist advantages. These tendencies were in contradiction to local sentiments and provoked hostilities and sometimes violent reactions. In operations, the colonial forces were deliberately heavy-handed in response to security infractions. Along these lines, cantankerous relations between troops and communities developed as the forces always safeguarded British interests.

The counteraction against the Egba uprising in 1916, the indiscriminate firing at unarmed women in suppression of the Aba Women's Riots of 1929-30, the maiming of coal miners at Iva Valley in 1949, and the brutal post-independence operations against Tiv Riots in 1965 proved this mindset. Post-independence, the armed forces further combined their roles as the enforcers of state power mongers and dominance.

Historically too, the personnel and rank structures were malevolently affecting towards white officers. Although these forces were unable to attract the right calibre of British military experts, they were populated by mediocre journeymen, drunkards, debtors, felons, and adventurers willing to risk living in the wilderness of the mosquito-infested Dark Continent.

The incentives for service in the colonial forces were quite enormous and attractive. As a result, hordes of poor, landless, nameless run-of-the-mill types flocked to fantasy lives driven by brutality and bloody-mindedness superintending over miserable and bewildered African ragtag armies.

These brutes were set apart by facility and demeanour from the main body of African troops to reinforce the mystique of white pre-eminence and apartness. The British rabbles were not only contemptuous in their routine exchanges with their African colleagues, but distasteful in all ramifications as it was always an officer corps of white British folks and subordinate troops of Africans.

This impertinence was extended to boarding and recreational facilities. In the future, when Africans gained commissions, the officers exhibited discriminatory tendencies along cadre and rank of services. The newly commissioned African officers ran an identically crude and exasperating version of superior-subordinate regimen akin to a master-servant relationship. This was reinforced by the proliferation of facilities like officers' messes, soldiers' clubs and other facilities set apart.

Notes
(1). For an account on European contact with Africa: https//wasscehistorytextbook.com/
(2-9). https//wasscehistorytextbook.com/
(10). For an account of slave trade see: Mintz, Steven: Historical Context: Facts about the Slave Trade and Slavery: The Gilder Lehrman Institute of American History.
(11). For accounts of European Exploration of Africa: Mazrui, Ali A: European Exploration and Africa Self-Discovery Cambridge University Press: November 11, 2008.
(12). Insights on British naval squadrons: www.historicuk.com : Jessica: The West Africa Squadron. March 4, 2023.
(13). Insights on British naval squadrons: www.historicuk.com : rain, Jessica: The West Africa Squadron. March 4, 2023.
(14). For an account of shambles and partition of Africa: https//wasscehistorytextbook.com/
(15). For an account of rivalry: https//wasscehistorytextbook.com/
(16). For accounts of the origins of NA see: Abdulrahman, Suberu chi: The Nigerian Army as a Product of Its Colonial History: Problems of Re-building Cohesion for an Army in Transition: International Affairs and Global Strategy. Vol.53, 2017.
(17). Haywood, Austin HW and Clarke Frederick AS: The History of Royal West African Frontier Force, Gale and Poden, 1964.
(18). Ikime, Obaro: Merchant Prince of the Niger Delta: The Rise and Fall of Nana Olomu, Last Governor of the Benin River: Heinemann, London.1968.

(19). Danladi, Anthony Ali: The Dilemma of Colonial Transportation on The Lower Niger and Benue Rivers 1879-1960: Jebat: Malaysian Journal of History, Politics & Strategic Studies, Vol. 46 (1) (July 2019): 155-171.

Academy 1991

Nigerian Army Day Celebrations 2006

Chapter Ten

Officers and Oscar Romeos

For a start, NA personnel are categorized into officers and soldiers, the latter is also known as other ranks. Ordinarily, the expression might appear inconsistent but in military jargon, the term describes a member of an army usually of a rank below a commissioned officer. In the Nigerian Army, soldiers' ranks are graded into eight echelons, and further split into warrant officers and non-commissioned officers.

The Warrant officer is the highest rank attainable by a soldier and has four classes namely Army Warrant Officer, Master Warrant Officer, Warrant Officer Classes One and Two, respectively. The non-commissioned officers' segment has a second category namely senior non-commissioned officers, which included the midsection of the troops. The latter subdivision composed of staff sergeants and sergeants. Corporals and lance corporals were junior non-commissioned officers, and the rear was brought up by privates and recruits, in that order.

In contrast, a commission was an appointment to the rank of an officer including a second lieutenant or above. Of these, there was a collection of eleven ranks. The topmost was the Field Marshal. Others in this category included the four-star General, three-star Lieutenant General, and two-star Major General at the top hierarchy.

The mid-section of commissions was the one-star Brigadier General. The highest-ranked field officer was the Colonel closely trailed by the commanding Lieutenant Colonel. The lower rungs of field officers included Major, Captain, Lieutenant, and Second Lieutenant. Therefore, to all intents and purposes, the NA was an army of soldiers led by officers.

By Choice or By Compulsion

In general terms, a military force was categorized by its mode of enlistment, which could be voluntary or by draft. A voluntary army was a force where members freely enlisted because they wished to do so. Whereas, in a conscription or draft army, individuals were compelled by decree to join. Expectedly, enforced mobilizations threw up complications since it was impossible to compel folks to risk their lives against their wishes. Even more, conscription negatively affected armies, as they were beset with the challenges of low incentive and poor motivation against a backdrop of compulsion.

By extension too, such armies were more likely to foster venal attitudes by which they fought for recompense with little or no loyalty to the country they served. Overall, the product of voluntary armies tended to be more loyal and better motivated. All told, the NA is a voluntary territorial army, and a long-service force of regular officers and soldiers.

Joining the Army

Since there were multiple strands of personnel in the NA, it necessarily meant that there would be multiple entry points into the service as well. In the colonial era, recruitment into the WAFF was at Zaria, Enugu and Ibadan. Typically, recruits were trained at Nigerian Regimental Training Centre (NRTC) Zaria, for a six-month basic training course.

On the other hand, officers were trained overseas until the establishment of the Royal Military Forces Training College (RMFTC), Kaduna. Since then, RMFTC and NRTC, the latter-day Nigerian Defence Academy (NDA), and Depot NA have been the primary posterns in the army, for officers and soldiers, respectively.

No Going Back

Depot NA was established in 1924. It is the primary unit tasked with moulding recruits into fighting soldiers. It serves as a pivotal installation that retooled raw civilians, magicians, impersonators, charlatans, shamans, alarmists, and extremists etc. It was a leveler outfit that demystified the posterities of aristocrats, failed robbers, debtors, clerics, witchdoctors, occultists, pimps, regionalists, witches, sorcerers, groupies, and peasants etc.

The unit expertly deconstructed trainees manifestly populated by the amalgamated interests of cartel capitalism, provincialism, partisan power mongers, and more. These combines were exorcised of all pretenses and phobias and delivered as soldiers adjudged satisfactory and operationally adept.

However, after the Nigerian Civil war in 1970, for a long time, the unit was moribund as there was no new enlistment into the NA until late 1979. The first batch of resumed intakes was trained in 1980. This set of trainees ushered in the 79NA series of soldiers.

However, while the training hiatus lasted, the relics inherited from WAFF i.e., physical edifices like training sheds, recruit lines, and officers and troops' quarters became derelict. Its woes aside, Depot NA was unique in a recruit's life because it epitomized a place of formative change for individual soldiers, as it was the first point of entry into the military as a trainee member.

When Depot NA resumed training, it could be seen that it took in visibly untrainable charges. It was such that, recruits were barely educated for a modern army. Even worse, during training, recruits were poorly clad in skeletal military kits and accommodated in ramshackle hovels in the name of hostels.

Besides, the training support for this key unit was miserable and recruits were fed poor workhouse portions during training. Amidst these drawbacks, intensified tribal hegemony and machination seized control. Lately, the unit became an infamous enclave for money laundering and diversion of resources. Despite this disagreeable situation, Depot NA still trained soldiers, except the quality of its products gradually deteriorated into low-performing soldiers due to nepotism, racketeering, and extortion from within and without that overwhelmed the recruitment and training process.

Nigerian Defence Academy

As already stated, WAFF regiments were typically led by a white British officer corps that superintended over Black African troops. Although Nigerian elements in WAFF were very committed, of proven gallantry and made sacrifices during British campaigns in German East Africa in 1916 and Burma from 1943-1945, none received a commission as officers until Warrant Officer Wellington U Bassey got commissioned on 30 April 1948, as the first Indigenous officer.[2]

However, all these would change by 1953, when the Regular Officers Special Training School (ROSTS) was set up at Teshie Ghana, in response to a shortfall of officers in the British chaperoned WAFF. The school's curriculum was designed to train officers from British West African colonies. Accordingly, officer cadets drawn from the colonies received basic training that lasted six months, even though the finishing took place at British military academies at Mons or Sandhurst. Thereafter, cadets were commissioned into the rank of Second Lieutenant.[3]

Moreover, WAFF focused on British security interests and not the concerns of the separable national forces in its fold. So, before independence, decisions were taken to address the dearth of native officers. To this end, the Royal Military Forces Training College (RMFTC) was established at Kaduna in April 1960, modelled after ROSTS and ran identical preliminary training of officer cadets. The college was renamed Nigerian Military Training College (NMTC) in 1963 when Nigeria became a republic. Post-independence, a review of the trajectory and conspicuous inadequacies of the existing structures demanded an expansion of the armed forces. Thereafter, NMTC was renamed Nigerian Defence Academy (NDA) in 1964, with its core curriculum revised from elementary orientation and upgraded to a full-fledged training of regular officer cadets for the Armed Forces of Nigeria.[4]

From its start, NDA was a joint services military academy. Therefore, the citadel trained officers for NA, NN, and NAF. The first set of instructors was seconded from Indian Armed Forces and the first regular course ran for three and a half years.[5]

Apartness

Enlistment into the service was different for each of the named categories of personnel. Although it was possible to transition from being a soldier to a commissioned officer, a reversal of status was not permissible. As a result, it became an obsession for soldiers, to aspire to a commission.

Professionally, all got instructed in various aspects of war and soldierly traditions. However, the first placement and orientation determined the mindset of each, i.e., one as a leader and the other as the led. This was central to the countenance and deportment of both. The beginning also marked an ever-increasing dissonance between the two, that in time bred discontent.

In the Bargain

In the bargain, there were distinct types of commissions into the NA. Each kind was related to peculiar circumstances or operational exigencies. There were principally five types of appointments and commissions namely Temporary, Executive aka Quartermaster, Direct Regular Combatant, Short Service Combatant (SSC), Direct Short Service Combatant (DSSC), and the Regular Combatant (RC) commissions.

The terms and conditions of each commission were spelt out outlining their limitations in responsibility and command. However, over time, the non-implementation of policies, so often significantly blurred the distinctions between the different types of commissions and created tensions. The RC and SSC were combatants and so trained to lead and fight battles while the others were non-combatants.

Short Service Commission

The Short Service Commission was made up of two strands namely SSC and DSSC. The main difference between the two was a factor of the academic qualifications at the point of entry because then, the SSC component accepted high school leavers while DSSC took in university graduates. Upon graduation, the trainees were granted the rank of Second Lieutenant and Lieutenant, respectively.

Both commissions were combatants and therefore eligible to command troops in the field. Nonetheless, they spent a shorter duration in training and the length of service was limited to no more than fifteen years subject to extensions. Both commissions were typically granted for fifteen years of which ten were on the active list. It was thereafter renewable for a period not exceeding five years. Even more, SSC officers also had the choice to convert to RC or DRC to enjoy a longer career.

Regular Combatant

The Regular Combatant was a thirty-five-year tenured career commission that was open to civilians and service personnel alike. On paper, it was the foremost commission. Regular officers were trained at the Nigerian Defence Academy Kaduna over a five-year period. In general terms, officers with this type of commission could reach all the ranks in the NA and were not subject to any limitations. However, the commission came with professional and mandatory upgrades before progressing to the next higher rank which in turn created venomous competition among contemporaries.

Enlistment

If any individual wished to join military service, they were expected to meet certain criteria to be considered in the first place. These counted in educational qualifications, physical fitness, and the right mental attitude. To join, whether as an officer or soldier, the prospective candidates had to apply for and get shortlisted to appear before a selection or recruitment board. The process started with a boot camp-like setting. At this point, candidates were put through mental tests and rigorous physical exertions to evaluate their suitability for military training.

Course Numbering System

The military had a course numbering system based on the batch of trainee enlistment. This system was meant to reinforce a hierarchy of seniority, as well as to set apart each set of trainees. Even more, it allowed that individuals could be on the same rank, but seniority could be discriminated by the date of promotion or course which was generated serially.

The basic information incorporated the year of training and the course serial. For instance, I am a member of 40 RC which could be expressed as the fortieth set of regular officer cadets trained since the inception of NDA in 1964. Similarly, 79NA/17, stood for the seventeenth set of regular recruits' intake trained at the Depot NA of the 1979 recruitment series. In this way, individuals applied to and were accepted on a particular course and were so identified throughout their service years.

Selection Board

Prospective officer cadets were chosen through a selection board. Once a decision was made to accept new intakes, the Chief of Defence Staff (CDS), instituted a selection board composed of a president, secretary, and members. Usually, membership of the board was drawn from the three services along with civilian representatives from the Ministry of Defence.

However, if the exercise involved only the NA, the composition of the board devolved to the office of the Chief of Administration (Army) at the Army Headquarters (AHQ). The board then went ahead to conduct medical screening, verification of documents, and rigorous physical tests. These along with other unpublicized factors were used to determine successful candidates.

Recruitment Exercise

On the statute books, the Education Department of the NA was the designated branch responsible for the recruitment of trainees. In the main, potential recruits were selected through a recruitment exercise. The administration department set up a board and like the selection board, its activities involved medical screening, verification of documents, and rigorous physical tests. However, over the years, the NA experimented with different outfits including the Directorate of Army Recruitment and Resettlement (DARR).

Eligibility and Localized Competition

By law, only Nigerians were eligible to join the NA and its sister services. An individual had to be an indigene of any of the thirty-six states and the Federal Capital Territory to be considered. Even more, the force was an equal-opportunity employer. Therefore, the competition for placement was confined to states and local councils for both recruitment exercises and selection boards.

In simple terms, each state was allotted vacancies that were open to its constituents to be fairly distributed across local councils. Nevertheless, there was little neutrality even in the localized allocation. This process only served to deepen ethnic propensities and hardened deep-seated animosity even within the same ethnic group. Hence, enlistment into the NA became saturated with deadly ethnic shiftiness.

To complicate matters, countless prospective candidates falsified their identities and claimed localities, councils, and states other than theirs. It was so obvious that such officers and soldiers had neither physical attributes nor the cultural traits of the localities of origin they claimed. So, deceit and concealment went into joining the army.

Moreover, due to the centralizing role of WAFF in the colonial times, many non-Nigerian elements got recruited into the NA. The presence of foreigners expanded significantly during the Nigerian Civil War with a large intake of the Godogodo (Chadians) into the NA. This practice persisted as the service was still populated by Beninois, Cameroonians, Nigeriens, and Ghanaians.

Women in the Nigerian Army

Colonial armies in Africa were mostly all-male institutions. Although imperial armies had cause to deploy women in war, it was a late 20th-century development. Even still, the roles of women during WWII were ancillary. For the most part, women in those armies were not deployed in direct combat roles until the late 1970s.

It was not a matter of masculinity or lack of roles for women, but it had everything to do with it as well. The fact was that not much was known about the impact of subjecting women to extended combat fatigue. Also, the tender constitution or gynaecological intricacies could be an obstacle.

From personal experience, when I lived among soldiers, there were no female personnel, because till then, none or few were enlisted. The closest mock-up of women in uniform in NA barracks were the Magajiyas or women leaders. These were not soldiers per se, but resourceful and garrulous spouses appointed to help in the mobilization of soldiers' families when it became necessary to do so. Funnily, they were always decked out in drab caricatures of military uniforms and ranks.

The military being true to its ethos, even when it was clear that women played vital roles in areas like policing, nursing, and catering, the NA remained effectively an all-male service. However, starting from 1974 recruitment of tradesmen and women, few women were accepted, and some progressed to commissions and were deployed in medical units and catering services. In the intervening time, starting from 1980, this exclusiveness was significantly altered when womenfolk were accepted on the 79NA series of regular recruits into the army.

The fallout of these new entrants was that it all but shook-up military discipline. First, it became known that there was an adverse reaction of the feminine circle to the arduous and sustained training at Depot NA. It was reported that the menstrual periods of female trainees went into abeyance during the training. Hence, female recruits got impregnated by fellow recruits, or instructors without knowing, owing to this temporary remission.

Additionally, special administrative instructions had to be drawn up to outline the relationship between officers, soldiers, and their female counterparts, especially on fraternization. It must be allowed that, for all the stringent rules and regulations, it was ever an epic phallic struggle. The reality was that there was still amorous attraction towards each other between female soldiers and their colleagues on one hand, and officers and female soldiers on the other.

There were guidelines which explicitly forbade libidinal transactions between officers and female soldiers, though in practice, both were locked in the forbidden entanglement. As an organization built on order, the all-male army was now challenged in an uncharted territory of passion and sensuality. With their airs of entitlement, superiors were faced with instances when arbitrariness would not suffice because the young female soldiers now excited luscious hysteria by which they contrived to grab military good order by the balls.

The pervasive prospects of carnal attraction were expected; so, cautions were pronounced by which it was forbidden for an officer to cavort or marry a soldier of either gender. Soldiers could marry among themselves but not across the lines. Nonetheless, it became known that couples persisted in illicit trysts and either way or in extreme cases, both gave up their careers.

But the struggle lay deep, not only within the individual but a system-wide obsession. The young female soldiers were pubescent girls with high sexual drive normal at their age. Despite their grouchy military demeanour, inside they were not any different from deflowered and giggly seducers. Due in part to the patronage system in place, some of them, not only eagerly toppled into the arms of fellow soldiers, but often officers, in the hopes of salacious favours and many unnamable benefits.

Another dimension to the conundrum was the improper deployment of female soldiers that further accentuated a sexist slant to their potential. Most young female soldiers were deployed as tea girls, office orderlies, orderlies to spouses of senior offices, batmen, and other such duties at close quarters that stimulated intimacy. Consequently, an elaborate system of sexual exploitation and abuse, which was mutually beneficial to both parties evolved.

Even with the deterrent measures, randy pairs or groups granted themselves carnal pleasures and other incentives including monetary rewards, material gifts, accelerated promotions, and commissions as officers, as complementary bestowals for making the service both rewarding and pleasurable. Along the line too, decisions and policies were twisted or tweaked to favour partners in sex-fueled gambols that manifestly undermined moderation and the good order of the service.

It was now bare, that scandalous superiors had traded away good order under the influence of demented bacchanal escapades. So, the young female soldiers, with feline legerdemain, became serially insubordinate to their superiors and projected the authority of the very senior officers they carnally chaperoned. They became arrogant, condescending, and untouchable on account of these illegal liaisons and libidinous deployments.

Matters were not helped as captivated senior officers became overtly protective and indulgent of their acolytes. Even without the hints of untoward activities that subsisted, female soldiers and officers were given to blackmail. They would refuse lawful orders and turn around to plead sexual harassment or persecution. As these could not be easily proven, it was a matter of conjecture and discernment to decipher abusive liaison from duplicity.

This disagreeable trend did not go unobserved and soon enough, tales and rancour were infused into the system. It became such an emblematic and endemic affliction that the authorities froze further recruitment of women into the army to review their future roles. Consequently, from 1990 through 1991 regular recruitments, women were not accepted. This was followed by intermittent enlistments from 1992 through 1999 only to be suspended again in 2000 and 2001 but reversed in 2002.

In the officers' corps too, no women were accepted for training as regular officer cadets at the Academy as all women commissioned into the Nigerian Army were granted Executive or Direct Regular Commissions and trained mostly at the Infantry Centre and School at Jaji. I had already retired from service when the first batch of female regular officer cadets were selected in 2013. For those who had undergone training at NDA, the anxiety about introducing female cadets was understandable, especially given the corporeality of the training. This could only be achieved by a radical review of cadet training.

Even still, during enlistments, the core Muslim northern Nigeria presented fewer female candidates, or none, for consideration. It was a right that was routinely declined. Unfortunately, in its place, gigolos, pimps, paedophiles, libertarians, and head-hunters appropriated those vacancies to barter for sex, money, alcohol, and tobacco.

As at the time of writing, the army had expanded to include a newly formed Nigerian Army Women's Corps (NAWC). It is possible that, all the experiences over the years may have been synthesized and evaluated hence the bold decision to carve out an entire corps dedicated to women. Otherwise, the degree of perversion, exploitation, group orgy, and abusive mindset associated with the recruitment, training, and service of women inflicted material damage to the good order of the service.

Manipulations

At the superficial level, the army was an equal opportunity employer, by which all and sundry were accommodated in its fold. However, the proceedings that played out during enlistments bespoke of tribalism, regionalism, chauvinism, opportunistic nepotism, and second-sighted stacking that was deepened by power mongers, sectional champions, and speculators.

Owing to the manner sundry primitive proclivities were affected during enlistment exercises, being accepted into the army was no longer a factor of stipulations only but superfluous considerations of pedigree and inequity. Noticeably, relations, children and wards of serving and retired servicemembers dominated the candidature at selection boards and recruitment exercises.

It was clear that the process became thoroughly fraught with misgivings in a situation where formation commanders nominated the local boards. Similarly, officers, and soldiers of the formations, serving or retired, civilian employees of the army, touts, commission agents, canvassers, and petitioners had more than passing interest in the process. Consequently, the work of the boards was not made any easier by the pressure mounted on all sides.

Ironically, at the outset, when the British imperialists recruited Hausa and Yoruba soldiers to conquer constituent parts of colonial Nigeria, the troops were composed of lowly characters. People felt these hordes were beneath the attention of the highborn. Even more, civilians perceived soldiers as uneducated and reprehensible lot. This was partly because those who ventured to serve returned with anti-social behaviours like terrorizing markets, drunkenness, drug abuse, intimidation, being disorderly, and frolicking with gangs of troublemakers.

This contemptuous sentiment towards soldiers was universal and not confined to any region as respectable families would neither allow their children nor wards to join the army. For instance, among the Yoruba, it was more prestigious to package sons off to legal Inns and Temples of England and afterward lucrative corporate careers. Meanwhile, the Igbo people were more enamoured to commerce and deep mercantilism through a rigorous system of apprenticeship.

The Southerners in general embraced erudition and the new economic order but appeared ignorant of the mechanics of state power. The instruments of coercion and state power embodied in the embryonic structures of the post-independence Nigeria lay with the supposedly poorly educated forces at arms. When the Southerners eventually joined the service, they were knowledgeable in western elucidation and democratic ethos, but uncharacteristically oblivious and conceited about low-level troops. As a result, southern Nigerians for all their sophistication did not decipher the latent mechanics of power epitomized by the Nigerian Army and its sister services.

At independence in 1960, there were about eighty-two Nigerian officers, and a sizable proportion of which were of Igbo extraction from the southeast.[6] This ethnic imbalance within the officer corps contrasted with that of foot soldiers where northerners predominated. The composition showed an overwhelming majority of hard-core fighting men of Northern origin with southerners often deployed in the services as clerks, artisans, and drivers but fewer combatants.[7]

The commanding role the army was to eventually play in national affairs could not be understated. The Northerners had correctly discerned that, in no distant future, it was the elements in the military that would rule the wobbly country. To nurture this agenda to the region's advantage, two individuals stood out namely Alhaji

Muhammadu Ribadu, the national Minister of Defence, and Alhaji Tanko Galadima, the Minister for Army Affairs in the Northern Region.

It is pertinent to note that, the latter ministerial portfolio existed only in the Northern region. Whereas other regions of the Nigerian federation paid scant attention to military establishments; the Northern leadership understood its strategic importance. With foresight, the region had foreseen the shape of things to come and most significantly, noticed its tenuous position vis-à-vis other regions. In this way, deliberate attempts were made to address the obvious imbalance.

Even more, for a long time in the Northern Region, careers consequent on Western education were the exception rather than the rule. As colonial control became entrenched, a handful of educated members of the ruling class were either drafted into colonial service or the army. For most young people though, personal ambition had nothing to do with it because decisions were taken by village and district heads and the emirs with fervent advice and support of colonial bureaucrats.[8]

The duo of Ribadu and Galadima embarked on extended tours of schools persuading students to consider future careers as soldiers. Such visits and reassurances to young people to join the army were widespread then. One typical example was the then Provincial Secondary School, Bida, where the entire class of 1962 was drafted wholesale into the army and would later produce generals like Garba Duba, Sani Sami, Mamman Magoro, Mamman Vatsa, Ibrahim Babangida, Sani Bello, and a host of others who became very senior military officers. Consequently, because of a failure to grasp the mechanics of power, the South was left with the short end of the power baton.

A Short List

All shortlisted candidates assembled at a designated venue at the start of the selection board usually NDA. However, because of the substantial number of candidates, states were split into batches and screened over a period of three weeks. On arrival at the venue, each candidate was documented and issued a numbered apron called chest number by which they were known throughout the selection board. As an insignia of identification, it was worn always.

Afterwards, candidates were also lodged and grouped by states of origin for ease of mobilization and mustering. The potential officer cadets and recruits were then put through a series of checks counting medical screening, document verification, physical exertions, written tests, critical thinking, and oral interviews.

Medical Screening

The army job was defined by muscularity and so individuals expecting to join needed to be healthy. This was critical since training and later operational demands were of such intensity that persons with pre-existing health conditions could become casualties. Medical screening therefore took precedence over the whole enchilada. Thus, no candidates were allowed on any physical apparatus until certified to be of sound health by the medical team of the contemporaneous board.

The cocktail of medical checks included vital signs of which high blood pressure was a drawback. There was also an eye test and physical examination for flatfoot and umbilical hernia (big navel). Shockingly, the posterior end was thoroughly scrutinized for tell-tale signs of pile or evacuation deficiencies.

Likewise, the array of checks covered urine, faecal, and blood plasma samples. The authorities insisted on exhaustive medical screening because it was central to a trainee's survival during training. This was the only aspect of enlistment that was not easily manipulated without consequences. However, spin doctors still found ways to sneakily deploy medical screening to prune down the number of candidates by unfairly dropping others to create vacancies that were filled by minions.

When the medical teams were all done with provisional results, a list of candidates that had scaled the hurdle was declared. Nevertheless, the pruning of candidates rather than mark progress precipitated petitions by influence peddlers, bitter enders, and revisionists. Most often, there were demands for a review of the results. In this way, the medical teams were overstretched throughout enlistment exercises.

Even worse, it was at this point that staff cars and orderlies were shamelessly deployed in support of lame candidates while their fellows grumbled endlessly about how the children and wards of the high and mighty were insulated from competition. Such candidates walked about with sprightly steps and self-assuredness. Yet a close interaction with them revealed neither brilliance nor unique gifts except latent fear and anxiety like others.

This practice was even more gross with recruitment exercises as wolves and vultures invested the venues extorting money from desperate potential recruits and their parents. These conspirators demanded and got sexual gratification from female applicants, a widespread practice that cut across soldiers and officers. Curiously, disqualified candidates with the right links would then be recalled to the utter bewilderment of fellow candidates. In this way, with twisted and cooked proceedings, the exercises wobbled forward.

Qualifications

The minimum academic qualification required to be accepted into the army was a General Certificate of Education Ordinary Level for prospective officer cadets and a Junior Secondary School Certificate for soldiers, an upgrade from the First School Leaving Certificate demanded in the past. Since NDA was of a university status, over time the documents submitted by candidates were duly authenticated by the West African Examinations Council.

As for the recruits, it would appear not much further screening was undertaken. In fact, at a point, due to the scramble to attend higher institutions among qualified soldiers, it was encouraged to accept candidates with poorer results in the hope that they would concentrate on the army job when recruited. So, apart from result slips, other documents inspected included a Certificate of State Origin, Certificate of Birth, or the much-maligned Declaration of Age presented in lieu of the former. But even this simple activity was complicated by candidates with multiple credentials.

Physical Exercises

Once the medical teams cleared candidates they went through physical exertions. These included a 3.2-kilometre run, twenty push-ups, twenty sit-ups, ten beam heave repetitions, a monkey bridge, and of course, a timed charge through an obstacle course.

Written Test

To mark progress, candidates wrote a test which was typically a multiple-choice type meant to confirm the aptitude of potential trainees. These quizzes were straightforward enough, but still many had to be propped. It was amazing that enlistment exercises revealed the malediction of poor education among Nigeria's younger generations. It was baffling to see candidates with excellent grades on paper huffing and puffing over simple quizzes.

Sand Model Exercise

Also, during the selection board sand model was introduced to potential cadets. The model was meant to evaluate critical thinking and problem-solving by individuals. It was more about planning with limitations, during which candidates were presented with scenarios to proffer the best workable solutions.

Facing the Board

The last segment of enlistment exercises was facing a board. By now, the candidates had surmounted all the other hurdles and came face to face with the core board members. It was a physical sighting by the board and marked the very final stage of enlistment exercises. From this point, one could start counting himself as a potential officer cadet or recruit.

The Results

For potential recruits, the entire process was abbreviated when results were announced, and the successful candidates camped preparatory to reporting to Depot NA. However, in the past successful candidates got notified at the state recruitment centres. Afterward, potential recruits were dispersed home to allow them time for personal administration before resuming training.

However, this policy was changed due to incidences of tinkering and other untoward practices by interested parties. It was discovered that conspiratorial individuals altered the final list while in transit. For instance, several so-called successful candidates were never at the boot camp at all.

Therefore, a new policy was adopted whereby recruits were given letters of appointment and reported to an intermediate location for another round of screening to remove persons clandestinely inserted. Besides, by not announcing the results instantaneously, there was an opportunity to cook the final list.

Another aspect that affected the outcome of recruitment was the general lists. It was a list based on privileges and other unwritten codes.

These lists were drawn by senior officers, formation commanders, state recruitment officers, clerks, typists, emirs, warrant and beaded chiefs, witchdoctors, and a coterie of others who shared this exclusive right with their spouses. By the time these humongous lists were assembled, little was left of the original list.

In the end, regardless of all the shenanigans by vested interests and boorish power agents, the outcome of the enlistment exercises still incorporated villagers, peasants, mechanics, butchers, truck pushers, touts, and a full complement of aristocrats and proprietors of the army and Nigeria by extension.

Thus, the assortment of recruits and cadets was so ridiculous as to elicit questions about the diligence of the processes. The boards that sifted through thousands of candidates accepted cadets and recruits of all shades including the old, young, imbecilic, brutish, and unenlightened thugs all in one breath. While on the other hand, it also handpicked the finest, most humane, and intelligent crop of young people around. Hence the good, the bad, and the ugly were all fused into the making of NA officers and soldiers.

Notes

(1). Recruitment of Nigerians into RWAFF see: Morris, Emmanuel Nwafor: Recruitment of Nigerians for military service during the Second World War 1939-45. Journal of the Society for Army Historical Research (London, England) 98:276-303: November 2020.

(2). On composition of WAFF officers see: www.GlobalSecurity.org:West African Frontier Force.

(3). For a history of ROSTS Teshie see: Ebo: The Development of the Army Officer Corps in Ghana 1956-66. https://journals.co.za.

(4). https: nda.edu.ng.

(5). https://nda.edu.ng.

(6). For an account of officer strength see: Abubakar, Ubale: Career Management of Officers in the Nigerian Army (1970-2014).

(7). For an account of ethnic imbalance see: Suberu, Ichi Abdulrahman: The Nigerian Army as a product of Its Colonial History: Problems of Re-building Cohesion for an Army in Transition.

(8). Kole Omotoso: Just Before Dawn (Spectrum Books, Lagos, 1988).

Second Lieutenant 1993

Chapter Eleven

Commencement

After three strenuous weeks at Kaduna, I headed home to bide my time and await the outcome of the selection board. By early August, the final list of successful candidates was published in newspapers nationwide. But then again, I was unaware of the publication until I got to a friend's place. The situation was remedied by my consuming habit of reading old newspapers and publications. I instinctively picked up a two-day-old National Concord newspaper and stumbled on the list.

I hurriedly perused the publication and saw my name listed as a successful candidate. I was selected as a member of the Fortieth Regular Course of NDA. I could proudly cackle because I was neither propped, nor sponsored by any individual, cabal, community, nor an ethnic group but was selected on merit arising from a personal decision to join. Luckily, the commencement date was still a couple of weeks away and I made frantic preparations to report for training.

A Homily

The euphoria of being selected notwithstanding, I had to go to the village and inform my aging parents of the coming training. It was during this visit that I had a lively discussion and a definitive advisory from my father.

"My son, you are joining not only an armed but an implacably grumpy group. Be guarded in whatever you do. However, you must discern that not every order given to you should be obeyed, and equally that not every order should be disobeyed." He grumpily and figuratively declared sage-like.

I was truly baffled by this advisory because my father was never in any uniformed service. So, I pondered the basis of his two-faced homily. But then, as a true father, he could not mislead me, so I took his words to heart.

Uncannily, it took a noticeably fleeting time for our discourse to divulge its import because I had barely spent but a couple of hours in a military camp when I began to grasp its systematized brew of predatory duplicity and distastefulness garnished with institutional randomness. Hence, from the very beginning, I responded pragmatically to orders, knowing they could be issued either validly or illegally. To survive this system meant acquiescence and like amount of defiance to navigate the intricacies of a forceful society.

10 September 1988

To resume as a regular officer cadet, no demands were made except your physical presence on the appointed date. But then again, I had to get myself essentials and toiletries. Ever guarded, I headed to Kaduna one day clear of the resumption date. So, as early as 0900hrs, on 10 September 1988, I walked through the coffin-topped gates of the Nigerian Defence Academy into the bizarre world of army job.

Dreamland

As young cadets, we were received at a front office by the Academy gate with little or no ceremony and led to the QM stores on the ground floor of an old one-story building, which we came to know as Dodan Barracks. I perused the surrounding area randomly, because as candidates we were allowed limited access to the premises and spent more time at the candidates' quarters outside the precincts of NDA.

The first set of rules in this new town was puzzling. Every call and response were shouted even when it was pointless to do so. Moreover, nobody moved on their own until asked to or shepherded, and always in bands attended by an ever-present and swelling number of pesky escorts. There was an assortment of instructions and protocols to be conversant with and adhered to, in a process of conversion that was hurried.

The Academy, as it was commonly called, was a cluster of old but freshly painted sundry structures and buildings standing singly or arranged in quadrangles. There was an open parade ground, a network of roads and walkways hemmed by freshly whitewashed curbstones. The farthest point within its boundaries was about two thousand-five hundred metres. It was unnerving to be thrust into the heart of a cloistered setting and exotic culture. As for the gaudy painting everywhere, I would discover at the tail end of my first year that it was an item on the training package of the Academy.

Worst Offenders

At the QM stores, more of my fellows joined up. First termers, we were officially designated, but within the hour on arrival, we had been labelled and addressed by a thousand or more names. From the stores, we were issued the same basic military kits in a large rucksack, a bucket, and caboodles. We discovered later that much of the gear that was supposed to be included in the package was not, such items as military boots. We had just been introduced to a system of hoarding by the QM staff. At last, all was now set, and we were to be marched to the lines, as living quarters were called, a simple act that proved to be a long haul.

Just before we reported, we were all individually assigned cadet numbers and allotted to training battalions in such a well-ordered arrangement on its surface. However, while being issued bits and pieces at the QM store, we sighted second termers, our upper-class adversaries, hanging by and very impatient to start the drive.

The first fatwa upon resumption on our ill-fated group was being instantaneously declared as worst offenders, in the peculiar parlance of officer cadets. When all was set, the skinniest of the lot stepped forward and bellowed in a high-pitched declamatory whine.

"Unfortunate Nigerians, crabs, clowns, stones, couscous" He fired rapidly. "Sir" we all chorused. "Welcome to the Academy of your dreams" he broadcasted imperially. Of course, it was a dream come true, but we never expected to be derided for achieving that for which we wished.

"As you all can see, you baggers, (a meaningless word), are the worst offenders. You saw Ahmadu Bello University (ABU) Zaria, Ibadan, Kano, Jos, and all the other ABUs but you chose to come to my father's Academy to do cadet."

For a starting, it was quite off-putting. I never knew before now that the Academy was a family business owned by the father of one of the cadets. Also, I could not see whatever thing, nor did I understand how we became offenders with the array of Nigerian universities conveniently aggregated to ABU. Nevertheless, it was just the opening act, and I needed all my expansive patience to overcome this measured baiting.

"This is not a threat but a promise." He persisted in his shrill voice. "By the time my course mates and I finish with all of you civilians, you will all dash back to your villages." But again, so far, nothing in our individual nor collective conduct nor countenance was untoward to elicit threats and promises. I must confess that I did not expect such an adversarial debut.

"Now before I open my mouth, everybody pack your 'kaya' and fall in by the road there go." Kaya was Hausa for luggage. What now followed was a staccato of commands in Hausa and English in a jumbled order.

Historically, the use of the Hausa language as the lingua franca of the NA was adopted over time and undoubtedly owed its origins to Glover's Hausa Constabulary of 1863. Over the years, as the force evolved, the succeeding WAFF became a multi-ethnic regional force. However, because the Hausa language was widely spoken across West Africa, it lent itself handily as the medium of instruction and communication for recruits during and after training. Although pidgin, a form of argot derived from a combination of English and local lingoes came to be spoken in the barracks, the Hausa language persisted within the army. But I digress.

We all reflexively obeyed his instructions of which the next set was not only unexpected but uncalled for. "Now squat down, carry your kaya on your head, hunch on." We were heavily laden with our personal belongings apart from the new military kits just issued moments ago. To hunch or frog-jump was a wearisome activity on its own without encumbrances, much less with loads. Soon enough, the offenders jettisoned debris all over the place.

Unfortunately, our "sadistic" escorts insisted every bit be borne by its owners. By now there was panting and heehawing. While we agonized, our teasers enjoyed the spectacle. I do not recall when the torment abated, but graciously we were delivered to the rooms.

Nevertheless, we were not allowed to settle in but were ordered to quickly change into blue shorts (salala), a white vest, and stockings on brown canvas and form up in an open space. This flimsy outfit would be our main apparel for the next sixteen weeks. In the intervening time, I saw that cadets were housed two to a room, each with his cabinet or wardrobe. I thought this arrangement quite impressive given my experience of crowded university hostels. Within the hour, I had become an offender and internee by choice, and for the next five years, two weeks and a day, I would remain within this citadel.

From the moment we arrived standing upright in the morning, all later movements were on crouches. On being formed up under any guise, we were inundated with countless physical activities including push-ups, forward rolls and endlessly hunched (frog-jumped). Graciously, it was lunchtime. It would be my first meal as a cadet, as it was past breakfast time when I reported in the morning. The route and movement to the feast at Cadets Mess was very tiresome as it was a combination of doubling and hunching with countless unscheduled stops at the instance of senior cadets coming in the opposite direction. At the Mess, we were articles of curiosity and the butts of bawdy jokes. Day One was a Sunday and I did not see any friendly face that day and by now I deciphered that there was a combine to cripple us.

My Wedding Day with my Best Man
Lt James Rotgak Danyil 1995

Being Decorated Major Yola 2002

Chapter Twelve

Refabrication

By accepting a placement as an officer cadet, it implied the individual would be refabricated to fashion out a military officer. It was a challenging rite of passage. Nonetheless, by proceeding one day at a time, we got to the end. Even so, it was a profound exertion, given the diverse circumstances from which we were assembled, it was tasking to both the instructors and trainees alike.

From a general outlook, it was plain that the elements on the courses incorporated all shades of characters and the key to sorting out this puzzle lay with a progressive training outline from the beginning, to disassemble and re-form, precast young adults to create the desired product.

Rifleman and Junior Leader

The basic training at the Academy was directed at producing officers for the Armed Forces of Nigeria. However, to reach that high status, it was pivotal to go through the paces of grounding as rudimentary foot soldiers. This was essential because, a foot soldier, or the rifleman, was the backbone of all land forces, as they skirmished at close quarters with enemy forces.

Though, as a force multiplier, individual foot soldiers were grouped into sections. A section was the basic fire team of manoeuvre. Apart from technical attachments like mortar, antitank and sniper teams, a fire team was the smallest organized operational component, particularly of the infantry.

A section typically composed of a ten-man team of six riflemen, a pair of general-purpose machine gunmen, a grenadier, and a team leader. However, on its own, a section could not produce sufficient firepower in most combat situations and was therefore grouped to form platoons.

A platoon in turn was the primary fire unit and manoeuvre element and was composed of three sections in conventional deployment. It was designed to engage the enemy at close quarters either on its own or as part of a larger force, usually a company or battalion.

In any case, massed riflemen armed with light weapons and allotted limited ammunition scales were the mainstay of a fire unit and skirmished mostly with their opposite numbers in direct combat. Normally too, riflemen had other tasks on the battlefield like carrying or general load bearing for accompanying items such as binoculars, extra ammunition boxes, mortar rounds and the like for a unit.

Therefore, the tactical or operational doctrine as conceived was simple enough because, during encounters, riflemen were expected to bring rapid aimed fire against enemy targets within resources. As a result, the character and skills needed from infantry soldiers counted in physical hardiness and instinctive agility. For the leaders, there was a need to have the ability to motivate troops in the face of danger.

At its face value, this goal was so easily attainable. However, it was not only emotionally draining but physically challenging. Therein, lay the sum of cadet training at the Academy, which was calibrated to produce an infantry platoon commander, or equivalent in the other services, a fire-eater, with the basic attributes of a rifleman in addition to being a junior leader.

Training Cycles

In the main, there were countless oddities to be mastered in basic military training. It was unbelievable the number of rules, regulations, mumbo-jumbo, procedures, skills, and a myriad of inanities that an individual was expected to distil and grasp within an impossibly short time. In general terms, the process of transforming trainees began when training cycles were formulated every year and riven into quarterly projections and weekly training modules.

The Forecast of Events

First in the scheme of work was the Forecast of Events. This document was, to all intents and purposes, a calendar of the training year in view. The worksheet captured the projected training activities and schedules for the year on a single planner. Also, due to a need to operate seamlessly in the future, and the many skills and competencies that had to be imparted, all possible scenarios and dynamics were factored in and laid out in long-term plans that fitted snugly into annual training cycles. Whereas the planner captured the prognoses for an entire year, its implementation lay with quarterly projections and weekly training programmes.

The Weekly Training Programme

Training activities at the Academy were driven by a weekly training programme. A timetable published unfailingly by Fridays in the Academy Routine Order (ARO), was built on a five-day week, i.e., Mondays through Fridays. Although flexible, once published, it became the guide for that week as daily proceedings were outlined therein.

It was the responsibility of each cadet to be conversant with the schedule, although copies were handed to course leaders. These covered all aspects of training, outlining details like the time to wake up and time to retire to bed, and over time, all cadets caught the general drift and could easily predict the training events.

The Shout

Taken together, the hectic and annoying first day at the Academy counted to nothing. The next morning, Monday 11 September 1988 was the official commencement day. As a first day, it was like all other days except when there were intensifications, of which there were and often so.

A typical day in a cadet's life started at about 0500hrs by which time shrieking awakened all from slumber. These hollering or yelling, called shouts, were a practice by which the most junior course, aroused or summoned the rest of their colleagues, to an impending activity with synchronized howling and were as numerous as the activities as they came. The first of the day was the wake-up and the last was the lights-out shout.

We were introduced to the system of shouts by our immediate seniors in a style peculiar to cadets. First, we were woken and rounded up, then led into the baths to be drenched and marched afterwards to a central spot in the battalion quadrangle for the shout. The shout itself was an uncomplicated affair but being sodden fully clothed was not a particularly stimulating way to start a day, especially in the biting harmattan cold in Kaduna at that time of the year.

For effects, the same fate befell us each time we were prompted by our seniors to this routine activity or any at all. The only way to stave off the calamity of ice-cold drenching in the early mornings was to self-wake. As an aside, first termers slept last and woke-up first.

The nights were dreamy, fitful and forever interrupted. After a couple of days, all shouts were dreaded especially wake up because nights were oddly short and daytime unduly long. Undeniably, the start of each day was expected but not when we had just gotten into bed, only to be awakened to embark on another rigorous day. This would last for the duration of the training, as lack of adequate sleep, and or sleep deprivation became a general affliction from which all cadets universally agonized.

Muster Parade

The first activity of each training day was muster parade usually convened at about 0515hrs at the Academy Parade Ground or covered up at the expansive Drill Shed on rainy days. The entire cadet body was formed up according to courses and by training battalions. Each course turned up dressed in conformity with its scheduled training period. Everyone, for none, was exempted from this assembly, except individuals on leave passes or medical confinement. This routine went on in a loop, from Mondays through Fridays but varied during the weekends, when cadets were mustered by battalions in the lines.

These parades typically lasted for twenty to thirty minutes, during which every cadet was accounted for before dispersal to different training areas. As a rule of the thumb, every assembly at the Academy was an official parade, and the muster parade marked the first, in a series of confirmatory physical checks on each cadet throughout the day, for the duration of the training period.

All through each training period, the same checks were repeated. Checks. Always checks. First periods could be Puttee Parade, Morning PT, Weapons Training, Equitation, Drill, and Breakfast, which took place simultaneously at different training areas. During muster parades though, on the sides, as the reports were being compiled, background activities took place concurrently like hunching, langa i.e., hopping on one leg and forward rolls. It was also a time to grab a culprit who may have eluded reprimand but could not dodge the muster parade.

Training Areas

The whole shebang at the Academy was about training, energetic training, and more training. The entire layout of the citadel was one vast training ground with designated training zones including sheds, observation stands, parade and sports grounds and others that fittingly accommodated the training packages.

Training Periods

The training time at the Academy was split between academic and military modules. This was because apart from being trained towards a commission as officers, we were concurrently studying for undergraduate degrees. Thus, Monday through Thursdays were taken up by academic lectures while Fridays were devoted solely to services or military training.

The training periods were scheduled between the courses in turns, with each programmed for an alternate first period during the week. At about 0600hrs, the training periods began and lasted an average of forty minutes. In the interval between 0630 and 0745hrs, every course was expected to have been through with first periods and breakfast.

The academic lectures then commenced at about 0800hrs and ended by 1400hrs with a fifteen-minute mid-day break between 1145hrs and 1200hrs. Lunch was by 1400hrs, and afterwards, there was a 90-minute gap leading to 1530hrs, provided one was not a culprit (an offender) and if no extra event came up. You could take a cat nap, which was rare, but by 1600hrs, it was evening games, except on Wednesdays which were programmed for club activities.

Puttee Parades

As first termers, the Physical Training Wing became like a second home, and puttee parade was a staple, particularly during the first four weeks into training. Much as I tried, I could not figure out the concise definition of the term as it related to the activities to which we were subjected. But whatever the literal meaning, it did not take long before we felt its excruciating impact.

Puttee period always took place at the Sports Ground under the supervision of PT Instructors. With hindsight, it was meant to remove the undue love of one's body, a deprecation against narcissistic vanity because, on resumption, we had lovely and glossy skins, but all that would disappear rather quickly. The parade involved crocodilian crawling, barrel rolling, hunching, heavy lifting, forward and backward rolls as well as seating on the head and more in sludgy conditions that left us caked in red mud.

With PT instructors, puttee parade was timed and controlled but when dispensed by cadets, it became a prolonged torment. Even worse, because we were clad in vests and shorts, our exposed body parts were soon covered in festering bruises and lacerated skin. By the third day, we collectively broadcasted putrid body odour and stank badly from lack of proper washing which persisted for the next four weeks.

PT instructors had their peculiar vernacular, just like each wing of the Academy. The exercises were short but systematic as they went from the neck through the chest, shoulders, hands, and waist onto the feet. After the ubiquitous checks, we were split into groups and assigned to instructors.

Instinctively, once in a group, we formed up. After a demonstration of the exercise in view, the instructor would then continue thus:

"You out dia go" They randomly pointed out a cadet in the ranks. "Ajuwaya (as you were) too slow. When I calls you, you moov shap as if faya touches you. Fall in, in front dia go. You are the leader, the rest of you follow your leader." The exercise then began and could be interrupted abruptly by the ever-observant instructors.

Each of them had his peculiar style. The one would go ahead by yelling something like: "Physical yourself…fut (foot) fut fut." Meanwhile, he was always out of step. The other would halt the exercise midway "Stooop, you dat lousy cadet, don't come here and show us your carubility." Someone at the rear of the formation snickered. All of us were dumbfounded as to the meaning of the word 'carubility,' that is, if it was an English word at all. At which the instructor would rebuke thus:

"Who laughs there? If I catch, caught, or rather catches you will be in hot soup." Oh dear, we were buffeted with so much English grammar. From the skin-gashing groundwork, we were gradually familiarized with other apparatuses like beams, wooden horses, monkey bridges and the other arrays on the obstacle course.

Marching to Beating

Most folks are captivated by martial music and smart soldierly marching. The drum rolls tingled in a manner that elated even the most unexcitable persons. It was beautiful to behold soldiers executing flawless and coordinated movements. Ironically, the marching part was the most draining of all in making a soldier out of a civilian.

Even so, there was more to marching than just music and synchronized movement. Every movement, especially by a group of military men was a drill. These were constantly repeated patterns of movements or tasks, in marching as in manoeuvres and weapons handling. Marching was iterative in the sequences of tasks or exercises performed until completed flawlessly.

The Drill Wing was the only training section of the Academy commanded by an SNCO. Its staff consisted of the Drill RSM assisted by a Sergeant and a retinue of NCOs. Drill sticks and canes were a vital paraphernalia of instructors, which they were allowed to ruthlessly deploy. With physical chastisement within sight, it was an extraordinary feat to grasp the chaotic locution of the habitually garrulous lot.

During drill lessons, we assembled, formed up, did the necessary checks, and handed in the parade state. When it came to authenticating parade states, drill instructors were very meticulous. Funnily, one of my course mates distinguished himself as an unparalleled course senior. He was trusted by the instructors because he managed to be present at all drill periods but was dubiously efficient. An immensely helpful colleague, he ensured he inverted reports by booking those on parade absent and vice versa. It was a trick that worked always as the instructors never unraveled this deliberate mix-up.

After the reports, came the warm-up entrée. We marched in and around the parade ground at a furious pace to a timed cadence of a side drum and halts were always abrupt. Most cadets missed the halt command which excited copious deployment of drill sticks and canes.

During the introductory drill lesson, the instructors split the assemblage into manageable sizes of eight or ten that were marched off to a corner of the vast parade ground. The first drill lesson went along these lines:

"Skod tode an gon to introdus you to atteshun. De popos it is tot, is to inabu a shoja or gru of shoja to kom to atteshun in a smat shojaly mana. Fo di popos of introkshun, it is bin divad into fats an nombad. Is dia eni kweshen? Ubanka, diaris no kweshen. If diaris no kweshen, kontinu to luk dis wei as awi demontret di muvmen on di koman atteshun wan" which translated to:

"Squad today am going to introduce you to attention. The purpose it is taught is to enable a soldier or group of soldiers to come to attention in a smart soldierly manner. For the purpose of instruction, it is divided into parts and numbered. Is there any question? Your father, there is no question. If there are no question, continue to look this way as I will demonstrate the movement on the command 'Attention One.' This monologue was delivered in a rapid staccato as to be almost unintelligible. The instructors rambled on still:

"On de wod of koman atteshun wan, I res ma leg ha, pontonot, hans ba de sad, ma nil fuli ben and tous pontoon danwed" which meant:

"On the word of command 'attention one' I raised my leg high, point to note, my hands by the side, kneel fully bent and toes pointing downward." It took supreme efforts to understand the drill instructors' language. Most unhelpfully though, there was no room to seek amplifications as this interrupted their rhythm especially as these were crammed recitals, and with each distraction, they had to be parroted all over again.

Drill periods were practical sessions. The second part of the lesson was a run-through of the two-sequence attention. Amusingly, midway through the period, by which time, fatigue and hunger had set in, one could not place specific commands against calls originating from the multiple squads on all corners of the expansive parade ground. It was also at this point that the instructors proved their dexterity at the use of drill sticks and canes on cadets to coax alertness and comprehension.

There were various phases to drill lessons. Over time, apart from basic foot drills, we learnt cane, rifle, and sword drills. We were also trained on colour party, silent, funeral and quarter guard drills along with a host of function-specific ceremonial drills.

Drill Square Test

Drill sessions were vital to the gradual evolution of cadets into smart officers and going through its paces culminated in a Drill Square Test.

It was the first obstacle to be scaled to confer a new status. Recall that our dress code until then was a flimsy shorts and vests on canvas shoes. Apart from poor cover, it made first termers easily identifiable at a distance.

The test was administered about eight weeks into training. However, it was preceded by a great deal of preparations. These included intense pressing of over-starched khaki uniforms, and military boots brushed until they reached mirror-like reflections. Passing the test conferred the privilege of joining other cadets in wearing full uniforms as well as giving the military salute to officers.

The only snag to these feverish preparations was that we had not been issued military boots. As earlier noted, when we received our initial military kits at the QM store, essential accoutrements were missing. We could not therefore be expected to be fully prepared for this all important test. However, our roommates were tasked to get us borrowed boots. In any case, we were not deterred by the indignity of being examined during our first military test in borrowed footwear.

A Metallic Feel

One could not certainly begin to carry-on like a true soldier until after a touch of the cold metallic feel of a rifle. It was logical that on the very first training day, we were introduced to a rifle. After the bruising puttee and energy-sapping drill periods, Weapon Training (WT) was the next in line. The emphasis was on personal weapons which were the basic weapons of an infantry soldier in battle, but we trained on different classes of weapons too.

The range of weapons included pistols, rifles, submachine and light machine guns as well as lobbing ordnances such as grenades, shoulder launchers and smooth-bore mortar guns that were deployed in close support. At the right time, we progressed to heavier calibre weapons organic to infantry units like heavy machine guns and anti-tank guns.

We also got instructed on heavy calibre fire support weapons like artillery guns, tanks, mine warfare and demolitions as the training advanced. However, instructions on the latter were theoretical, not until the finishing stages of our training, when tours were organized to field units for firepower demonstrations and exhibitions.

On the first day at the WT wing, we all marched to the Academy Arms Store, and each trainee duly signed for a rifle. It was the Belgian Fabrique Nationale Self Loading Rifle (FN SLR), calibrated at 7.62mm with an effective range of three hundred metres which could be extended to eight hundred metres when mounted on a tripod. Although antiquated and not operationally dependable like the Kalashnikov AK47, it was the main assault rifle in the inventory of the NA then.

When we collected the rifles, a first feel for some of us, we held onto them like babies and converged at the WT sheds and formed up. After yet another check, we were split into squads and allotted to WT instructors stationed by the open training sheds. The first lesson then began thus:

"See wan mumu hia, see as e hol di bindiga, yu tink sey na wokin stik?" The lesson had started with another great put down and the opening salvo translated to: 'Look at this fool, look at the way he is holding a rifle. You think it is a walking stick?' By now, it was getting clearer by the minute that curses and caustic language were part of the training and I needed to be reconciled to these obscenities. All after the grimness, the lesson proper began thus:

"Skod bifo yu is de fabri nashanal sef lodin rafu. Bifo, I go ito namin de fats, a we fes tich yu de sefly frosudua. Dis is to inabu yu to yus de rafu sefly amon kwamrads."

To wit: "Squad before you is the Fabrique Nationale Self Loading Rifle. Before I go into naming the parts, I will first teach you the safety procedure. This is to enable you use the rifle safely among comrades."

No longer bothered by the gibber from all the instructors, I reckoned it was the right way to start because poor weapon handling could lead to tragic consequences to the handler as well as his comrades. The instructor then indicated: 'Dis na de tiriga, sefly ka, magajin ka, magajin, magajin slo and kwakin handu. Eni kweshon? Pe atteshun. De fes tin to do wen yu pik a rafu, mek shua de tiriga is at poshishon sef, rimu de magajin and kwak shap and hol, inspet de shamba, mek shua e dey emti, retun the wokin fas fowod, tun de sefly ka to fayarin poshishon and fres di tiriga. riton di sefly ka to poshishon sef and mont bak di magajin. De rafu is kiliya and sef"

For all the rapidity of its delivery, the much the instructor said was: "This is the trigger, safety catch, magazine catch, magazine, magazine slot and cocking handle. Are there any questions? Pay attention. The first thing to do upon picking up a rifle is to ensure the trigger is at position safe, remove the magazine, cock sharp and lock, inspect the chamber and make sure it is empty, send the working part forward, turn the safety catch to position fire and press the trigger. Return the safety catch to position safe and mount back the magazine. The rifle is cleared and safe."

The instructor then named the parts of a rifle and their functions from the butt to the muzzle tip. Although we started on the FN SLR, the module was expanded over time to include other weapons like Kalashnikov AK47, GPMG, Submachine gun, CETME G3 rifles and the entire spectrum of infantry platoon weapons listed earlier.

The presentations also took trainees through stripping and assembling during which weapons were disassembled into modular tads and coupled back. This came along with cleaning and overhauling. The introductory lessons were rounded up with different firing positions. It was clear that the design of WT lessons was to impart personal skills on weapons handling and remedial actions in case of stoppages and malfunctions while running the weapons.

Equitation

Within the week too, we were introduced to the Equitation Wing at the Academy Stables which housed about twenty horses. The Equitation lessons trained cadets on horse riding and horsemanship, i.e., riding skills and taking care of horses.

This was an unexpected area of training for me. Yet, it soon became understandable because mounted troops had played central roles in recent histories of European armies. Although the use of horses i.e., cavalry, was old-fashioned, it was still extensively used during massed and ceremonial parades.

Field Craft

As a land force, the NA's doctrine of training and operations was dominated by infantry manoeuvres. In mechanized or motorized armies, troops were deployed along armoured fighting vehicles, self-propelled guns, and guaranteed air power projection and other protective gizmo. Since NA troops were composed primarily of riflemen, survival in the field therefore became a central preoccupation that could be attained by giving time, effort, and committing to memory of battlefield details. This was the art of field crafts.

Field crafts were tactical skills needed to deploy stealthily during the day or at night in harmony with the terrain. These skills combined description of ground and judging distances, indication and recognition of targets, understanding why things were seen, and the art of camouflage and concealment. These also included mastering navigation while overcoming obstacles to execute tactical movements and manoeuvres.

Instructors

The subjects taught during training were wide-ranging. In the hectic introductory days, the first set of trainers commonly encountered were soldiers until we began exploring tactics. The rehash of their comical locutions was not meant to ridicule nor question the knowledge and suitability of the instructors. It simply denoted a general trend in Nigerian military forces as commissioned officers had formal education, while there was a low-level schooling among soldiers.

The pool of trainers at the Academy was drawn from both ends of the services. The NCOs could be stupefying on occasions but were proficient at their trades such as WT, Drill, PT, Equitation, Signals, and sundry subjects. They ran hands-on modules, while commissioned officers took on the more abstract components and field training exercises.

Foundations

Most military-related training activities were introduced during first periods in the run of the week and overseen by SNCOs. By scheduling, nominal military-related training took place from Mondays through Thursdays, and these were typically taken along with academic lectures. However, Fridays were dedicated exclusively to military training by each service. This was the point at which active interactions between cadets and commissioned officers occurred. Even more, the Academy ran two academic semesters and one service or military training term.

Officers instructed tactics with a focus on the platoon in the field accentuating battle drills, the phases of war like advance, attack, defence, and withdrawal along with ancillary operations like harbour in defence, demolitions, patrols, ambushes, and raids.

To ensure balanced instruction beyond basic training as an infantry soldier, the teaching was expanded to incorporate aspects of employment and deployment of combined arms. These were teeth arms and combat support services like armoured, artillery, engineers, medical and other logistics mishmash that went into warfighting.

The bent of instructions inculcated a command-and-control attitude in the trainees, especially in battle drills and the instinctual actions taken before being invested in a battle. Even more, since we were being trained to become subalterns, instructions included section and platoon battle drills.

The operational doctrine was to be able to function two echelons down in deployment. Thus, it was expected that a platoon commander would be directly involved, as far as marking out the trenches or giving guidance during deployment, down the rung as the position of the individual rifleman.

Chapter Thirteen

Training Formations

During my time at the Academy, it was deemed of a university status organized into an Academic Branch and a Military Wing. The Academic Branch was superintended over by an Academy Provost (the equivalent of a vice chancellor or president of a university) and was usually a civilian egghead. The military division was run by a Director of Military Training (DMT).

Both branches were coordinated at the Academy HQ through directorates of military training, administration, logistics and finance. These were complemented by service branches including army, naval and air force wings. At the end of training, cadets got first degrees in different disciplines and a commission into the Armed Forces of Nigeria.

Preparatory Wing

When we reported to the Academy, my course was not integrated directly with fellow cadets but held at an intermediate accommodation at the SSC quarters. Several reasons accounted for this decision, but it was primarily due to the large strength of the course. It would appear there was inadequate bed space within the existing lodgings. Therefore, by an off-the-cuff plan named Preparatory Wing, the SSC quarters became our temporary abode despite being allotted to the four regular training battalions.

Besides, over the years there were reported cases of desertion by young cadets, especially during the early weeks into camp, as some new entrants could not adjust to the distressing physical and awkward cadet routine. Although casualty, withdrawal or dropping out were expected while in training, new entrants leaving in droves had attracted the attention of the authorities because left unchecked, such leakages vitiated the meticulous tasks of selecting, training, and staff projection.

Cadets Brigade

Military forces are organized into units and formations of manageable sizes for ease of mustering, scaling of firepower, deployment and effective operational command and control. For illustration, the NA is structured into divisions, brigades, battalions, and the like smaller sub-units. Of these units, the battalion was the smallest with a commander and a staff of officers (in charge of personnel, operations, intelligence, and logistics) to assist.

A notch higher was a brigade which typically consisted of two or more combat battalions or regiments and allied support units. It was smaller than a division and commanded by a brigadier general or a colonel. The hub of training at the Academy was a formation of a brigade-plus status.

The Cadets Brigade composed of a Headquarters, four training battalions and two companies namely Abyssinia, Burma, Dalet, and Mogadishu battalions for regular cadets, with Colito and Tamandu companies for SSC cadets respectively. The latter two were sited outside the perimeter fence of the Academy along with their segregated training areas.

The HQ and administrative offices of training battalions were at cadets' lines. Typically, they were under a commanding officer with a complement of staff officers, which included an adjutant and company officers. Unlike field units though, it was always skeletal operational staff, never more than five officers at any given time, and all were drawn from the pool of instructors already posted to the Academy.

Cadet Leadership Appointments

In my days at the Academy, there were at least seven hundred cadets at any given time. For administrative expediency, the Academy was split into training battalions and staffed with equivalent cadet appointments. Although policies were formulated at the Academy HQ and coordinated by HQ Cadets Brigade, to a greater degree, the controls, implementation, and checks among trainees were the responsibility of cadet appointments of which there were two levels namely the central all-academy and battalion appointments.

These appointments included Academy Senior Under Officer (ASUO), Battalion Senior Under Officer (BSUO), Academy Cadet

Adjutant (ACA), Regimental Sergeant Major (RSM), Regimental Quartermaster Sergeant (RQMS), Cadet Sergeant, Cadet Corporal and Cadet Lance Corporal respectively.

The ASUO was the topmost cadet appointment akin to a brigade commander. He mustered and accounted for cadets and the general good order of the Academy. The appointment to this position was tenured and rotated every quarter of the year among the four BSUOs at the Academy.

In a field unit, the adjutant was an administrative officer or assistant to a commanding officer. He managed personnel and ensured that a unit ran smoothly by coordinating information and activities. In the same vein, the duties of ACA were not any different from those of the corresponding counterpart in the field. The tempo, rhythm and alertness to parades and general state of discipline in the Academy, lay with the forcefulness of the ACA.

All other appointments were replicated in the four regular training battalions and SSC companies. It was these appointees that coordinated cadet training by cadets and accounted for members of a battalion and ensured general good conduct. At the right time, a BSUO was eligible for appointment as the ASUO which was rotational.

Considerations for Appointment

Countless considerations went into the selection of cadet leadership. Apart from individual drive and outstanding personal qualities, supercilious permutations also came into play. There was the interplay of official and eccentric factors that determined the choice of candidates for appointment. These included prior military background, personal brilliance, and indeterminate commendations.

Ex-Boys and Ex-Jams

When we resumed training, we were from sundry backgrounds. While many of us came in as raw civilians, others were products of Nigerian Military School Zaria, the so-called Ex-Boys and Air Force Military School, aka Ex-Jams. These categories of cadets had undergone quasi-military training for five years before entry into the Academy. In a way, they were better equipped for leadership in the cadet ranks. Of these, a number were quite exemplary and in equal terms, the most wayward cadets were drawn from their ranks too.

Another distinctive set of cadets were the other ranks. It was known that soldiers, airmen and sailors who had already undergone basic military training in the services were on the courses. Such prior training came in handy, as they were acquainted with regimentation, military etiquettes, and traditions and thus perfectly placed to assume leadership positions.

Furthermore, the progressive assessment of cadets from the first and later years were factored into choosing individuals for positions of leadership. Thus, an individual's overall performance, personal qualities, carriage, and general service knowledge were crucial to being appointed.

However, often unmentioned were the twin tribulations of ethnic machination and the chicanery of eye service that came into play in selecting cadet leadership. These and other considerations overarched merit and capability, which tainted the selection process.

It must be appreciated that ethnic jingoism, which was so pervasive in our national life, also thrived at the Academy. The contending power blocs exemplified by the noxious contests between the North and South of Nigeria, as well as countless factions impacted the Academy. Worse still, bigotry of all shades counting for instance, religious and sadly perverse sexual orientation also reckoned.

The Academy policy instituted a balanced and objective process, but regrettably, it was subverted by elements within the authorities with active collaborators from cadet ranks. In this way, each of the contending ethnic blocs and various interests impeded fair play.

Along these lines too, apart from reflections on suitability and capacity, the exercise devolved to preferment as nothing was based on merit and the unqualified superseded. Still, a corps of cadets keen to be identified as capable descended into the most obsequious charade imaginable, which was known as patching.

Patching in cadet parlance, referred to conduct by which a set of cadets exasperated all, to stand in the good stead of their seniors and the authorities. In the end, not only deserving cadets got appointed to leadership but a mishmash of ethnic gaslighting, religious charlatans, and incurable yes-men. In time, these portents known all through the Armed Forces of Nigeria as eye service, took on a vicious life of their own and endlessly plagued the credibility, fairness, and capability of the services.

It was apparent that Nigerians loved power and would do anything to grab its handles. From the beginning too, these scheming cadets knew the importance of placement and preferment. So, in this way, cliques and cabalist aggregations became established incredibly early in the day. These would later develop into ruthless power mongers and bruising shove for favours and appointments.

Wedding day $ November 1995

Chapter Fourteen

Academy Routine Order

Being selected to go through cadet training was the easier part of the bargain, as the greater challenge lay with enduring the associated packages. The pattern of activities was divided into two uneven parts, i.e., sessions with instructors and intra-cadet mayhem. Although both segments were official, the former's activities were determinate and structured while the latter were nebulous and capricious.

As earlier noted, there were two classes of instructors at the Academy namely commissioned officers and SNCOs. While the officers took on the conceptual framework of high strategy and field tactics, SNCOs were engaged in imparting direct skills to balance the abstract bent of the former.

Instructor Deportment

The demeanour of instructors at the Academy was a harbinger of the kind of colleagues we met in the field. They came in various shades and characters both brilliant and daft. Collectively, they exhibited extreme haughtiness especially the SNCOs that were inclined to overstress the fact that they were instructing future officers. It was a relationship dominated by terseness and condescension as they reckoned little of their cadet charges and treated them with patronizing brashness.

Instructional Sessions

For each branch of study, lessons were presented that constituted the body of knowledge that trainees had to grasp. The opening sessions consisted of the general principles as well as associated cross-cutting themes taught over time. Also, attention was paid to all aspects of the desirable branch, as these were exhaustively covered and recapped to ensure full comprehension.

Not for once disremembering that the Academy was a military citadel, most themes were about war and the art of war. Others incorporated Map Reading, Signal Communications, Minor Tactics, Equitation, Military Law, Man Management, Methods of Instructions and General Service Knowledge in no order but all coequally important.

Tactics

Fighting a war was a chaotic encounter. Even so, there was a method to it. Hence, the resort to the art of organizing and employing fighting forces. This covered all actions before, during and after an engagement, either near or on the battlefield. Every dynamic was based on the best use of firepower, mobility and manoeuvre, force protection and fire discipline to achieve shock action, i.e., to make the enemy incapable of coherent response.

Apart from these considerations, the fighting doctrine of a force was a factor of the military technology available to such a force. For instance, motorized, mechanized, or armoured forces etc., were trained, and fought differently due to the mechanics of the technologies incorporated.

Apart from military technology, the dominance of a particular fighting arm also dictated the tactical bent of each force. Such allied fighting arms like infantry, artillery or tanks defined the strategic training of forces. In the NA, the infantry was the dominant fighting arm which influenced the overall training at the Academy.

The tactics segment was expectedly inclined towards the infantry but incorporated joint arms strategies as well. The scheme of study included battle drills, movement and core military operations like advance, attack, defence and withdrawal and other operations such as harbour, patrols, raids, and ambushes. It was a general orientation, but any skills not imparted in training was left to be experienced in the searing furnace of operational eventualities on the battlefield.

Military Law

As earlier conceded, the army was a grunt job characterized by meanness, coerciveness, and arbitrariness. By its disciplinary system, it was a doctrinaire society. Given the stiff-necked fashion and egotism with which rules and regulations were imposed, universal acquiescence was not achievable. It must be understood that individuals made up armies and not all complied unquestionably with instructions. So, rules and regulations were decreed for institutional guidance, good order, and proper conduct of personnel.

At the onset of training, Military Law was introduced especially because servicemembers were also subject to civil law as articulated in the so-called doctrine of compact. These laws were encapsulated in statutes that set up the services outlining administrative instructions, customs, and traditions of individual services, fighting arms and units etc. It was a fascinating area of the service because in implementing its spirit and letter, it exposed the whimsical tendencies of individuals.

Method of Instruction

Method of Instruction dealt with transmitting knowledge. It functioned on the assumption that personnel who were knowledgeable on subjects should be able to instruct colleagues on what they knew in the easiest realistic manner. By implication, this meant all military personnel were potential instructors or teachers.

General Service Knowledge

The trainees were destined for different services, but the primary training was universal at the onset. This was chiefly as infantry or foot soldiers in battle. But then again, the army was not composed of only the infantry as there were other arms like armour, gunners, sappers, and other specialized fighting arms. So, as the training progressed, it became essential to introduce General Service Knowledge (GSK).

GSK inculcated an awareness of the employment and deployment of organic and support elements of all fighting arms and joint operations. It dealt with the size of sub-units, units, formations of support elements, sister services as well as operational doctrines in combined all arms fighting and joint operations.

Field Exercises

It was previously noted that instructions were primarily class sessions amplified by field exercises. On the other hand, not all subjects taught were run-through in the field except map reading, signal communications and minor tactics. There were two types of field exercises namely Tactical Exercises Without Troops (TEWT) and Field Training Exercises (FTX) of which the conduct was based on the nature of the subjects. For effects, they were graded and formed the basis of the performance evaluation of individual cadets.

TEWT

Tactical Exercises Without Troops were scenario-based exercises (SBE). During these outings, conflicts were simulated that necessitated the deployment of troops. The trainees had to proffer workable courses of action to given operational situations. TEWTs were mostly about minor tactics, map reading and signal communications.

The defining character of TEWT was the locale of an exercise which could be within the grounds of the Academy, or at any of the abundant training spaces. However, Map Reading TEWTs were held both within and outside the Academy grounds due to its requirement for elevated locations like Mahuta and Kakau Hills.

FTX

Field Training Exercises (FTX) were not any different from TEWT except for the locations and mock-ups. Like TEWTs, they were also SBEs but with added requirement to run through battle procedures. Battle procedure was a recurrent activity that began with a warning order, through battle preparations, reconnaissance, issuance of orders, movement and deployment, skirmishing, exploitation, reorganization, and a final withdrawal or advance.

All these were notional encounters, but the trainees were deployed in role-play as commanders, troops and vice versa. Over the years, as our training progressed, these field exercises morphed into camps with more elaborate activities at training areas away from the Academy like Afaka forest or NDA Training Areas at Kachia and Jos.

Additionally, study tours to training schools of the various fighting arms or corps of NA were occasionally scheduled. During these visits, there were static displays and demonstrations of firepower by live firing as part of field exercises. The main training camps were Camps Initial, Adventure, Kura, Farauta, Kurata, Pre-Highland, and Highland.

Confusion

Having spent about ten weeks at the Academy, we had presumably gotten adequate elementary military orientation, and it was time to get outdoors. Our first FTX was at the Afaka Training Area. This training area was a vast expanse of shrubland stretching from west of Nigerian Air Force Base parallel to Mando settlement with the School of Forestry as its southern boundary. Its northern end was fringed by the Kaduna International Airport and the NDA new site.

It was an Early Start Day. This meant all activities for the day were unusually earlier. Wake up, breakfast, assembly, and forming up at the front of Cadets Mess all took place before 0700hrs. We also turned out in the right attire for outdoor exercises which was Full Service Marching Orders (FSMO) less big packs.

Even before we formed up, the vehicles detailed to convey us were already parked at the assembly area. These were an assortment of transporters which included two buses, and open-top trucks, which cadets derisively dubbed as cadets and horses. It was pathetic that the authorities never contrived to provide any comfortable means of transport other than those rickety cargo vehicles. It would appear the operative mantra was more utility and less coziness. After the reports, we awaited the arrival of officers who would lead us to the exercise area.

The first officer to arrive at the assembly area was the sponsor or lead for the exercise. He came laden with bulky envelopes from which he distributed the exercise papers. We were expected to read ourselves into the scenarios as the sponsor handed out more papers on the current situation, which were the so-called requirements.

I collected copies but because it was early dawn and poorly lit, I could not read it and stuffed the papers into one of my pouches and snoozed off, erroneously assuming that there would be enough time to go through the papers later. Perhaps, if we had been given the exercise papers on time, we may have understood the situation better. However, because we were a mixed bag of trainees, our knowledge of outdoor exercises differed substantially.

One key area of deficiency for those of us "raw civilians" who had never experienced an FTX before, was the joint curiosities of what to expect and what was expected of us. For all the tedium that went into our premier field exercise, all we needed was to understand the whole thingmajig about scenarios and activities that went with it.

The opening salvo in the bush was a random question from one of the instructors directed at the cadet nearest to him: "Why are we here?" The cadet intuitively answered that we were out for a "bush exercise."

What followed was an invective-laden outburst about the lack of seriousness and lackadaisical attitude of cadets.

Of course, we were on an outdoor exercise, but he needed to add there had been cross-border incidents by the Niagara Army that encroached on our territory and that we belonged to Jamaku Army. Also, we were there to launch a series of patrols and reconnaissance to confirm the veracity of the intelligence received.

Even more, as part of the pre-planning to conduct patrols, we were expected to make sand models as well as prepare and give out operational orders. For these orders too, there was an Orders Notebook with formats which was filled-in related to the nature of the operations projected. Although these were tasking and time consuming, they were the nuts and bolts of field operations as they were repetitive routines in all phases of war.

In retrospect, I felt these key elements were not properly communicated in the lessons. So, on the eve of the exercise itself, there was a proliferation of orders formats which we exchanged among ourselves. By now, I began to observe a strange method of instruction characteristic of the army, which I would later encounter repeatedly.

For such primary military skills, it was not too much of a task to schedule lessons and introduce cadets to the basic procedures for induction into operations. It was indiscreet to presume the trainees would guess the procedures before and during the FTX proper. I do not recollect if this was done at all, preparatory to the first field exercise. But later, I recognized an inverted system of training where exercises preceded rudimentary instructions.

Novices Boxing

Once again, we were introduced to another novel aspect of cadet training. This time it was novices boxing. Whoever incorporated pugilism into the training module was a genius because what played out during the bouts was melodramatic spectacle. It had never vaguely occurred to me that young people who came into majority could not throw or deflect punches in self-defence.

The build-up to the week of the event simulated preparations of amateur boxers. Our seniors led us through a rigorous week of grueling training during which, swathed in ponchos, we ran long distances with clenched fists held on guard. We also tried to perfect the feign, bob, and do the shuffle. We all later assembled at the Sports Complex where everyone was weighed in, matched and mixed across the four training battalions by weight. I got classified as a heavyweight and by noon we all knew our opponents.

When it was time, we were festooned in head and groin protectors, gloves, and a mouth guard. This made the hands bulky and with a mouth guard in place, it felt like bits in the mouth of a horse. Apart from adding to bulk, it was clumsy. Each match lasted two rounds of three minutes, but it passed more like hours. The bouts took place at the Academy gym which had a standard boxing ring.

Lord have mercy. When the bouts properly started, the spectators were treated to a repertoire of boxing styles which included 360-degree hooks, back punches and swings, some individuals ran round the ring to avoid blows, turning away from the encounter and a funnier part was when others resorted to "dambe", the traditional Hausa boxing.

On the first day of novices boxing, nine Burma clowns fought, and of these, seven lost. Then all hell broke loose. In fact, from the gym, we were marched collectively to the lines as a course, not segregating those who fought from those who had not and treated to a twelve-hour overnight drenching at the height of the cold harmattan.

It was during this night that I discovered that no matter how freezing, water, if continuously poured, felt warm. However, to be intermittently speckled, felt like a thousand needles driven into a person. A worse finding was that, due to the cold, we broke wind uncontrollably.

Finally, it was the time for my bout, and I fought in a combined state of rage and fear and eventually knocked my opponent down. When we started again after the mandatory count, I attacked again with another barrage and the fight was stopped. It was a victory by knockout in my favour. At the end, I was so dazed that when I went to dinner, it took an effort to masticate as my jaws were locked from the mutual pummeling.

Camp Initial

Camp Initial was the first full-fledged FTX that young cadets customarily went through at the Academy. The camp was designed as a low-level field exercise to put young cadets through their paces on navigational skills i.e., day point-to-point, night march, map-reading skills, night, and day patrols.

As the refrain went, cadets trained cadets and even more. However, by cadet reckoning, the training regimen for the camp was overstretched by its competitive drive. This translated into a very frenzied pre-camp training schedule that lasted almost five months from when we were assembled on the course.

Following our release from our ten-week stay in the preparatory wing and on being integrated into the main cadet lines, our seniors took charge, as each battalion already had standing Camp Initial Teams in place. The main activities in the camp were pitching and striking of tents, night navigation, day point-to-point, night and day patrols, kit laying and fit-for-fight (FFF).

Initial Camp Training

The entire excitement about Camp Initial was even the milder stuff compared to the persistence and vigour with which our superiors approached its training. The pre-camp training built up gradually but when it peaked its intensity was long and sustained, and its vim and vigour were not only physically demanding but emotionally draining.

It took a supreme effort to drink from so bitter a cup. It was also the season for absconding because younger cadets who could not cope with the blistering pace of the build-up deserted or dashed. It became an intolerable practice, as our seniors barred us from engaging in normal ball games except those strenuous activities related to the impending camp.

At the Academy then, working days, excluding weekends, were divided into three segments namely first periods, academics, and evening games. Typically, first periods were taken with SNCOs and never lasted more than an hour on average from the assembly before the event to dispersal post-event.

The academic session was dutifully spent typically with civilian lecturers being instructed in line with our various scholarly pursuits. This took much of the day by six hours and was a more relaxed segment by temperament. However, by noon this would be overtaken by the scorching evening games.

Evening Games

Evening games were a daily staple at the Academy. There was the weekly central Cadets Brigade and battalion-only evening games. During the former, one could expect to play ball games though with the latter, it was always endurance and more of it.

As a first termer, every impending midday was ushered in with disquiet. From midday until lights out by 2100 hours and beyond, about seven hours of each passing day and more during weekends, were taken up by intense training activities. It was during these intervals that all the different dimensions of the venomous intra-cadet relationships manifested.

Endurance Routes

There were many endurance routes that cadets plied daily. The shortest of these went from the Silver Jubilee Gate through Officers' Quarters by 241 Mammy Market and back into the Academy by MRS gate. The second snaked from the Ribadu Cantonment first gate and looped through Engineers Mammy Market by the Barracks Mosque and through 81 Barracks into the Academy by the MRS gate. It was longer by a factor of about three to five kilometres.

There were also more endurance routes known as the "44 Routes" which went short of or by the railway through Unguwan Kanawa to 44 Hospital roundabout. Of course, there were other branches to this route too. We could turn right at the roundabout and ply the shorter of the 44 routes through Kurmin Mashi and back into the Academy.

Of the second and third 44 routes, one went in front of the 44 Reference Hospital and meandered behind Kaduna Polytechnic, while the longest version passed the front of the polytechnic by Kasuwan Barchi and hit the Kaduna Bypass at Asikolaiye and finally returned to the Academy at the rear gate of Ribadu Cantonment, about twenty through thirty kilometres. Of course, the latter route being the longest always registered lots of droppers.

Camping Kits

When the pre-camp training began, we were clad in normal fatigues and lightly kitted but over time the appurtenances increased immensely. Later, backpacks with blankets, filled water bottles, shoe brushes and polish, and mess tins (canteens) with a rifle in tow. By the time we hit the endurance routes, we were harnessed with over fifteen to twenty kilograms of weight. For effects, our participation in other physical activities was curtailed and we began to receive special attention.

Navigational Skills

One of the cardinal pillars of pre-camp training was imparting navigational skills to young cadets. This involved day point-to-points and night marches. The practice was for individual battalion training teams to go out on recce, plot the bearings and follow up with the actual exercises.

The day points-to-points and night marches were held over a vast training area covering the then sparsely populated Mahuta village, National Eye Hospital, Afaka forest and across Mando settlement stretching as far as the Nigeria Air Force Base. The vast distances were not a problem but the sundry activities during the navigational exercises.

For an exercise proper, the trainees were coalesced into a single team, with three key lead appointments namely a guide, pacer, and recorder. At all times, the recce team that plotted the course always drafted a navigation chart. This was usually a three-columned table with a start point, bearing i.e., direction of movement, distances to be covered and the terminal point or objective, typically prominent landmarks, or features.

Before then, we were familiarized with the use of prismatic compasses as navigational aids during introductory map reading lessons. Moreover, we could judge distances, and everyone was expected to master his paces astride a hundred-metre distance. So, during point-to-points or night marches, the guide led the navigation, while the pacer judged distances and the recorder took notes on the objectives.

Under normal circumstances, navigational exercises were scheduled during weekends, especially on Saturdays. Of course, we got prior notice of the impending exercise. Thus, after the routine toilet washing during the early hours of the morning, we marched to the Cadets Mess as a group and hurriedly wolfed down our breakfast and reassembled in front of the mess for the final checks before setting out.

A Posse

A typical posse that set forth included the Officer-in-Charge (OIC) usually a fifth-term cadet, or his Second-in-Command (2i/c) and seniors co-opted on the team. There were also the ever-present second termers, who expectedly made up the larger proportion of the supporting team. The trainees were heavily laden, though at the initial stage, we went out without rifles, but as the training progressed, it was included.

The party marched out through the southern end of the Academy across Nnamdi Azikiwe (Western By-pass) and headed to the extensive land earmarked for the National Eye Hospital. The points from the beginning were conspicuous and easily identified objects. Traditionally, a knoll at the Mahuta settlement was commonly used by all the training teams as the first point of navigational exercises. The hill was not so massive but was easily visible from the southern end of the Academy given the open terrain.

Finding Your Direction

The basic technique on the march was to figure out a bearing, get aligned to an intermediate or visible feature, close the compass, and start dashing. Onwards to the next point, the same procedure was repeated until the distance was covered and an objective positively identified. However, there were bound to be obstacles on the way, and these could be bypassed by systematically detouring and re-aligning the march by lateral distances.

Apart from all these niceties, we had to contend with the presence of our seniors, especially the second termers, that accompanied the posses during marches. By this time, all the hounds were unleashed once we left the confines of the Academy. From a force of habit, they promptly procured cudgels, long whips, and other scourging accessories with which they descended on us in a frenzy of flogging that spurred us on a feisty dash to the objectives.

Oh dear. The beating was administered indiscriminately irrespective of whether we kept a blistering pace or not. It was of such intensity that on occasions, we completely missed or overshot our objectives. In such situations, we often retraced our steps and once the point was identified, the interval between recording and plotting a new bearing was spent in a mix of frog jumps and press-ups. The routine was repeated throughout a march and by the end of the exercise, a combination of hunger, exhaustion and blisters in our heavy military boots would have taken its toll.

During the return leg to the Academy, it took supreme efforts to maintain a walking gait. Drained of energy and dog-tired by now, we haggardly dragged ourselves or crawled back to camp. As a rule, straggling was not allowed. So, we had to march back as one compact group from when we set out.

On the other hand, night marches were not any different except we never ran so hard but sustained fast paces. The beatings were unceasing, and it was a miracle that we went out and came in without casualties or any accidents given the number of dry water wells that littered the training area. Although we heard stories of a cadet who drowned during a night march, nothing untoward happened throughout our training. Over time, before the Camp Initial proper, we mastered the routine.

Other pre-camp trainings included setting up and dismantling a tent (pitching and striking), and kit laying by which each cadet displayed all the military paraphernalia in the packs. The last aspect of the training was the dash back or fit-for-fight (FFF). During the mock training, we set off from the Academy and trekked to Buruku village, about thirty kilometres along Kaduna-Birnin Gwari Road and took off back to the Academy.

By the time we finally got into camp, all the trainees were in top physical shape. Although, Camp Initial was a military boot camp, it counted as a major competition in reckoning towards the Academy championship. We were warned over and over that we had to come tops come hell or high waters. Funnily, just before we set off for the camp, the BSUO in a final address reminded us that if we came back without the trophy, we would chew nails and that he had already set up a Disappointment Committee to receive us in case of failure.

So, after many months of demanding preparations, we finally got into the location of the five-day camp. The campsite was the Afaka general area, the site of the new NDA. We quickly set up the camp and were settled in by a heavy downpour on our first night out. In the end, because the real exercise was led by officers and instructors, the run-through was a whimpering denouement to the preparatory cacophony preceding the camp. In comparison, it was obvious that the hard preparations made the actual exercise look rather tame.

Fit-For-Fight

All the events scheduled like pitching and striking of tents, point-to-point and night navigations, patrols and map reading etc. held as planned without incident and we went in for FFF which was the last part of the camp. It was the thirty-kilometre dash back to the Academy. However, just before we were set off, the PT officer stepped forward and delivered an ominous address.

"I know that you all prepared for this day. I do not have any doubts in my mind that you are of sound health, capable and in prime physical state. However, let me be candid with you and advise that, if you are carried away by the spirit of competition and you overreach yourself, and God forbid, if anything happens to you, the army job will continue."

Accordingly, we were set off after this gloomy speech and about two hundred of us took part. Initially, we were road bound but soon enough, we veered off into the bushes to make our way back to the Academy. Already, we were familiar with the general area because, during the pre-camp training, we had repeatedly crisscrossed the entire expanse of Afaka forest.

Kit Laying

On arrival at the Academy, we assembled on the SS Parade Ground for the last phase of the camp which was Kit Laying where cadets and civilians were already assembled. Each trainee was expected to have hauled along in his backpack and pouches certain military items. For each missing item, points were deducted.

So, despite our stellar performances in the camp and most especially during the dash back, we all watched helplessly in horror as our efforts were technically nullified by missing items during kit laying. Our worst nightmare had materialized as Burma battalion lost the 1989 Camp Initial trophy.

Chewing Nails

After the results were announced, we knew for certain that we were going to have a difficult day. The BSUO's speech on the day of departure came back in full force as the Disappointment Committee received us. We hunched to the frontage of Burma Mainlines and continued to do many funny things until the BSUO came after an endless wait to address the culprits.

"Clowns" He called out imperially. "Sir" Our now thoroughly tired group chorused. "Hehehehe" He laughed noisily and adjusted his impeccably pressed uniform. "Gentlemen clowns, what was our agreement" he inquired rhetorically. We all drooped our heads downcast. He spoke angrily and tersely ordered we be led away and not allowed to see peace. To which our seniors especially the second termers waiting in the wings gave an uproarious cheer and then split us into groups and the afflicting began.

It was while this hounding was ongoing that the deputy commandant of the Academy appeared suddenly and saved us from further punishment. But our seniors that were directing the whole thing were now in real trouble. The senior officer was horrified, but to the cadets, this event was a normal daily occurrence. In the fallout, there were rumours of relegation or outright withdrawal. The conductors of the macabre orchestra were eventually charged for the offence of brutality and tried by the CO but mercifully, a lesser punishment of extra duty was awarded, more like a mild reprimand.

Camp Initial also marked the end of the most energetic training directed exclusively at first termers as a group. Although there would be other correspondingly demanding modules, the intensity was not as sustained. At this point, we had completed the rudimentary and critical phase of transitioning from raw civilians to soldiers who could be deployed in combat.

Final Official Puttee

Having successfully concluded the first boot camp, the next big struggle was to attain the right to wear the No.4 dress, i.e., the officer's jacket. Our superiors had so far denied us the privilege of wearing this dress. I could not say how it felt for others, but I eagerly awaited the day I could get into a jacket. We were denied this craving because we had not earned the right to do so, not until we had undergone the rites of Final Official Puttee (FOP).

In any case, there was nothing final nor official about this puttee apart from the fact that it was a sanguinary cadet-conceived ritual. It was not any different from other activities with cadet oversight which involved an excruciating practice short of outright cruelty. The ACA gleefully proclaimed that the next Saturday would be FOP Day for our course. This announcement was received with riotous cheering which was utterly confusing.

In truth, FOP was an event to be experienced rather than explained. Accordingly, as early as 0600hrs that Saturday, we all assembled in front of the Cadets Mess. While awaiting the arrival of the ACA to declare the show opened, judging by the mien of our superiors and rigorous activities like hunching, forward rolls, and press-ups, during the build-up, I could discern that this FOP business would inflict a bodily toll.

Finally, the ACA arrived and was received with yet another deafening jubilation. It was not a speechifying event but just to assure clowns of the fact that every other senior cadet had undergone the same rites and officially declared the ceremony opened. We then stripped our tops and marched uphill towards the North Gate of the Academy in the general area of the Faculty of Science block which was the starting point.

In the beginning, about two hundred initiates huddled tightly while the rest of our seniors were formed in a file formation facing inwards. All the proceedings took place within the narrow confines of the file formation covering about hundred and fifty metres, with the finishing point in front of the Cadet Mess. We all waited anxiously for the call to start.

When the event was finally flagged off, the word start sounded more like dash. Every one of the initiates except yours sincerely, backed off but I stood my ground and stepped forward and went into the very first forward roll of the day. Then all hell broke loose with whippings, scraping with stones and grass stubs, rubbing of boots all over the bare torso.

All these afflicting was accompanied by taunting, screams and the signature thuds of the inner plastic helmets registering on bare backs and buttocks unmistakably. It was clear that the whole kernel of FOP was an ordeal. It took ages to get through the cauldron, akin to going through distinct stages of affliction as the plaguing intensified with each passing stage.

Worse still, I spent more time at certain points than others. Also, I had wrongly assumed that getting to the end point marked the end of the thingamajig. The other strand of thought in my mind was that this whole thing was a test of bravery. I endured and finally got to the last station in front of the Mess. But unbelievably, I was sent back to the starting point to go through all over again. In fact, I was being inducted to the fundamentals of military perfidy.

Once again at a very dark hour, out of nowhere, a guardian angel appeared. Just as I was halfway through my second run of the deadly circuit, the Commandant, who was about on an unscheduled weekend tour of the Academy grounds happened in on the grisly din. There was pandemonium and the whole proceeding came to an unexpected halt.

The Kahuna Stops FOP

The Commandant was visibly furious and demanded explanations from the organizers of the sham event. There were lame excuses about tradition. But he was unimpressed being himself a product, in fact, the premier corps of cadets, of the same Academy. He further explained that if for anything, it was to be overseen by PT instructors and not intended to demean or dehumanize fellow cadets.

Tempers and anxieties ran high but once again the culprits who were too many to be relegated or withdrawn, were let off-hook with caution. A few initiates were hospitalized but I survived with lacerations all over my body and excruciating pains for the next two weeks.

An Assertive Clown

Later that day, at lunchtime, one of our course mates boldly wore his No. 4 dress to the mess. Along the way, he was accosted by his seniors who soiled his uniform and ordered him back. They claimed hypocritically that since the FOP was inconclusive, the course was not eligible to dress as such.

It was a typical manner of derogating rights and privileges when it was convenient for superiors whenever and wherever it served their purposes. After much haggling among our superiors, it was eventually declared that the course was eligible to be decked in No.4 dress. It was a grim and hard-earned victory.

A Compassionate Sister

Immediately after the FOP, an admin day, read, a free day, was declared. It was then, I sneaked out on AWOL (short endurance we called it), to visit my elder sister in Kano City. As usual, and as with all cadets, since we collectively suffered from sleep deprivation and at any given opportunity, we tried to grab enough sleep as we could. So, during that brief visit, I fell into a deep slumber.

However, my short blissful sleep was soon interrupted by my big sister who was beside the bed shouting. What was the uproar about? In my deep sleep, half nude, she saw my scalded feet and torso covered in grazes.

"What is wrong with your feet? What are these bruises all over your body?" It was a monosyllabic interrogation, so, I took time to address her concerns. The blistered feet I explained were because of the heavy military-style boots and the scrapes all over me were on account of the FOP ritual but she was unimpressed.

"The military job has no refinement, but I did not expect them to maim you alive. It is not worth it. You should consider leaving that place." She counselled compassionately, but she conceded it was my decision to make. Besides, I explained that since I joined voluntarily it was important to ensure that I went the whole hog, lest I be labelled a cowardly individual unable to withstand pains. It was a rational advice all caring sibling would give their own. I never withdrew but completed my officer cadet training.

Hard Labour Serenaded with Music

By mid-August every year, the Academy was seasonally serenaded with the sounds of martial music. The NDA Band massed and was fully engaged for about four weeks. During these periods, Army cadets would have been through with Camp Highland, the last FTX. At the same time too, their Naval and Air Force counterparts returned from specialist finishing schools which marked the commencement of preparations preceding the Passing Out Parade (POP).

The ambience over the Academy was enveloped with martial music and a flurry of activities as preparations for POP got into top gear. There were rehearsals in the mornings and afternoons and other activities which included Beating the Retreat, Awards for individual brilliance in sports and Dinner Night.

While all these took the forefront, in the background intense manual labour ensued, which was volubly baptized Interior Economy. It was the last competition towards the Academy championship during the training year. I found the name quite bizarre because the related activities had nothing to do with neither an interior nor economy.

It consisted of mostly hard manual labour deployed to sweeping, brushing, weeding, scrubbing floors, washing toilets sparkling clean, laying kerbstones, and thereafter painting them in garish whitewash. Those who have had cause to visit the Academy during POP would attest to the gleaming appearance of its grounds. The preparations for Interior Economy lasted two weeks and the competitive assessment itself took place just a week before POP.

It was not just the intensity of the activities involved but the unrelated but embedded irritations in an already wearisome condition. We were constantly drenched in puddles and discommoded by rigorous physical exertions for no reason whatsoever. No excuse was mandatory except the overriding desire to make things difficult for everyone, especially the juniors.

By now, we were rounding the bend of our first term with renewed hope when by July of that year, candidates for 41 RC assembled for a selection board. This marked progress, as it was certain that soon enough, we would be endowed with a junior set behind our course.

Pluming

Eventually, the first term ended. For the year, the main event of note was our first break as first termers which coincided with the Yuletide season. There was Camp Initial and its associated training activities and of course our FOP. The highlight of our first break was "pluming," i.e., going home to your folks in military uniform in the beautiful hat of the Academy with a plume.

I vividly recall my first break. As part of the preparations, we needed new uniforms. It was at this point that a course mate informed me that his roommate, an Academy appointment, had a No.4 dress he wished to dispose of, and I was invited to buy. It was not a voluntary transaction, as an old apparel was being forced on me.

This dress was not made to my fitting, but I had no choice. The worst part of the whole shebang was the bargain that followed. I was hopeful for a discount on account of its being used because the going price for a new pair of uniforms was fifteen Naira. I asked to pay less but he insisted, or rather decreed, and I could not decline the transaction. It was an extortion in its most unadulterated form.

Well, I had the dress refitted at an added cost to me. I also ensured that it never made my expeditions during the break any less exciting, especially the photo ops with my beloved mother and the heroic visit to my village. It was a momentous homecoming, the memories of which endures to this day. Subsequently, I did this for every break until the third term when I ceased.

Owerri 1997

Chapter Fifteen

A New Set of Subordinates

By September of each training year, as the most senior corps of cadets were being processed out, another replaced it. It was the same for our course as we saw off cadets of 36 RC Army and Air Force (36 AAF). Incidentally, 36 RC enjoyed a special status in the history of the Academy due to some adjustments.

Up to a point, upon graduation, trainees were awarded a Nigerian Defence Academy Certificate of Education (NDACE). However, in 1985, the Academy was upgraded to a university status beginning with 36 RC. After the review, it was discovered a number on the course, were considered ineligible for conferment of a degree on account of academic deficiencies.

The pertinent question was how they got selected in the first place if the same entry qualifications were demanded of all. This meant a dubious compromise and double standards. In any case, the trainees found to be ineligible were loped off a year earlier than their fellows who got degrees.

In September 1989, 41RC reported for training at the Academy. It was a momentous step forward for me, a year out of five cancelled. I was so excited as I was being addressed prefixed by the moniker of senior. I was immediately drawn to the young cadets because I knew I could be useful in assisting these young entrants to settle in without the habitual cackle.

Not long after, I was officially seconded to 41RC Preparatory Wing, and then 42RC, two years in a row. I had an opportunity to be impactful without being vicious. Even worse, I was converted to a demonstration cadet before my subordinates.

Like every young person, I was not without rough edges. For instance, I would sneak out often to grab a bottle or two of beer. Thus, while I was all over trying to positively inconvenience my subordinates, I was often plucked right in their front and made to do the same things I was asking of them.

The intention was to undermine me before my underlings. However, I absorbed the aggravation calmly and once released from those intermissions, I would resume with intensity right where I had been interrupted. It was a learning process and a situation that I met repeatedly while in service. It was a widespread, adverse, and deplorable propensity, of superiors to habitually chasten subordinates before their underlings.

On being nominated as part of the team to groom 41 RC, I forfeited the post-POP break. At the Academy, breaks were a rarity massively prized because they were time to grab uninterrupted sleep. Nonetheless, I was thrilled by the simple act of adding a second bar to my shoulder.

The preparatory wing ran on a hectic schedule. Apart from mustering and keeping an eye on our younger charges, all of us in the team had to follow our official schedules unfailingly. We conducted the cadets, from wake up through muster parade to the point they set off to their first training periods and ensured, they collectively left the lines by 0745hrs to other training activities.

By 1400hrs, when the official instructor-led training ended, we were at the Cadet's Mess to assemble them back to the lines for the next phase of activities, which began at once. It was always jogging, not just leisurely jogging but hard synchronized running, technically baptized endurance. We all had to endure regardless of seniority. In drilling the others, we also went through the same paces. How so true. Our days always 'technically' ended by 2100hrs with night checking and lights out.

The 41 RC Preparatory Wing was officially dissolved by December 1989 by which time, all cadets were integrated into the various training battalions. The training team was also dispersed, and we had to move back into the lines. For me, it was another momentous change, as I was moved from one training battalion to another.

Chaos versus Serenity

It was clear from the onset that each of the training battalions had its peculiarities. Our seniors told us while at the prep wing to specifically pray against being deployed to Burma Battalion. Although there was nothing untoward about the battalion but for its conflated tradition in all activities. Shortly afterwards, we were allotted to training battalions and providentially, I was deployed to Mogadishu Battalion.

When we reported to the Academy, there was bed space shortage in the regular cadet lines. Although Tamandu and Colito lines reserved for SSC cadets were available they were not taken. Eventually, those bed spaces were made available to regular cadets but there was still a shortfall.

Finally, the day we were integrated into regular cadet lines, those allotted to Mogadishu were balkanized, ten each to Burma and Dalet Battalions, while the balance was retained. So, from excitedly accepting Mogadishu, I was being herded to Burma instead. At the battalion gate, one of my mates was inconsolably transfixed and it took persuasion from the BSUO to get him to enter the lines. So, in my first term, I trained in Burma Battalion.

Burma Battalion was organized on the principle of dissonance and ran on a doctrine of exasperation. As a training and competitive unit, it was eternally optimistic but never won any Academy championship in a long while. It was easily decipherable because the battalion suffered from overtraining that led to underperformance. It was a hyperactive unit and its preparations for cross-country competition, for instance, exemplified its overtraining. It was the most physically demanding competition and the racing circuit traversed over fifteen to twenty kilometres of smooth and rough patches. The pre-competition training was more rigorous than the competition itself.

It was undoubtedly doubly difficult for Burma Battalion. Its cadets, especially half-battalion, were captured at the Cadets Mess during lunch and marched to the lines. From there, the solemn and mostly downcast group were led to the start point. It was typically hot afternoons and the meal taken had barely digested. When finally set off in the blistering sun, the bowels convulsed, and the cadets threw up. Keeping their heads to the side to ensure that the vomitus did not splash on them, they kept running. It was always grim.

In contrast, Mogadishu was quite dissimilar to Burma, both in temperament and organizational character. In this clime, there was no ceaseless tormenting of subordinates. When a parade was shouted for, in less than ten minutes, all assembled including the BSUO, and events were snappily conducted and dismissed.

Additionally, Mogadishu cadets were very protective of their subordinates. They would be formed up and marched to the mess for meals and shepherded back. Meanwhile, Burma cadets could be delayed until they forfeited their meals.

Furthermore, in Burma, after a shout, we all dashed back into the lines until physically dragged-out room after room. We all knew from experience that, if one came out earlier than necessary, there were inconveniences including hunching, hanging by the drainage, or pulling through Burma Tunnel, a claustrophobic culvert.

The Burma Tunnel

The legendary Burma Tunnel was a ring culvert linking the drainages from Burma to Abyssinia Battalion. Its diameter was just big enough to accommodate the biggest cadet. Halfway through this hellhole was a pipe connected to electricity that always mildly electrocuted at the slightest contact. This was an obstacle that could be crossed repeatedly irrespective of the hour of the day or night on the slightest excuse.

Although, there were funny things ongoing as soon as any corps of cadets mustered, the tendency for things to get out of hand was more pronounced in Burma. I was constantly reminded that I was in Mogadishu and not Burma each time I arrived late for parades. It was a learning process all over again.

Of all my new experiences in Mogadishu, the most intriguing was collective obedience and the powers of superiors. Right from the point of entry, hierarchy was pronounced and reinforced. In Burma, if you wanted to puttee a cadet; you made extra efforts to get at him. You needed to pack (i.e., to accost) him instead of issuing a reporting order.

On the contrary, in Mogadishu, a senior could issue a reporting order which was typically obeyed. Time after time, I was in default, as I could not keep to this new system. From my Burma mentality, it was only reasonable that if you chose to inconvenience me, it should come at a price and be mutually disconcerting.

Sandhurst and Others

About this time too, ten of my course mates were screened towards a nomination to attend Sandhurst Military Academy in England. A lot of my colleagues were aware of these opportunities, especially the Ex-Boys, and so worked assiduously towards being nominated. As usual, I was completely ignorant of such prospects.

Later, I understood cadets were shortlisted based on their performances, specifically in the services. I knew that I had high scores in academics but as for the military subjects, it was different for me, due to the system of learning by rote. So, when eventually the nominees were chosen, it was most unexpected because they never remotely represented the best.

Finally, two out of the lot made it to England. One, an ex-Boy, was clearly of problematical cadet because just within the brief period of our stay, he had shown a shifty persona. So, it was not unexpected, when on account of truancy, he was withdrawn from Sandhurst and the Academy. It was a desirable course to attend because it ran for only a short eighteen months instead of the usual five years at the Academy.

In later years, more openings were offered by the United States Military Academies for the Army, Air Force, and the Navy. These were long-standing bilateral provisions that were revived after a lengthy hiatus. Comically too, this set off deadly rivalry among cadets who were bent on outdoing each other, in order, to be considered for a placement in those foreign academies. It was the same unfriendly jostling that characterized service in the field. Worse still, in one or two cases the cadets selected for training overseas absconded.

Camp Adventure

In our second year, the next FTX was a newly introduced Camp Adventure. The camp held at the Citizenship and Leadership Training School, (Mountain School) at Shere Hills, Jos. It was then I noticed that, as young people, we were at the prime of our physical fitness. We surmounted the obstacles at the school at a dash and made a joke of the compass match within the camp and over the hills.

Only two activities in the camp stood out namely, watermanship along with rappelling and abseiling. We learned rafting at a dam in the vicinity of the Mountain School, while the rappelling took place at the top of a scenic rock called Gog and Magog. Unfortunately, the instructors did not forewarn us about the descent. On the first day, a sizeable number of cadets did not pad their shoulders properly enough and got a deep branding by the ropes used for the descent.

Tragedy

As officer cadets, we were so full of life that death or dying never remotely crossed our minds. All year long, we endured physically exerting activities. Graciously too, we enjoyed good health apart from mild irregular incidents of malaria or typhoid fever bouts. On a general note, the body of cadets was a healthy lot.

A tragic event in my second year was the loss of eleven Naval cadets of 41 RC onboard a capsized boat at NNS ONURRA-Onne. The authorities did not offer official clarification about the mishap, and we fell back on speculations and tittle-tattles as there was no commemoration. Normal activities continued as if nothing had occurred. Always, when we lost colleagues, it was mercifully away from the Academy.

29SSC

On January 5, 1990, we received another set of subordinates at the Academy. This was the 29SSC which was composed of Ex-Boys and graduates a sizable number of whom I knew from my university days. This course deserved a mention here because its arrival fourteen months into our training became contentious during our service years.

The terms and conditions of regular and short service commissions were unambiguous. Each category had its pathway spelt out, but individuals and countervailing vested interests excited frequent policy somersaults that led to unnecessary conflicts and bile. I do not know who led the charge, but again and again, our seniorities were swapped. After a while, I deliberately ignored such official inconsistencies.

The arrival of 29 SSC also brought about analogies. The instructors attached to SSC Wing made it a point to connect their performances with ours. I was not bothered because I knew my journey was on a different trajectory and had no cause to get entangled with individuals trying to undermine others.

The crowning infamy of these unnecessary and vexatious comparisons was being drafted to swell their ranks during field exercises and endured the histrionics to the end. I could begin to see an evolving trend where the service was actively promoting showmanship.

22 April 1990

It was a bedlam on 22 April 1990. In the wee hours of that Sunday morning, there was an attempted military coup against the impostor military president, General Ibrahim Babangida led by one Major Gideon Gwaza Orkar. It was an attempt with far-reaching consequences for northern hegemony and military rule in Nigeria. It was not difficult to see especially given the ominous radio broadcast on that day.[1]

The coup we learnt targeted Dodan Barracks, the seat of power, on Lagos Island. For me, it was the first military putsch since I joined the army seventeen months earlier. In a long-winded broadcast, the ringleader portentously excised parts of Nigeria and made damning allegations against the government of the day.[2]

It would appear the attempt recorded partial success as there was no news about President Babangida, except his aide de camp (ADC), Lt Col UK Bello, who was killed when he responded to the mutiny. There was a confused reaction. In Kaduna town, there was an eerie silence with little or no response from HQ First Infantry Division in the city.

Later that day, a retinue of bizarre events unfolded. First, was a counter-coup broadcast on Radio Nigeria Kaduna by Maj Gen Hassan Usman Katsina, a retired former Governor of the Old Northern Region. A former coup plotter himself, it was difficult to figure out under what capacity he made the broadcast.

The GOC had abdicated responsibility at such a critical time. Later, the Colonel General Staff (Col GS) of the division, also made a counter-coup broadcast on Radio Nigeria Kaduna. It was probably at the prompting of General Hassan, who may have realized his indefensible and awkward broadcast.[3] For us cadets, a better part of the coup day was spent in limbo. It was not clear if the insurrectionists had succeeded. However, by mid-day, news of its failure started filtering in, and of the arrests of culprits.

It was a rebellion orchestrated by mid-level NA officers from Nigeria's South-South region. For Major Gideon Gwaza Orkar, a Tiv from Benue in the Middle Belt, his participation in the putsch was in the least out of character. Unfortunately for Major Orkar, his accomplices had already absconded at the time he was making his brave speech.[4]

In the evening of the same day, a thoroughly flustered president who had earlier dashed into hiding was on national television with a retinue of showy armed escorts. The attempted coup had failed and what followed were reprisals, bloodletting and secret killings that lasted well over a decade.

All Cadets were herded to the drill shed and formed up, where a series of checks were instituted. Although it was unexpected that cadets would take part in any attempt to overthrow a government, we were nonetheless, placed under gating (curfew). In any case, after the initial checks, several cadets were absent, but a deadline was set by which time absentees would be sanctioned.

"Yeeeees …. We have won. We have won." rented the air as a section of cadets of northern origin jubilated. By then, it was obvious that the coup had failed, and I was in a quandary because my fellow Tiv had led the unsuccessful attempted coup, but I did not feel responsible.

During the checks, a particular officer cadet was consistently absent. Very soon too, when the names of the insurrectionists were broadcast, his elder brother's name featured prominently. However, by the last check of the day, this suspected cadet was on the ground. Although his movements and whereabouts, were suspicious, he was not questioned any further but was eventually withdrawn from the Academy two years down the line under questionable circumstances.[5]

Under a Spotlight

In my second term at the Academy, I came under a bright spotlight on account of my sterling performance during the Hockey Championship. I had learnt to play this beautiful game by watching soldiers at 81 Barracks Kaduna. Later, in my high school days, though not played at my school, I joined students of Mkar Teachers' College, where I honed my skills and by the time I got to the university, I was well-rounded in the game.

During the Hockey championship, I took the Academy by storm as I put up a supreme display, so vastly different from the whacking pattern played by cadets. I dribbled, danced, feigned and forcefully orchestrated a series of victories and the Hockey championship for

Mogadishu Battalion. I had my glorious spotlight as I became a star but for the short duration of the competition period only.

Battalion Training Team

For all the pains and harshness that I endured during Camp Initial training, I was still attracted to the excitement of being outdoors and joined the Mogadishu Battalion Camp Initial Team. It was a close-knit team that was dedicated and given to sacrifice. The work of the team was very demanding.

For us all, it was akin to getting trained for the first camp all over again. There were days dedicated to long endurance, pitching, and striking of tents, day, and night marches. We typically set out on recce and plotted the routes, marked up the objectives and prepared the charts.

Due to the engaging workload of official training, the team's schedule was tailored to conform to the activities of the week. We reserved weekends for day marches, but any night of the week could be used for night marches. Despite my sacrifices and active role as a trainer cadet, I never received an official cadet appointment, not even the lowly Cadet Lance Corporal

Sad Battalion Party

The Battalion Party was one of the many cadets-inspired traditions. As the name implies, as the year wound down, just about a week before POP, celebratory parties were initiated and funded by cadets across all the training battalions. I remember vividly an encounter during my First Term in Burma Battalion. The levy was Five Naira only per individual. I had no cash at hand but due to the persistent harassment by the senior cadet in charge of collecting the dues, I could not stand it any longer, I had to take a loan of Five Naira from a colleague to go on AWOL to Kano.

I went on a forced visit to my sister, and graciously she gave me Twenty Naira. I came back the next day and was able to pay back the loan and my dues and still had Five Naira left on me. Being driven to borrow money, as well as being forced to sneak out of the Academy without permission was not a palatable encounter.

The highlight of this party tradition was that cadets were allowed to receive visitors in the lines, wear mufti and keep late hours. It was an annual event that was eagerly anticipated especially for the female visitor component. So, during my second year, it was yet another season of Battalion Party. This was 1990 and the course due to pass out was 37 RC. I promptly dropped my contribution without the hassles of being inconvenienced.

The 1990 Battalion Party commenced as scheduled simultaneously in the four battalions. There were visitors and all including ladies. In fact, at the Mogadishu party hall, one of the staff officers, a Major came visiting. This officer was accorded special recognition as he was served bottles of chilled Gulder beer and chicken laps. I observed that he was obviously very famished as he greedily wolfed down everything on offer like an orphan.

Everyone was having a swell time when suddenly a fire alarm was sounded. It was an unexpected distraction on the only free day taken by cadets. Perhaps, an emergency may have cropped up. But it was not. It was the Cadet Brigade Commander (CBC), a reptilian fossil of an individual, who emanated from wherever to upend our joyful moment.

We had to hurriedly abandon the partying and change into military fatigues and form-up as usual at the muster point. It was then that the CBC arrived with the abovementioned staff officer in tow. I could not think anything of the imp, except the hunger I saw on him. It was a chaotic fire alarm.

Our guests, both male and female were still milling around. So, while we were still assembled, the CBC instructed the soldiers on guard duties to round up all the visitors including scantily clad ladies that came for the party. Now before we realized what was happening, a lot of damage had already been done. For each non-cadet apprehended, they were cajoled into identifying whose guest they were. It was such a shame.

I had also invited a young lady to be my date for the party. When the fire alarm sounded, I took her to my room and got dressed for the parade and left her behind. However, when I realized what was happening, I dashed back to the lines and stealthily sneaked her out through one of the many clandestine exits cadets had created to steal out of the Academy and rejoined the chaotic parade.

Later during the parade, the CBC was fulminating and raving about indiscipline of the crop of cadets at the Academy. It was disheartening to see that the perfidious staff officer could neither pacify nor prevail on his principal. The man persisted with his imprecation and threats and by his antecedence, all the cadets trembled at the prospect of what was to come. It was menacing and in the next couple of days his dire threats materialized.

The cadets whose visitors were apprehended or found in their rooms were charged and received accelerated trial and withdrawn from the Academy. Of these victims of the party fallout, about seven were POCs and over twenty others were withdrawn on account of the Battalion Party. It was not only an unjust decision, but it also amounted to a monumental waste of state resources and the time of the withdrawn cadets.

I contemplated the whole scenario as it unveiled, and I knew it was by some providence that I had escaped similar fate. I also privately questioned the draconian sanction of the command as the penalty dwarfed the offence. I thought deeply, why no moderating voice was there, to plead the cause of those beleaguered officer cadets. Not even the Commandant? the father figure to cadets?

It was not the law. There was nothing on the statute books that qualified a common tradition, an annual event at that, to constitute the basis for sacking cadets. The charges preferred against them were not substantive provisions but a concoction of semblances. Sadly, those individuals that had dutifully endured years of arduous training and some were due for a commission in about a week's time.

Why were those so-called offenders not given a lesser but equally tedious reprimand like relegation? If they spent an additional year at the Academy, that would still be drastic enough. But all compassion and redemption were denied on account of one individual's sanctimony.

The vengeful senior officer's negative energy had overwhelmed and driven the decision to wrongly cast adrift fully trained military men. It was an arbitrary and impulsive decision that ruined most of the victims. It was also a gross violation of their human rights. The decision to withdraw was questionable. It was a sore turn of events, but we were helpless.

With my Family at Obudu Resort 2012

Matriculation University of Ile-Ife 1982

Chapter Sixteen

Second-in-Command

I got to the Fourth Term at the Academy with a lot of relief. Technically, we were the next most senior course, and by implication, there was less inconveniencing except from Fifth Termers and Instructors which was far from the truth. Our superiors contrived to make our lives very difficult as we were held responsible for the misdeeds of our subordinates, even when we were not remotely connected.

To sum up, it was a lesson in how not to assume any reliefs or privileges from your immediate boss. In the military, the system was designed for only one top dog at a time. Overall, it was the toughest year to weather because of the continuous torment, and any little slip, one could be summarily thrown out of the Academy.

Camps Kura and Farauta

At the point 30 SSC reported at the Academy, we had already spent 46 of 60 months or 184 of 263 weeks of our training spell. By then, my course was done with all field or outdoor exercises. The last two, namely Camps Kura and Farauta were held before the course reported. By this time, we were in our services term about a couple of weeks shy of our fifth year.

At this point, we were potential white men, in an apartheid system that ran at the citadel. By any means, therefore, I was a lord beyond the knowledge of, a lower sixth course, in a nominally five course Academy.

Unguwan Antai

During Camp Kura, we bivouacked at Idon, a village by a rail crossing, about twenty kilometres due north along Kachia-Kaduna Road. The FTX itself was routine, and nothing was out of place. The last leg of the camp was a dawn attack. Afterwards, we were moved back to the derelict NA Camp at Kachia.

While at Kachia, no organized activities took place, so we drifted about for most of the day. Finally, by late afternoon, we were assembled and driven out of the camp. We thought we were on our way back to the bivouac at Idon, but it was oddly too late in the day to head back. The vehicles were then halted by a hill abutting the highway. We disembarked and the Exercise Sponsor then stepped forward.

"Gentlemen cadets, we are now going into the next phase of the exercise. It is an ordinary compass march which you are all familiar with." He paused for the message to sink in. For us too, it was nothing to get fussy about since point-to-point was neither new nor strange.

"You will remain grouped as per battalion. We expect you to set off as a group and assemble as a group at Idon Village. You must take care not to get injured or lost." he rounded up. It was such a plain speech as to conceal the enormity of the challenge before us.

The sponsor then handed us charts showing distances, directions, and objectives. Each group was to march on a different route, but all had to go through a common point at Unguwan Antai settlement. By the time we were through with the day-cum-night march, Unguwan Antai village held a special place in our training folklore.

The first group was set off at about 1700hrs, and others at five-minute intervals. With about one hour of daylight available, our group made quick progress and was able to nail the first two objectives in rapid succession. However, darkness soon overtook us but graciously, the moonlight was exceptionally bright but that was not enough to shield us from the difficulties that befell us that night.

As all the teams soon discovered, the distances on the charts were plotted off the map and therefore did not match what was on the ground. For instance, by the time our group got to our third point, a conical-shaped knoll, the team had spent about two hours trying to cover a supposedly 4000-metre stretch.

We asked for the direction to Unguwan Antai village from the herdsmen we found in the surrounding area, and we got treated to a pastoralist idea of time and space. It was not too far from where we were at, they insisted. Just by getting around the butt of the hill, the settlement was on the horizon.

By now, my team was neither using a compass nor a chart. We just hit a worn path and spent about an hour trying to get to the other side of the hill. Next, it took another two hours to reach Unguwan Antai. By now, it was past midnight. Again, we asked for the direction to Idon, but now we did not bother about distances. The village was the last leg of the night march, and it took another four hours, and finally we arrive in Idon at the break of dawn.

We headed to the camp as the teams arrived in disjointed groups. The exercise had taken a toll. Apart from physical exhaustion, most cadets arrived with bruises, sprained ankles, shredded fatigues, broken shoes, and all. It was a remarkable sight. We had spent about twelve hours on the march, and it was the longest throughout our training as cadets.

Mufti

Those who have been at jobs requiring the use of uniforms appreciate the overwhelming and invasive ability of military fatigues. As a cadet, I spent the first three years festooned in one form of military attire or the other, every day. The outcome was that cadets were poorly clad during events that demanded the use of mufti.

So, in the Fourth Term, a new policy was enunciated that authorized trainees to wear mufti during weekends. This well-thought-out policy improved cadets 'sense of style. However, as with all other things, cadets found an ingenious way to make the new mufti policy an ordeal. The use of ties was encouraged but our superiors made a sport of undoing ties and insisting they be knotted back in their presence which was always a struggle.

Academy Lords

The Fourth Term ended on 13 September 1992, and we became the Academy Lords. It was a case of one day at a time, and finally, we reached the status of the most senior cadets. It was a long and tough journey. Having reached this standing, I became more measured and guarded in every step I took. For, it was the last lap, so it was important to ensure that the illusive finish line was crossed. Naturally, the final year was less bothersome because the workload was reduced as we had already gotten a degree in our areas of academic specialty and concentrated solely on military training.

In the Army Class, a corner of the board was specially dedicated to a countdown. Every passing day, whosoever arrived earliest to the classroom, took it upon themselves to update the regressing numbers. From 365 days on resumption, the days receded gradually until the last 28 days when we were fully engaged in the activities preceding POP. The remaining part of our training sessions now consisted of consolidation and reinforcement of all the knowledge that was imparted in the preceding years. So, nothing new cropped up but there were expectations that we would have mastered the plethora of military erudition that we had gotten so far.

30km Dash Back

Another training event of note was the thirty-kilometre Dash Back, which was an aspect of Camp Farauta. The take-off point was by the same Kachia hill to 1 Division, Base Ordnance Depot at Agunu. Along the line, villagers had graciously lined the route with clean water and at several points, peanuts, which came in very handy. It was a characteristic display of the generous spirit and discernment of the poor. This dash back too was done with and at the end, I looked lean and hardened.

Camp Kurata

We had gone through all the basic FTXs except for the last two that were scheduled in the final year. However, when an understrength 30SSC started training, we were drafted to swell their ranks during exercises scheduled for their course. To do this, someone crafted a "Camp Kurata," a new-fangled hybrid field exercise, which was a combination of Camps Kura and Farauta.

Camp Kurata which took place at the same Idon location was a routine camp. However, the instructors took to comparing our course to the 30SSC, for whom it was a main event. In the opinion of these instructors, 30SSC were better trainees. How they arrived at such a rubbishing assessment, could not be understood. It was better recognized as constant attempts at exceeding each other, because of the different commissions for which we were projected. Incidentally, SSC officers formed the bulk of instructors in the camp. The whole thing was distasteful. Perhaps, if our consent had been sought, we could have declined to join because after so many years fatigue had crept in.

Moreover, during Camp Kurata there was a failed experiment with Meals-Ready-to-Eat (MRE). The catering staff typically cooked in the field. Even more, cadets augmented their meals with snacks like biscuits, bread, garri and groundnut cakes aka service support. But along the line, someone tried to institute snacks or MRE as field rations. The basis of this experiment was unknown, but I remember, at a point in the Academy, cadets were issued canned rations manufactured by one Jobitex company.

Shortly after the samples were distributed, the Director of Military Training (DMT) came around talking about its virtues and the need to adopt its use. To reinforce his disjointed accounts, he said most developed countries' armies subsisted on MRE. But he forgot to say if Nigeria was yet a developed country, much less a developed army.

So, when we got to the field, the Catering Officer, a lady very adept at concealing her inefficiency by shedding copious tears and feigning offence, experimented with a localized MRE, with the connivance of the DMT. She made bread toast and other stuff packed in bags and had them shipped to the camp. In their haste to execute the heist, they forgot that the packaging of meals designed as MRE had a delicate science behind it.

These bread-based meals were prepared the previous night before the camp. By breakfast time, we were confronted with an unfamiliar menu. In fact, by that time too, it had already gotten rancid. All we could do was suppressed grumbling.

Primarily, it was wrong to try a change of menu so drastic and so hurriedly. Worse still, the initiators did not contemplate the science of preserving processed foods. The fact that they overlooked the lots of manual and physical activities we were engaged in, was a display of poor judgement or outright wickedness.

The trial was a woeful failure. Later, bags and bags of spoilt food were brought out for unsolicited distribution. Of course, I did not get anywhere near the putrid odour that emanated from those curst bags of a costly experiment. Later, the Catering Officer, was all over the place trying to mitigate a situation that should not have been allowed in the first place. When field meals were eventually served, the rations were halved because of the shortage of funds on account of the failed experiment.

Meanwhile, in the camp, 30SSC cadets had contrived to assume equality with us. It was unheard of. When we queued for meals, they were pushful, claiming rights. They had committed a cardinal military offence. The unwritten rule was that superiors gorged themselves fully before subordinates deigned to get near the serving point. It was an unpardonable offence.

So, all after the phases of the exercise, the trainees were dropped off at a bivouac, to spend the night by ourselves till dawn when we would embark on the return trip home. It was a night of clearing of doubts. The magical thing about the resolve was that it was unplanned, save an opportunity presented itself. Collectively, we were determined to leave a lifetime impression on the course.

During the night, we engaged them in push-ups, hunching, forward rolls, barrel rolling and singled out the recalcitrant ones in the lot for special treatment. What followed was general beating that attended any iota of resistance as we ensured they slept minimally that night, and when we were satisfied that justice had been served, we let them be.

By the next morning, we set off. But still, once we got to Television, a suburb of Kaduna, we were dropped and set off on yet another dash back to the Academy. It was the most tiring of the series because of the poor feeding during the camp. It would be the only outdoor exercise we took part with 30 SSC. Three months later, they graduated and were commissioned.

The DMT was a lively man who loved to engage us in lengthy discussions. After Camp Kurata, he came over and opened a floodgate and was prepared to absorb any reproaches directed at him. Unfortunately, cadets were not forthcoming. We had endured lots during the long training, but this unpleasant experience at the last camp stood out awfully. Perhaps, the DMT knew, as he had visited during the exercise and just wanted to be told the hard facts, so the authorities could make amends for the future.

Unfortunately, fellows just kept mute and displayed a semblance of normalcy. It was not. We had all felt the pangs of hunger worsened by the intense physical activities during the camp. More so, we openly grumbled within our ranks and yet everyone kept mute. As I was wont to do, I spoke my mind freely too. The crux of my observation was that the change in diet was too sudden and that the portions served were too small, considering the rigorous demands of the camp.

Not bothered by his likely reaction, I said what everyone else did behind, during our grumbling sessions. It was heartening to note that my outpour elicited not a scowl but extended guffaws from the very senior officer. I believed he had expected feedback, but he got negative quietude. I never understood this attitude as a cadet and during my years as an officer. It was an act of cynical concealment of emotions in aid of self-preservation.

Chapter Seventeen

1993: A Long-Awaited Year

From 1988, the magical year of 1993 took like eternity but finally arrived. It was the longest waiting period of my life. Five years was a long time in an individual's life especially when it was combined with relentless pressure and demanding physical exertions, time moved very slowly indeed.

It was yet another home stretch for me of my many pursuits. By 1 January, I had spent 224 of 260 weeks at the Academy. There was a balance of 36 weeks left before the commission. Just being around by that year was such a great accomplishment. It was the magical year on which my dreams were anchored particularly with the prospects of a presidential commission as well as getting started in life having spent the past twenty-one years in one form or the other at school.

There was a palpable infusion of excitement and caution. The destination was now so close and within reach. But inexplicably, I became a nervous wreck because I was not as confident as I was, at the onset of the journey now that I approached the end. During my years here so far, the unpredictability of events at every turn as a cadet had taught me that, it was not being so near the target that counted but bagging the ultimate trophy itself. I still had to trod on with added caution and expect that my blessings thus far would abide.

Even more, 1993 was a pivotal year in Nigeria's history. It was a remarkably turbulent year. On the national scene, the political terrain was in the throes of military rule led by a conceited and unpredictable manipulator. The pseudo-military president had taken the country on a seven-year-long ride in the name of a transition to civil rule. Regrettably, the leader of the junta deviously sabotaged his best efforts until he eventually got trapped in his own web of deceit.

The Nigeria National Guard

By week 225 of 260, in January 1993, yet another course assembled at the Academy, and was composed of a special corps of cadets. These were not normal cadets of Nigeria's military forces but the pioneer set of a brand-new paramilitary force, the Nigeria National Guard (NNG). The arrival of these trainees brought further complications to our already harried course.

Although the Babangida junta survived the Orkar Coup scare, it was shaken to its foundations. While the regime may not have pointedly declared any intentions to hang on to power indefinitely, its body language, frequently altered transition programme and the political tinkering signposted an opposite perception.

Therefore, a clandestine attempt to perpetuate the regime was to revive an old idea of founding a new counterforce to the nation's armed forces in the form of the NNG. As the nebulous transition to the Third Republic floundered, the ruling cabal doubted the allegiance of its colleagues understandably besmirched by its antics.

The whole doodad about NNG started well back in 1989. When first mooted, it was projected as a paramilitary force directly under the presidency. However, there was an uproar because the new force's roles would overlap those of the police and army and might become a ready tool for political intimidation and persecution.[1]

For a start, a couple of police mobile units were selected as the nucleus of the force. However, due to the unease the idea generated, the regime reconsidered its creation and the whole thing fizzled until after the 1990 Orkar coup when it was revived.

By late 1992, the junta's transition programme was not only disjointed but suspect. It was glaring as Nigerians had discerned a fraud. Without and even within the military hierarchy, there were tremors and widespread tetchiness. The discredited regime knew it had squandered its goodwill.

Although nominally a military regime, it was profoundly exclusionist in nature. As a result, servicemembers felt neither an affinity to the regime nor its impact and was alienated from its pretensions. It was clear that the regime preferred to cavort with scheming political jobbers, conjurers, snake charmers, ventriloquists, magicians, court jesters, alarmists, capitalists, and commission agents to the hilt.

As a first step, the regime tried to reinvent itself and lately created an Armed Forces Consultative Assembly. It was a talk shop, meant to capture the pulse of the military, that is, if their input counted at all. Its membership was composed of senior officers drawn from across the services.[2]

In addition, the regime tried to address the welfare of the troops. This was facilitated by a survey, where shared welfare interests were collated and led to selective schemes of furniture allowances, a revolving car, motorcycle, and bicycle loans euphemistically referred to as IBB spirits.

Nevertheless, on the sides, while the regime halfheartedly placated its impoverished constituency, it simultaneously plotted strategies to address any insurrectionist tendencies. Subsequently, the NNG caper was dusted off the shelf for implementation. The first commander of the NNG was one Colonel Abdul Mumuni Aminu, a serial coup plotter, along with officers poached from the three services which formed the core of the new force.[3]

In a definitive policy broadcast on 21 April 1993, its commander proposed that NNG would be deployed on Nigeria's borders and that its duties would neither encroach on those of the army nor police.[4] There were plans to set up additional units including "ground intervention, paratrooper and marine service squads".[5] For operational purposes, the country was provisionally divided into four zones namely: the North West, North East, South West and South East with bases at Kano, Bauchi, Akure, and Umuahia respectively.[6]

Training NNG Personnel

Every perceptive individual understood that the whole NNG hubbub was motivated by sinister intentions to undermine the existing forces at arms. It was meant to perpetuate the junta in power and at the point of the force's revival, there were widespread misgivings about the endless political transition of the military regime.

When the force was established, it had a skeletal organizational framework but zero infrastructure and had to be built from the scratch. Ironically, for an organization that was meant to methodically weaken the standing armed forces, began life by cannibalizing or being grafted on the existing services. Beyond independently recruited pioneer operatives, they could not offer training that was different from the normal army type.

Consequently, most of its formative activities copied the design of the army. Hence, its rank and file were sent to Depot NA for basic military training, while its potential officers were sent to the Academy as cadets. So, in January 1993, NNG Course One reported to the Academy for training.

When the course reported, as per Academy tradition, they were the most junior course. It was not a matter for argument. It should have ended there, but it never and spilt over into the field. It was also glaring that there was no provision, in terms of training modules, for the kind of force envisaged.

Perchance, as a counterforce, it was being given a peek into basic military training before been possibly enhanced with specialized training later. But since the force was grafted onto the existing armed forces structures, an impromptu arrangement was made to accommodate NNG cadets, if they were to be called by that name. Ordinarily, the issue of NNG needed not have been given too much attention, but their arrival brought about a near collapse of the established order at the Academy.

For a start, the orientation was that when the force eventually became operational, it would be a superior force to the existing armed forces. How they intended to achieve such a tall dream remained to be seen. So, the lot was aggressive and disruptive. Unfortunately, the odds against them were overwhelming in both strength and establishment.

Secondly, NNG cadets lived apart from the main cadet body and were accommodated at Candidates Quarters next to the Mammy Market, on the fringes of the Academy. In that way, they never grasped the constraints of cadets' regulated lives. Even more, our interactions with them were always caustic, especially at shared common services like the Cadets Mess.

For instance, they were always improperly dressed, a habit; that no regular cadet could be found in breach of. Invariably, offenders were sent out of the mess. As the most senior cadets at the Academy then, we never got entangled with these elements of an undefined organization. So, the vexatious lot persistently gnawed at the abundance of our collective patience.

Again, the course had a litany of claims that they were not military cadets and could not be subjected to military absurdities. Many of them felt that as university graduates, they were superior to cadets who were mostly school leavers. In fact, they completely missed the essence of the Academy.

While we endured these shenanigans, the younger cadets raged. One afternoon, an NNG cadet, who was notoriously untrainable, got into a brawl with First Termers at Cadets Mess. I intervened and cautioned against his unruliness, but he persisted. Therefore, I urged the incensed younger cadets to clear his doubts and stood by to supervise as he was given a thorough physical shakedown. While he was being re-educated, the duty officer, walked in and demanded an explanation for the chaotic situation. Being true to myself, I absorbed the younger cadets of culpability and accepted the fact that, I had orchestrated the chastisement due to the disorderly conduct of the NNG trainee. The duty officer ordered me to report to the Quarter Guard alongside the scoundrel. The officer returned two hours later and released us. Regrettably, this rowdy NNG cadet, as an Ordnance officer stole arms in his care and sold to dissidents.

Over time, there were so many incidents involving NNG trainees, which soon got to the attention of the authorities, and an All-Academy assembly was convened at Ribadu Hall. The Commandant addressed this tense assembly and demanded to know the cause of the constant altercations between the regular cadets and NNG1 trainees.

This time though, many cadets spoke out. They demanded to know the status of the course at the Academy. More importantly, it was suggested that they be integrated into the Academy community instead of being at the fringes. All the concerns voiced, were promptly addressed and rectified.

Sierra Leonean Cadets

In March 1993, the Academy received a batch of twenty cadets from the Republic of Sierra Leone Armed Forces (RSLAF). It was about the same time that contending issues were afflicting that country. By 1993, the country was being turbulently led by a 27-year-old Captain Valentine

Strasser. Not long after, the country degenerated into a brutal civil war, on a scale never been seen anywhere on the globe. The presence of these cadets also gave us an insight into the acrimony and intransigence with which the Sierra Leone war was fought. Those individuals drawn from diverse groups that constituted that republic were so argumentative and cantankerous. They could hardly agree on any matter.

Such an unruly lot, they squabbled and fought among themselves and everybody incessantly. It was clear that some of them were actively involved in the quagmire back home before being shipped out to Nigeria for military training. There was no need to integrate them into the regular cadet community and were left at the fringes of the Academy.

Unfortunately, down the line, Nigeria got her troops ensnared in the conundrum when ECOMOG mission in Liberia escalated and incorporated firefighting in Sierra Leone. This humanitarian interposition bled the country in a war notorious for its limb-severing viciousness.

Pre-Camp Highland

The first camp of 1993 was Pre-Camp Highland held at the Kachia Training Area. It was supposed to be a normal outdoor exercise but again things were complicated by being joined with yet another junior course. It was not that I had any personal misgivings about being trained with other courses. I just felt that each time we took part in such exercises, we got undermined. Just like the 30SSC, we endured yet another bout of negative appraisal. I thought, if after over four years at the Academy, we were still being compared to trainees of four months standing, then the system of training itself was questionable.

So, when we got to camp, we went through the normal phases and by nightfall, we dug into a defensive position. We knew the drill by heart and seamlessly performed all the specified actions. Sensibly, NNG and our course was each deployed as distinct units under separate commands, so each group went through its paces without the other.

Defensive Area

Typically, when troops occupied a defensive area, the positions were reinforced step-by-step on a timeline called priority of work. It was a technical activity. The order of events proceeded from split locking of weapons, i.e., siting the machine gun and rifles, towards the direction of likely enemy approaches. This was to ensure the ability of sub-units to fire across the frontage as well as support each other known as overlapping and interlocking of fire.

Afterwards, the trenches were positioned to conform with the deployment and carved, with a parapet developed. All these were to exact dimensions which ensured immediate protection from direct fire. Later, the overhead protection was reinforced, and the trenches gradually evolved into bunkers.

Apart from a reinforced main trench, communication trenches were dug when a defensive position was held over a lengthy period. These were interconnected networks of lateral and rearward radiating trenches that allowed undetected movement of troops, within the defensive position. This too, was dug to a dimension, which we had been taught during our first year.

Even so, carving a trench was always a handful business. For instance, in the dry spell, hands blistered from the rock-hard ground and during the rainy season, trenches in the initial stages of development could be transformed into muddy quagmire. Either way, it was a very physically demanding task.

Funnily, the instructors never got tired of playing grisly games with trainees. While making the rounds to ensure compliance, they casually demanded a trench repositioned by a couple of paces outwards or inwards. This normally translated to excavating a new trench all over again.

Now our story properly began at the Kachia Training Area. When we reached the defensive area, it was a pitch-dark night and drizzling and not ideal to excavate trenches as the location was inundated by mud but against all odds, we managed to produce trenches. That night, I dug modest communications trenches in both directions. It was normal, as we were expected to develop them over time.

Early in the morning, the instructors started making the rounds and expressed displeasure at the level of our defensive work. The worst characters in the group were instructors attached to the NNG Wing. These were a motley of SSC and cynical RC officers who were incurable pessimists. Things turned invective very quickly as instructors were incapable of agreeable language. We were directed to go over to the NNG positions and see the extent of the work done and were formed up afterwards.

From the impromptu address of the exercise sponsor, it was clear that he was swayed by the dissing of officers from the NNG Wing. Full of bombast, he forgot that at this stage, we were fully trained and could not be easily unsettled by his posturing. Meanwhile, the homily was just a preparatory diversion to the main purpose of the assembly.

While the assembly was ongoing, all the instructors got armed with cudgels and sticks. The sponsor then ordered us to press up. While at it, those beasts, in the name of instructors, descended on us, beating on us until the DMT arrived and stopped it. The senior officer was visibly angry and said so. Just two months before commission, and these goons imagined that they could beat cadets into becoming better officers.

This vicious assault was incited by officers from the NNG Wing, and the ringleader was an SSC officer. It was obvious he was not happy with his commission, especially as he may have been discriminated against. I guessed at a point in his career, he was sent on a short infantry course to the United States of America where he fashioned for himself, an exaggerated pseudo-American accent. We found his antics comical and sensed that he suffered from low self-esteem. For all these, he nursed a grudge, collectively against our course and finally delivered that morning as he exceeded himself lashing at the trainees.

After the gruesome parade, I casually strolled over to the defensive position occupied by the NNG trainees, to see for myself the works that earned accolades for them and damnation for us. It was hogwash. Instead of trenches, it turned out they dug a series of graves and deep drainages. A trench, we were taught, was not just an excavation of indeterminate depth but incorporated a firing position within a certain dimension.

The NNG trainees did not adhere to any of these criteria. For them, it was all about meaningless digging, just to placate bloody-minded and sadistic instructors. All these came about because they went through the same humiliating treatment in prior field exercises. It was unfortunate because the mindset of these instructors was about trench warfare. Whether it was pleasant or not, the Pre-Camp Highland was rounded up, and we returned to the Academy.

Chaotic Cadet Appointments

I never bothered to mention that during Pre-Camp Highland, NNG trainees were so disrespectful to our course as their superiors. Well, it was not a time to drag over seniority when the ultimate trophy was within sight. However, we got a shock treatment.

During the after-exercise review, the lead officer of the Wing, suggested that NNG trainees should be accorded a status of Fourth Termers, the next most senior cadets. It was such a bizarre proposal; we were so horrified no one commented. These were strange times indeed. How was that possible in the first place since seniority in the service was based on who came first. So, if we were to treat them like the next most senior, what about those contemporaries we had spent years with at the Academy?

The next action was equally bewildering as they were given equivalent cadet leadership appointments, in their ranks, without clearly delineated lines of authority. As expected, they soon started dishing out orders to other cadets who were their seniors by the established hierarchy. Of course, 44RC, the most junior regular course at the Academy then, violently resisted such gross insubordination.

Knocking the Table

The Cadets Mess was equally a training ground. The head of a table, known as the high table, was reserved for the most senior and the other end was occupied by a mister vice, the most junior. Although the mess was one of the toughest places to be, at any given time, it was still a venerated practicing ground for military etiquettes.

In this way, dress code, seating arrangements, etiquettes and other traditions associated with ceremonial dining were practiced in a chaotic cadets' style. However, there was always order. For instance, cadets of the most senior course could knock a table, except their peers, all eating ceased, and junior cadets promptly hid their hands under the table. An information or instruction would be passed, and a second knock signaled the resumption of activities.

No junior could knock a table, even if only one of his seniors was around. However, a junior could knock, only at the behest of a senior. A knock was always with a cutlery set, rarely were bare hands used. However, knocking the table was abused by roguish cadets that disrupted the rhythm of meals. It took time to understand the importance of these rituals. However, the NNG trainees may have felt that they were linked to seniority and privileges. So, a day after they were conferred with leadership appointments, they may have reached an agreement, to disrupt the mess traditions.

They came to the mess, and a clutch went and sat at the high table. Nobody was surprised but the reaction was swift. The First Termers promptly re-arranged the seating in the mess without a high table. The response to this infraction was measured because, at this stage, there was no need for a precipitate response to orchestrated mischief. We knew it could end badly if we were not watchful of our approach.

But even at that, they overstretched their luck further. One of the so-called appointees stood up and knocked on a table during dinner. Lord have mercy. This was impunity overstretched. What followed was quite unexpected. Instead of garnering the desired attention, First Termers rushed him and handed him once-in-a-lifetime chastisement and all other NNG trainees present at the time were given vicarious treatment and would readily attest to the ferocity of the younger cadets' reprisals. It was a blameless reaction to serial and undeserved baiting.

Ordinarily, I would have preferred to be at the epicentre of disputations, however uncharacteristically, I walked out of the Mess with a typical cadet swagger, with my arms spread out. If I were found in the vicinity of this fracas, I might end up, either as an accessory or as a mastermind of that unchoreographed but brilliantly executed rebuttal.

This incident generated a lot of wind but graciously, the authorities, and especially his fellows, unanimously agreed that the perpetrator had overreached himself. There was nothing to prove on any part of the NNG trainees. It was traditional that, as the last set of trainees to arrive at the Academy, they were automatically the most junior.

Therefore, if they were granted appointments, it was solely for their wing and not the entire cadet body. It was the height of indiscretion and therefore strange and to what purpose he knocked a table when it was clear that, he had no subordinates, to pass instructions to, and at a wrong location.

The incident we witnessed that day was a harbinger of the things to come. We all instinctively knew that it was not a localized problem, but an existential struggle by entrenched interests to corral power, even at the expanse of national institutions. It was a ploy by a military cabal to weaken and destroy military cohesion from within. It was not my business as my main preoccupation was not depreciatory distractions but keeping an eye on the ball.

Notes

(1). http://www.fas.org.

(2). http://www.fas.org.

(3). https://www.refworld.org

(4). Radio Nigeria 22 April 1993.

(5). Radio Nigeria 22 April 1993.

The Sphinx Cairo 2023

Chapter Eighteen

In 120 Days

By June 1993, we were finally set to round the last bend of an arduous expedition. The only pending FTX in view was the Camp Highland. In any case, there was no marked change in the passion or tempo of the training except renewed anxiety of trainees always apprehensive about bagging the ultimate trophy.

Besides, June 1993 was historic in Nigeria's national life. While the month lasted, there were series of momentous events with far-reaching consequences for the ruling military regime. The most central was a decisive phase of the junta's convoluted transition plan.

The 1993 presidential polls were scheduled and successfully held on June 12. However, as the results were being collated, the process was first held up and eventually annulled on 24 June 1993. The decision to cancel elicited reactions with far-reaching ramifications on our national life.

Meanwhile, our progress was steady, and we kept faith. Nevertheless, there was an adversary within our ranks to contend with. Let me explain. All cadet appointments were invested with manifest powers, but so much of it was exercised over junior cadets. Although, it was a given that, we maintained a degree of decorum, in order not to mutually undermine our apex status at the Academy.

Inexplicably though, we had a powerful course mate who chose to exercise his derogatory powers over his peers. It was enigmatic, as no one could place a finger on the origins of such perfidious attitude that threatened our collective ambitions. Regrettably, this led to the painful withdrawal of some trainees. The only plausible explanation could be that the pretender was overcome by a diabolical desire to explore the limits of his powers.

First, in the subjective style of a despot, he promulgated a series of unpopular rules from which he was discharged. This actor orchestrated egoistical edicts, directed specifically at his peers. For instance, he forbade take-aways from the Cadets Mess. But, like all pocket dictators, he discharged himself from the same decree.

So that day, one of our fellows saw a junior cadet carrying a food flask. Without hesitating, he grabbed it and smashed it on the ground. The flask belonged to the pseudo-tyrant, unfortunately, this led to his withdrawal from the Academy. Even more, he did not confine himself to being exasperating but continuously banged fire alarms. Fire alarms were emergency summons that were not trifled with as he singled out his course mates and expended so much energy on physical checks to ensure none was absent. Not any one of us, had expected to be inconvenienced in our terminal days by a treacherous course mate.

This piece of symphony scored by a colleague was very perilous, in the least, and soon enough one afternoon, all regular cadets were unseasonably summoned to Ribadu Hall. In any case, this was the Academy, and it was nothing strange to be mustered at short notice and odd hours.

Nonetheless, the feel of this parade was not good. As we congregated, the hall was filled with animated chatter but as soon as the principal staff officers and instructors arrived; the venue transformed into a stillness that presaged a ruinous anticipation.

An "All-Academy" parade to was not an everyday occurrence. Something important was about to happen. After a long wait, it was announced, "gentlemen the commandant," to which all rose to their feet as the general walked into the hall. What happened was a noticeably short but factious encounter.

After the routine salutation, handing and taking over by the commandant, the general then made weighty pronouncements.

"Zentumen kazets, ozoo many op yu are nwot kwalipied to be called zentumen." he opened the address in his heavily accented locution. "Ayam also a frozukt op zhis nobu akazemy. I waz a kazet op NZA kwas wan. Ma lamba waz NZA sirii." He relayed. The hall was hot, and the kahuna was already sweating. It was a cue for all of us, to vicariously perspire profusely too, because the motions of this proceedings so far portended no good end. "I hab resibed many brips of kazets inbolved in many asks of indiziflin. It iz nwat only unbeleibable but kwat dizhatening. I somsaims, wanza, if it waz za same akazemy that I pazzed srou."

By now, we had gotten a handle on the general drift of the assembly. Nobody was bothered about the expression, but the sanguinary message that was about to be delivered. This assembly was going to claim casualties which in cadets' vernacular translated to a Cutting Parade.

"I unzastan, many kazets break za bounds. Lemme, por za sek of empazis wan, any kazets zat ah kwat brakin za bounds, zay will be witzron." It was said with finality. The commandant took a gulp from a glass of water offered. This animated assembly was no longer speculative, it was going to bite. "So par, za refots are nwot gwud. Zome kazets, am alzo sold are inbolbed in zrugs. Zis iz mos on-opisalaik and un-azzepsabu." The countenance of the general was gradually being worked up to the point of explosion.

"Iz will not hapin unzer my watch," the general reassured himself. "Ayam zuty bonz to maintain a saisen stanzard. Ip I cannot improob on was I met, iz wud be a dizsabis, to allow za stanzard to zrop. Foszarisi wuz not be kind to me ip I pail mazef and za sissem. Goin powod, zrassik actions will be saken to azzress gross indiziflin. I will faus and kwall on za CBC to kwantinu prom hia." To which he took his seat.

The adrenalin flow was now a rush. We had prematurely expected the homily to be concluded without further complications. How mistaken we were. It was now time for the CBC to escalate the parade. The commander rose to his feet with a file clutched to his side. After the necessary courtesies, he slowly and deliberately opened the file he held and studied it interminably as if he were not sure of where to begin. He cleared his throat. "If you hear your name, jump up" he began dreadfully. Nobody knew whose name would be called and what would befall them.

"NDA XXXX, Officer Cadet XXXX." For effects, the official designation and numbers were enunciated in full. A deeper silence descended on the assembly. We all intuitively understood that the names being called were not an honour roll, but a culprit lists. Even still nobody expected a mild reprimand but the forceful fall of the hammer.

The first person called out at that assembly was our course mate who had smashed a food flask a week earlier. The CBC proceeded from the most senior to the most junior. They were called out in a group and from the composition of the culprits, apart from my course mate, others in the group were a motley of perpetual absentees and dissenter cadets. In this group too, were cadets with cases of academic non-performance or poor grades while others had been relegated before for various infractions. All we could do was hold our breath, guess, and wait for the verdict to be passed, and it did not take long.

"These officer cadets are hereby withdrawn from the Academy. This should serve as a deterrence to others who wish to tread along the same path. Nobody is happy to see cadets dismissed but we shall be failing the system if we do not weed out untrainable charges." The CBC said with a finality.

After the CBC's remarks, a throng of regimental provosts (RPs) instantly walked in to march out the dismissed cadets. These unfortunate ex-cadets were treated to last minute military grimness by the RPs. They were ordered to attention and unnecessarily yelled at while being ushered out of the hall. In short, a lot of salt was being administered to these victims' injuries as they were not even given time to ruminate over the misfortune that had just befallen them.

We all knew instinctively that the ex-cadets were taken to the lines where military kits would be retrieved from them and subsequently unceremoniously removed, not only out of the Academy, but Ribadu Cantonment, the larger military installation hosting the citadel. We vicariously shared in their grief and while still engrossed in this drift, we were abruptly jolted back to reality.

"Now the next set of cadets" the CBC thundered on. We all wrongly assumed that the culling had ended only to be rudely jerked back into the second phase of a ruthless exercise.

"NDA XXXX Officer Cadet XXXX." The senior officer broke a sweat as he reeled off the list. As if on cue, we all perspired profusely all over again. Nobody was sure whose name would be called out next. After a long stretch and over twenty names later he paused. We all awaited his verdict.

"These officer cadets are hereby relegated." The CBC declared. "You should consider yourselves lucky that you were not withdrawn like your former colleagues a few minutes ago." he enthused.

"You are all advised in your interest to change your ways, or you could end up like your former colleagues." He ended his homily and nothing more was said afterwards, and the parade was dismissed.

The dispersing cadets filed out silently and sorrowfully. It was as though we were bereaved. In fact, it was more than a bereavement as all of us were gloomily reminded of how vulnerable we were. Over time, we knew that erring cadets were usually first indicted, and tried before punishments were awarded. But on this day, all these niceties were dispensed with, and sweeping sanctions were imposed. This precipitate action only reinforced how easily things could degenerate at the Academy which was a situation beyond our control.

Bukavu Barracks 1998   Ile-Ife 1983

Chapter Nineteen

Camp Highland

At long last Camp Highland arrived. There were many FTXs, and for our course some were duplicated. Although progress was slow, we still got there. For army cadets, Camp Highland was the climax of the long grueling journey to a commission. The camp reinforced the prospect of an imminent commission but on occasions though, some cadets returned from the exercise to relegation.

This camp was typically scheduled between late July and early August during the rainy season when weather conditions could be unpleasant. However, at this stage, we could contend with any weather as an insalubrious climate was not a factor per se. Besides, over the years, we had trained in all weather conditions. Therefore, the impending camp although special in our training calendar, could not be treated any differently.

A Build-Up to the Camp

While waiting for the departure to the camp, I did everything possible to fortify myself mentally. So, all I did in the days preceding the exercise, was geared towards ensuring I was in a decent shape. I got myself bits and pieces like a map board, talc, writing materials, two sets of uniforms and service support.

Additionally, there was a dash back component during the camp which counted to the Academy championship. So apart from routine preparations, we were also training extremely hard too. It was more like a rehash of our Initial Camp training. But this time, almost five years down the ages, we could not exert ourselves like in our first year.

Nevertheless, we still trained collectively before camp. I remember a cadet appointment talking to us about the importance of winning the championship. He could have as well been talking to himself because for me, it was not a competition but getting through with this interminable cadet training.

Postponements

Camp Highland was customarily held at three locations namely Jos, with a training visit to Bauchi and the finishing at Kachia. Collectively, we were anxious to get done with this FTX. So, it was a great relief when a departure date was finally confirmed and on the appointed day, we packed our stuff and formed up at the muster point in front of the Cadets Mess. It was a large entourage since it was a combined FTX for 40RC and NNG1.

Yet again, we never foresaw this link up and were left contemplating. Was this NNG thingy not designed to be distinct from the regular armed forces of Nigeria? There were so many unanswered questions. However, it was not my cup of tea, but a policy matter that was best left to the authorities.

On this morning at the muster point, there were a variety of vehicles including buses, cadets and horses and command vehicles. Everything was set and we loaded our luggage into one of the trucks. By 0700hrs, all was set. It would be a long drive to the Jos Base Camp and Training Area where the main activities of the exercise took place. The advance team for the exercise had already left. So, it was expected to be an early start, then the waiting to take off now began.

We waited and waited and waited. It was noon by now and mealtime, but we could not partake in lunch because apart from breakfast, which was provided for, it was expected that we would take our lunch and other meals at the Base Camp in Jos. Alas, by lunchtime, we had not taken off but luckily, we were still within the Academy, so we got something to eat and continued the endless wait.

All this while, nobody thought it apt to apprise us of the situation. We were left in the dark and it was obvious that there would be no movement that day. Also, because nature abhorred vacuities, rumours started filtering in to fill the void. The narrative was that the commandant, an avid gambler, had lost the money meant for the camp at card games. There was no way to confirm this wild gossip.

By late afternoon, the Exercise Sponsor came around to address us. Still, the looks on his face did not inspire any hopes. The kernel of his speech was that we should disperse and re-assemble the next day. The next day led to another next day and another. Finally, reason prevailed, and we were asked not to assemble anymore until further notice.

Until further notice excruciatingly translated into a week of waiting. All we could do was to go to our normal army class and wait out the days. It was an ordeal difficult to come to terms with. Fortuitously, our wait was over, and were finally ferried to the NDA Base Camp at Jos. The entourage spent the night at the camp and were dropped off early the next morning at the assembly area to start our final FTX as officer cadets.

At the assembly area, the problems of administering such an unwieldy number of trainees in camp became apparent. It took time to split the trainees into handy subunits. The FTX commenced with an Advance to Contact. The conduct of the exercise was by role play hence commanders and subordinate commanders were appointed. Everyone else not so appointed played the role of a rifleman and all of us remained in our groups and kept tactical cover.

After a long wait, we converged under the canopy of a big mango tree where the orders group prepared a sand model and issued orders for the advance. After the orders, which were critiqued by the instructors, we set off on the advance. The advance was in the general vicinity of Fobur, precisely along Foron-Korot-Fanlo axis. By the way, my subunit was so far at the rear that all actions on contact were executed without our participation. Besides, we had repeatedly done this thingummy. Although we were far from the action, we still assumed tactical posture and movement.

Finally, the advance ended, and we went into defence. As soon as we started digging in, a heavy rainstorm descended upon us. It was extremely cold with the legendary chill of the Jos plateau. Not only were we thoroughly drenched but our position became waterlogged.

The defensive area was a small high ground, and my company was deployed in the forward slope. We were paired for two-man trenches. After split locking, we marked out the trenches and begun digging in earnest. We had diligently done what was expected of us. This was evident because there was little or no adjustments to our trenches.

Despite our self-congratulatory posturing of having done well, we still had running battles with our instructors over trench dimensions.

Although there was no pre-agreement among us, somehow, we all stuck to our guns not to excavate neither graves nor dry wells nor pit latrines.

For a second time, yet again prodded by those eternally condemnatory instructors, they lined us up again and started the battering all over. Mercifully once again, a saner individual in the lot prevailed upon these bloody-minded officers to desist from further assailing the trainees. This indiscretion was the highpoint of the camp.

After which, we engaged in general routine in defence like stand to, area patrols and fighting patrols, and raids. Apart from these activities, we gradually hardened our defensive positions by transforming the trenches into bunkers and gun shelters with overhead canopies based on priority of work. On the morning of the fifth day, we carried out a dawn attack.

The attack marked the end of the tactical phase of the camp. So, we went back to our defensive locations and backfilled the bunkers and trenches we had excavated. Also, we picked our stuff and got set for the dash back to base camp. The exercise was held around Bokkos on the Jos plateau. When we took off, our first target was the Jos-Pankshin highway. On hitting the road about five kilometres beyond the Jos Airport at Heipang we oriented ourselves by the route

We continued along the route until just beyond the airport runway and branched off into the bush and headed on towards Government Secondary School Kuru. From this point, every individual plotted his bearing. I emerged at the highest point of Nigeria's railway system slightly west of the school on Jos-Akwanga Road. I headed into the hills again and navigated by intuition far behind Police Staff College and emerged west of National Institute for Veterinary Research at Vom along Bukuru-NIPPS road. From this point, I was road bound knowing that the terminus was the NDA Base Camp at the Bukuru end of the road. Graciously, I arrived my destination and successfully completed the tactical phase of Camp Highland without any incident.

As earlier noted, the dash back component of Camp Highland counted as a championship race. My fellows and I monitored the arrival of each cadet. With each arrival, there was high octane jubilation in the camp. We tallied the numbers and were hopeful of winning. Finally, the last Mogadishu cadet arrived, and the battalion completed the dash back first and were therefore set to win the camp championship. It was unbelievable that my training was gradually being rounded off. As an aside, I had not taken a bath in the past six days, unless being drenched by rain that kept falling during those five days counted.

It was a Friday, we bivouacked in tents and relaxed for the rest of the day. There was a campfire the next day during which we acted drama sketches. I had abstracted a prophetic drama skit about herdsmen-farmers clash which won the trophy. By now, we knew we were the unofficial Camp Highland champions.

On a Tour by Cadets and Horses

Sunday was our day off, but not a single person was allowed out of camp, and there was no official activity either. However, without being told nobody broke camp. I spent the day cleaning my dirty uniforms, web kits and grabbing enough good sleep preparatory for the visit to the Nigerian Army School of Armour at Bauchi scheduled for the next day.

In the morning, we got set for the Bauchi trip. This time, only cadets of 40RC made the trip. About ninety-five cadets were on the entourage led by a clutch of instructors. For this trip, a fifty-five-seater bus and two cargo trucks (cadets and horses) were detailed. However, since cadets and horses were meant for cargo, they had no seats. This was not an issue despite the long distance.

At this point, we could endure any situation, but I ruminated. Was this kind of unseemly arrangement, a harbinger of the things to come? We were projected for a commission in about six weeks, so was it proper to convey us in such an undignified manner? If it were within the confines of an exercise area, it could be fathomable. But was it not degrading while visiting a distant location? All these agitated my mind during the trip as the sun roasted us.

Finally, we got to Shadawanka Barracks our destination. It was a combined exhibition and ride-on-for-the-feel tour of Nigerian Army Armoured Corps. Our entourage was received by a team of staff officers. We formed up at the car park from where we could see an array of armoured vehicles on display with a group of instructors, officers and NCOs, waiting to give our group an exploratory expose of the vehicles in terms of roles and capabilities.

All these stuffs we knew theoretically. Now, it was time to see and feel those vehicles. However, the commandant was scheduled to address our group before we started, and he arrived shortly. The senior officer looked intensely at our tired group and perused the car park, and his opening statement shamed me utterly, if not all of us in the company. "The team leader and his entourage, gentlemen officer cadets, on behalf of myself, staff and instructors, I warmly welcome you to the Nigerian Army School of Armour." He started his remarks and grinned at us. "However, before I continue, I must register my concern." He paused to grow our anticipation. It was so easy to guess. "I understand that things have gone bad, but I never knew it was to this extent." He continued. "I never foresaw that gentleman officer cadets could be brought on a tour on those contraptions out there. I must confess that I find this development very disturbing." He paused once again.

We all dropped our heads in shame. What none of our instructors, staff officers or minders, pondered or took for a trifle, was being pointed to us by a deeply concerned senior officer. It was such a mortifying experience. I felt that, if there was any shortage of vehicles, they could have hired commercial buses to convey us in a more dignified manner.

"Well, let me not detract from your tour. I just wanted to make my mind known. Meanwhile, the school's staff and instructors are ready to take you through the exhibition and later a ride on the tanks and other armoured vehicles. Please enjoy your tour and once again you are welcome to the home of armour." The whole entourage was chastened.

The tour itself was brief and uneventful because of what we already knew from GSK lessons. We spent time gaping at those behemoths of armoured contraptions. Afterwards, the crew took us on a ride on the T55, a Russian main battle tank (MBT), French made Panhard armoured recce vehicles and a host of others. The tour was rounded up and we re-assembled for the closing ceremony. During the quick rite, we were handed snacks in small packages. Soon after we embussed and returned to Jos and moved camp to the Kachia Training Area.

Battle Inoculation

The base camp at the Kachia Training Area from its wear and tear was clearly an old facility. Although used extensively by countless military formations for FTXs, it was in a rundown state. There were structures meant for dormitory-style accommodation, but the roofs were blown off. Even still, the safety of those with roofs intact was doubtful as they were overgrown by weed and clearly invested with vermin and reptiles. As a course, we had been here severally but never slept over. However, on this occasion, we encamped but most cadets chose to sleep in the open.

By morning trainees mustered and marched to a flat-topped high ground with a steep forward slope that had a stand and unhindered lookout. It was aptly named Nigerian Army Table Hill. The exercise sponsor gave a short address and demanded for keen attention to audit the sounds as he inaugurated the Battle Inoculation and Firepower Demonstration phase of Camp Highland. The nomenclature could be confusing as it was not anyway connected with immunization.

The exercise was about live firing at a vast open military range in the hills surrounding Kachia Training Area. The goal was to get officer cadets acquainted with the resonances of individual weapons and the din of battle noise when fired all at once. It was also meant to demonstrate the effective ranges of weapons. As part of the inoculation too, cadets were also involved in individual live firing under close supervision of instructors. Due to the substantial number of trainees in camp, this took three days and by Friday everyone was done with live firing. On Saturday morning, we broke camp, and headed back to the Academy to a new status.

UNAMSIL 2002

Basawa 2004

Chapter Twenty

Passing Out Cadets

With Camp Highland done and dusted; our course attained a new status at the Academy. I could not tell whether it was authorized, but we took to addressing ourselves as passing out cadets (POCs), since we were at the terminus of our long tough training.

The balance of days at the Academy were spent unhurriedly. Although there was no serious programming, we still went to our army class routinely. While no time was given off, events were a little relaxed. The main activity was the after-exercise review. However, on the national scene, things got remarkably interesting, and the fallout was the collapse of the military presidency.

It was the third quarter of 1993, and the cumulative impact and reverberations in the nation and especially within the military were quite huge. The annulment of the 1993 presidential elections undermined a regime that had incessantly played mind-games with Nigerians. Even more, apart from international pressure, there were legions of local groups that advocated for a revalidation of the annulled election. In retrospect, it would appear there was even more exertion from within the president's innermost circle. The regime had simply imploded.

I was not bothered by the political mess created by power mongers. At that time, my interest lay with the DMT. The general was a former military governor and a minister. He was a jolly good fellow who enjoyed animated chats and banters with our young group. During our engagements with him, we discussed almost every subject under the sun, nothing was off limit.

The good-natured senior officer amused us to no end with his advisories on personal living and prudence as beginners. For instance, he claimed as a young officer, he had only one suit which he wore it to every occasion knowing he would encounter different sets of people. It sounded funny at that time, but as soon as we started, it was obvious that the general was closer to the truth than we imagined.

At every turn, he recommended that we got involved with gardening. Although it sounded implausible, he claimed he cultivated vegetables at his backyards and lived off the yield. The import of his homilies took long in coming but one way or the other, in the latter days, it began to make sense. However, we loved it more when he brought up discussions on the government of the day.

"Tell me your feelings. Tell me what you honestly think. The president is my friend. I will relay it to him and get you feedback." That was how he normally opened our conversations on the current situation in the country. At this point, there were political agitations and the military regime had run out of credible excuses to defend its nebulous transition programme.

I would not know if our friend extended his conversations to other officers and instructors. Nevertheless, being the tad in the matrix, it was quite safe. So, the general kept sampling our opinions and letting us in on the fact that even within the junta, there was disquiet, and that the president was having a tough time with housekeeping.

"Then he should just go." A courageous person suggested, and a gasp reverberated all over the hall. This was not an easy option in the face of the present challenge. But how could this be attained? An outright resignation was unprecedented, while a putsch was treasonable. In fact, the developing situation was not under control and if not properly managed could spawn the unforeseen.

"I shall be attending the next plenary session of the Armed Forces Consultative Assembly scheduled next week at Abuja. Be assured I will make your contributions known." The general kept mumbling.

We took his assurances with a pinch of salt because we doubted anyone could listen to lowly officer cadets' musings. It was such a preposterous proposal considering that this military junta was the most obstinate in Nigeria's political history. He closed the session for the day.

Those were idle days and the DMT filled them with exciting discourses. For my part, I began to admire the man on account of his taking us into confidence and discussing high state matters with us, an indication of the high esteem with which he held our group.

Not much took place before our POP rehearsals were scheduled. It would be an arduous three-week practice drill sessions preparatory to passing out. But we could not commence just yet until our naval and air force colleagues at finishing schools at NNS ONNURA-Onne and NAF Base Kaduna respectively, returned to regroup with their army counterparts at the Academy. This could take another week or more.

Mid-week, the DMT resurfaced again accompanied by soldiers laden with boxes, the contents of which were unknown. The soldiers dropped the boxes and left. His visage was aggressive, but we could read him, he just wanted to set a solemn mood to his revelatory interaction with us on that day.

"What have you goons been saying in my absence" he pounced on us unexpectedly. But instead of getting mortified, we all laughed out raucously, and an ever-friendly individual, he joined with a hearty laughter.

"Remember, I told you folks that I would mention our chit-chats to the president, but you did not believe me. You are typical Nigerians who do not trust your leaders." He paused to cultivate our curiosity and we were taken in by his gambit and eager to hear the latest developments.

"Well, there was nothing new. However, it was a momentous event and the president called for a dispassionate discussion of the situation without embellishment and we had frank interactions devoid of encumbrances." He paused and surveyed our faces. He was obviously relishing our undivided attention.

"The deliberations were long and forthright, and it would interest you to know that the trend and thread of discussions were not any different from our informal chats in this class." He volunteered. The heat in the class was intense and he broke a sweat.

He deliberately slowed his speech and continued. "In not-a-too-distant future, you will hopefully get a commission into the Nigerian Army. It was therefore important that you begin to appreciate the magnitude of the political and social problems the leadership of our dear country is grappling with."

"I must confess that I was impressed when the assembly deliberated along the same lines of your contributions, given that you had little or no insider information about the events that led to the current problems." Well, hell, it was a subtle way of lowballing our group. In my view, I aggregated the current difficulties to the sit-tight predispositions of African political elites.

"The president was a misunderstood leader. Like I said in the past, he is not only my principal but a friend. But then he was only human and may have made some honest errors. This may not be necessarily due to any roguish intentions or the so-called hidden agenda as Nigerians like to call it. But it was not enough to ascribe to him many attributes on account of an indiscretion." He paused. It was now a monologue.

The place was excited and all of us were talking across the classroom among ourselves ignoring him. By now, it was apparent that all was not well with the regime. From this expose too, we realized that the impostor military president was no longer absolute. Our little quips were in fact a fitting evaluation of the state of the nation that resonated with the larger populace.

"Soon you would receive commissions as officers of the Armed Forces of Nigeria, it would be such a huge responsibility, and you would be expected to articulate on national matters beyond the pedestrianism of the uninformed." The rest of his rambling was drowned by murmuring as he began to sound like a campaign manager to an unelectable candidate or more like a snake oil salesman.

The message was passed. Next, he ordered the boxes unpacked. They were filled with books, a tome, more like a hagiographical effort.

"Please, make out time to read this professionally researched book. It should provide you a rich background knowledge and distinct perspective about this great man." From the way he said it, it was apparent that he could as well have been a sceptic himself.

Remorsefully, this marked the last time we enjoyed close chats with so friendly a general. Soon however, on its heels, historic incidents unveiled, one after the other as the country was gripped in a delicate balancing act. The most momentous of these was the abdication of the military president on 25 August 1993. We took the news in its strides and by now we were preoccupied with POP rehearsals as our naval and air force colleagues had returned to the Academy to join us in our last days as officer cadets.

The next three weeks were spent at a punishing twice-a-day POP rehearsals. The programming of POCs was minimal except something special came up. It was noteworthy that we started officer cadet training with drills and marching and it was being ended on the same high musical note.

There was one more aspect of drill that we needed to observe and master. This was the Guard Mounting Drill. By now the tide had changed. In an ironic twist of events, we were being persuaded to go out in the evening to observe the motions of the drill instead of being corporally coaxed as usual.

The POP rehearsals were energetic and by the second week, we turned out very lean and ramrod. It was the last time any of us would be without a hog-belly. But even still, the excitement of reaching the terminus after a turbulent voyage was enough motivation to keep at it. The rehearsals and prospects of a commission were an incentive to look forward to.

Ours was a combined POP of 40RC and NNG1. However, by now, survival instincts had taken roots. I could not care less about who graduated or got commissioned. I was but an individual and what I thought was of no consequence now. Meanwhile, several events were lined up, some special in character and others routine. For instance, the evening of Beating the Retreat was combined with awards for excellence at sports. I was recognized as an outstanding hockey player. Although I felt I should have been awarded the Full Blues, instead I got Half Blues which meant I was the second-best hockey player of my generation at the Academy. I could not tell what criteria were employed to arrive at the choice but that I got mentioned at all was gracious enough.

During the POP rehearsals, 40RC were formed-up as the first four guards to the right of the parade and NNG1 made up the remaining two guards on the left. It was here too that the differences in our training became visible.

For us regular POCs, it was out of question, to fall on parade. Falling on parade due to numbness or exhaustion was forbidden. Although this could be forgivable during rehearsals , there were dire consequences for falling on POP Day as it would fetch automatic relegation.

Therefore, the practices were deliberately prolonged to ensure we endured standing long on parade. During rehearsals, drill instructors constantly reminded us that, if any of us contemplated falling at all, such individuals should not stagger but drop tangentially. On occasions, dropping could lead to serious injuries and near-death situations.

Since we were aware of the consequences of even staggering while on parade, we endured. Not one member of 40RC dropped but NNG1 trainees continually tumbled over throughout the rehearsals up to and including the POP Day. Perhaps because they could not suffer any consequences, they got away with it.

No Good Rumour

As the preparations peaked and progress was made, the D-Day speedily closed in. The balance of the Academy championship events like Interior Economy and Drill Competition had all taken place. Whatever events remained unfinished were already scheduled.

However, just a week to our POP, a distasteful rumour started filtering in. The speculation was that the ceremony was likely to be postponed. It was an idle chatter that was best discountenanced, but it persisted with each passing day. A few days later, a week short of the event, which was slated for 18 September 1993, the postponement was officially announced. The new date was tentatively 25 September 1993. No reasons were advanced as we were only presented with a fait accompli and worse still nobody was sure of the new date. This extra week would eventually qualify as the longest waiting period of my life.

Passing Out Parade

The waiting period was excruciating but time inched closer by the minute. We got into the new week and preparations once again resumed in earnest. The last event related to POP was Dinner Night. This too was held without incident except a new and interesting development arose.

A Decision

About five days to our graduation, the POCs were summoned by the CBC. We all assembled once again to another tense meeting. I personally never wished to attend such an assembly again ever. It was a short wait though. Soon enough, the CBC a brusque and plain no-nonsense individual arrived with an entourage from HQ Cadets Brigade in tow.

"Gentleman officer cadets, I called you here this afternoon to clarify certain matters that are hanging." He started his opening remarks. We all paid attention to his every word and gesture.

"The delay of your POP was unfortunate but its good you endured. Besides a week is not such a big deal." However, it was a big deal considering the tenuous nature of trainee tenure at the Academy, each day counted.

"Please be warned. You must be well behaved in the next few days. It is not yet over until it is over." He cautioned ominously. Nobody needed to be told this fact since the reminder was superfluous. So far, it was not an alarming assembly yet. So, I dropped my guard.

"Additionally, it was recommended to the Academy authorities that provision should be made to accommodate newly commissioned officers outside the Academy." This was to avoid ugly incidents where power drunk newly commissioned officers (especially SSC), that went round intimidating staff and regular cadets. Two days later we were paid a stipend to cover limited expenses and directed to stay out of the Academy, immediately after commission.

"Now to the main reason that brought me here." We all sat up. He paused. "When the Academy was founded, the law establishing the institution clearly stated that it was meant for training officers for the Armed Forces of Nigeria. The law has not changed and therefore it was completely out of place that cadets of NNG1 were brought here in the first place." Oh dear, so 40RC was not the focus of this parade. It was beginning to look good.

"Be that as it may, if the law were not changed, no NNG1 cadets would be commissioned in this citadel, you will all therefore go back to whosoever brought you here to get your ranks. To start with, immediately after this parade, NNG1 cadets must return all military kits in their possession."

For the first time in my life, I gloated over someone else's misfortune. These upstarts and their minders had diminished our long years of training at the Academy. From that point onward, NNG1 cadets were not allowed to participate in the activities preceding our

POP. Even still, they were not allowed to wear military attires and were issued the uniform currently worn by the Nigeria Customs Service. They were part of the POP but were not commissioned to any rank on the Pipping Night.

What transpired that afternoon was a subtle start at a systemic renunciation of the legacies of the former military president. It was an ironic twist of fate and a demonstration of the transience of power, because all that the former leader stood for, just a couple of weeks ago, was being completely repudiated. This was just at the level of the Academy, but the same tendencies were replicated at institutions all over the country.

Reverse Puttee

Customarily, a day to POP, cadets enacted a ruthless tradition. It was Reverse Puttee Day. On this occasion, junior cadets descended on the POCs as they lost their powers as the most senior cadets and took inverse order from the most junior at the Academy. To a degree, the kind of orders or physical buffeting an individual got was an apropos reflection of their personal interfaces with their subordinates.

My course was not particularly lucky because we had been programmed unto the very last minute at the Cadets Mess. While the event was being rounded up, the younger cadets especially first termers, had cordoned and blocked the exits. At the end of the parade, we forcibly charged through the barricades but not without receiving blows. This marked our last interaction with fellow cadets at the Academy.

Happiness Full of Agony

Finally, after five years, two weeks and three days, 25 September 1993 came. We marched on parade, but our joyful day was turned into a prolonged anguish. The Reviewing Officer for the POP was Chief Ernest Shonekan, the Interim Head of State, of the contraption instituted after the abdication of the military president. It was evident that someone had failed in their duty of advising the dignitary about the long parade and timing.

So, we marched on parade by 0730hrs and were expecting the reviewing officer by 0800 or 0830hrs at most. Then the waiting now started. It was a long wait. 0900. 1000. 1100hrs, still no reviewing officer. The massed band tried to relieve the fatigue by playing rousing musical interludes to no avail. Although we had had extended stretches during rehearsals, it was never more than two and a half hours.

The parade commander kept calling the parade to attention to ease the numbness and encourage blood circulation while standing in ramrod posture for over four hours. The only option left open to us was not contemplated. Drop on parade now and gain an additional one year at the Academy. In the NNG ranks, a score of POCs dropped face down. I was in the same pit, and more bothered about surviving on my legs, for the next couple of hours. Finally, at about 1130hrs, after four hours on parade, we heard the piercing wails of sirens, presaging the arrival of the kahuna. It was such an energizing relief.

The parade marched past in slow and quick times, and in review order. There was presentation of prizes and coronation of the champion battalion. Then the Reviewing Officer made a long wordy speech after which the parade hailed him.

Mercifully, the POP was ending. The parade wheeled right once more and marched towards the saluting dais for the final pass by which time the guards were dissolved into a file formation. Just metres out of the parade ground, the last but sweetest command by each individual guard commander was shouted "Passing Out Cadets Inwards Salute!" We ran off to the edge of the parade ground and started cheering wildly and embracing each other. At the edge of the parade ground, I waited for my closest friend, POC James Rotgak Danyil (RIP), as he stepped off the parade ground, I ran to him, and we locked in a long hold. Conclusively, the bitter hemlock of officer cadetship had been taken away from us.

Convocation and Prize Giving Ceremony

From the parade ground after an interval spent for photo-ops, eating, and resting a little, we all headed to the Cadets Mess for Convocation and Prize Giving Ceremony. If you recall, the Academy was of Deemed-a-University status, so during the ceremony we were conferred with degrees. At that occasion too, prizes for academic excellence were presented. It was gratifying to be recognized as the Best Graduating cadet of Department of History and Overall Best Graduating Cadet Faculty of Arts for the year 1993. I was given cash and a collection of books. It was a short ceremony and we soon dispersed to await the all-important Pipping Ceremony.

Pipping Ceremony

The grand finale of the POP was the pipping ceremony, (hanging in cadet parlance) it was customarily held at night after the parade. It was so-called because it was during the ceremony that an attestation oath was administered and finally our ranks were unveiled to crown the years of tedious training and exertion.

The dress code was No.3 dress, aka Mess kit and we were all nattily dressed. On that night, each POC was allowed a solitary guest. For that role, I chose my immediate elder sister, Comfort Ngusuur, to be by my side. She deserved the honour on account of her love and selfless support to me while I was at the Academy.

The events of the night started as early as 2100hrs when we all filed into the Cadets Mess along with our guests. The hall's seating arrangement left a space in the middle. This space was used, first for dancing, and later for the Pipping Ceremony when we all crowded in there to get done with the business of the day.

The decoration rites proper commenced shortly before midnight. The POCs were ordered to form-up and an oath of attestation was recited and as the clock struck twelve midnight, our guests were called upon to unveil the ranks that were earlier carefully concealed under our epaulettes. So, finally on the early morning of 26 September 1993, I got commissioned into the rank of Second Lieutenant of the Nigerian Army.

Finishing Touches

During the weekend, I hibernated at a low-budget guest house and reported to an empty Academy on Monday morning as cadets were on break after POP. We assembled at Ejoor Hall for our administration and there we got issued service numbers and branches of service. I was deployed to the Nigerian Army Corps of Military Police, MP for short.

Our last act at the Academy was return of cadet identity card and its being replaced with officers' badges at the NDA Intelligence Detachment. Afterwards, we were all released on two weeks disembarkation leave, at the end of which we were instructed to report to our individual service branch headquarters, all of which were in Lagos.

Chicago 2016

Chapter Twenty-One

In the Field

In the second week of October 1993, lots of newly commissioned young officers started trickling into Lagos. Every individual was left to his own devices as no provisions were made for the beginners. There was neither quartering nor board nor financial support which made the beginning quite bumpy. Luckily though, I squatted with a friend, which made it convenient and easing, otherwise, the destitution would have been unbearable.

An Opening Salvo

So, on Wednesday 10 October 1993, along with eight of my colleagues, we reported to HQ Nigerian Army Corps of Military Police (HQ NACMP), at Arakan Barracks for deployment. An opening encounter with a sullen staff officer in charge of administration was quite irritating. I had woken up early, considering the chaotic Lagos traffic, to be at the HQ by 0800hrs. Graciously, the grid-lock prone traffic was passable, and I got there at the nick of time. I was hoping to do the proper thing at the commencement of my service.

At that early hour, neither the Provost Marshal (Army) (PM(A)) nor his principal staff officers were on seat. We were received by a subaltern, who invited us to wait at his office, a rather spartan affair. Its central space was occupied by an old table and a rickety chair behind it for him and another for his visitors. For this sizable number of visitors though, more chairs were brought in.

I surveyed the cubicle. The cabinet looked like an inherited antique piece. Standing in a wall slot directly behind the table was a safe, a hand-me-down article from WAFF. The ceiling was aging and discolored from years of continuous leaking. In fact, holes were drilled at the most stained spots to drain out water. The building that housed the HQ was a mortal, wood, and corrugated iron sheets contraption and was in a parlous structural state.

The most conspicuous feature of the edifice, if you called it one, was layers of paint coats, gaudily superimposed on the walls. My imagination was running wild, but I reminded myself that I was neither a structural engineer nor on a mission to determine the integrity of the HQ building. However, I could see that all the structures were in urgent need of renovation. As the HQ of a major branch of the army, I had expected something better.

The waiting ended when we were ushered in to meet this senior officer, the Colonel Administration (Col Admin). It was evident that he enjoyed the awe with which he was held. He was a conservative you-must-all-worship-me type. When we finally met him, he enquired obliviously whom the pack was, and I volunteered that we were young officers reporting into the net. This was a signal communications phrasing saying we were new in town and reporting for deployment.

The man suddenly and inexplicably went berserk. He was unimpressed by my military jargon and started grumbling about young officers that were prone to being problematic. How he arrived at this bizarre assumption was inexplicable. I deduced that he was under pressure from a nagging spouse at home, or he was financially broke, and or he was used to being addressed regally by sycophantic subordinates, or a combination of all. Otherwise, his off-handed fulmination was most uncalled for on account of a vivid and perfectly apt expression.

Afterwards, I simply dismissed and marked him as a thoroughly resentful type. The truth be told, I was not in the business of being terrified of grumpy superiors and this irritant would not lead me to that state either, especially not on my very first day in service. This kind of negative megalomania I encountered all through my years in service.

For all his goofiness, this inflated character was not the final arbiter on the matter of deployment. He could only make proposals. Therefore, his ploy was typical of influence peddlers that expected the entire world to genuflect before them in the hope of gaining unearned favours and positions. Apart from being inherently vain, they did not need any reason to hate, but loathed for aversion's sake. On that Wednesday morning, he could not do more than what he was directed to, as he discharged us to reconvene on Friday by which day our first posting would have been determined.

Manoeuvring with Difficulty

In the next couple of days, I stayed indoors. However, it was involuntary because I was penniless and had just barely managed to come from home to Lagos. Of course, after a couple of days, I was flat broke and to worsen matters, hunger set in. Although, I had a couple of flat mates but for the shame of begging, or was it pride? I could not ask any of them to buy me a meal. From now on, constant hunger became my companion, at least, not until well after December 1993.

On Friday morning, I was dropped by a fellow who owned a car. I managed to put up a cheerful face since it cost nothing. It was at HQ NACMP that I got informed about opening a salary bank account, and to do some paperwork at the Officers Pay Office (OPO). I was in a quandary. However, I stilled myself and went on to the office to listen to the impending travesty and it truly turned out to be a sham.

Mother Unit

A mother unit was the first unit of primary assignment at which an individual began his military career as a freshly commissioned officer. It was very central for a young officer, because the initial grooming, more like finishing, as an officer, took place there apart from the frenzied and often disjointed orientation at the Academy. To a greater degree too, it impacted not only the individual's career accomplishment, but it had a direct bearing on his relative material stability. This much was known by the army authorities, as some military units and locations, were officially designated as hardship units.

To all appearances, postings and appointments were routine administrative matters based on fairness and vacancy. However, it was known that it became a rationale for incessant lobbying and chicanery, into which thingies and jumbles were addled. It was such a pervasive act, but incredibly parties involved in the travesty, i.e., those in authority and the beneficiaries blatantly flaunted the malfeasance.

So, once again we converged at the office of the Col Admin. This morning too, the senior officer was late to office. In the interim, we sat out the time and speculated about the units. Finally, he arrived and called out the units and I was posted as an Instructor to the Nigerian Army School of Military Police, Basawa-Zaria (NASMP). It was the training arm of the MP. Although, I had no specific place in mind as I was prepared to serve at any unit, still, I was aghast that I was posted to the school.

Typically, for each branch of the service, they were operational units and a training school. It was normal for young officers to be deployed to operational units, where they got a feel of their branch of service. Thereafter, they went on a basic or young officers' courses for specialized training at the schools during which they were grounded in the nuts and bolts of the branch.

This was important because the focus at the Academy that churned out fresh officers was infantry generic in nature. The corps thereafter provided the basic orientation to its young officers in alignment with its working traditions, operational doctrines, capabilities and constraints.

From the foregoing therefore, it was customary, that no newly commissioned young officers were posted to the schools. This could not be done until they had taken at least a course at the school. But here it was, at the very first instance, I was sent out of the Academy straight to a specialist school as an instructor on what subjects I knew nothing about. It was a deliberate mischief, but it was not in my character to whine over charades.

Salary Account

Again, I was required to open a salary bank account, but I had no money. I had no money to feed myself much less to open an account. I do not even remember, how I got back to Ebute Metta from Apapa that Friday. However, I remained holed-up in the room. There was nowhere I could go for reprieve, but I equally knew that I could not survive lying on my back.

Accordingly, my mind went to work as I mentally scanned for any associates resident in Lagos. But I was uncomfortable with a score and settled for a young lady working at the airport area at Ikeja. But first I needed to concoct a reason for my situation. This could be any except the fact that I embarked on a new career penniless.

It was going to be a lie, so I kept it simple. Therefore, I decided that I should lose my wallet and all during a ride in one of those overcrowded and unsightly Lagos buses called Molue. A pickpocket obviously removed it, which sounded plausible.

Nonetheless, I still had no transport fare to transit from Ebute Metta to Ikeja to put my machinations to test. There were two options, i.e., either beg to hitch rides, to at least two connecting stops or trek fifteen kilometres to my destination. I chose the latter because I was still agile, and it was the least awkward alternative. It was unpleasant but I felt that the physical chastisement of ambling over such a distance would vitiate my perfidy. My simple scheme was now iron cast, so I laid low through the weekend until Monday morning when I set forth.

So, early in the morning, I took off when the sunshine was not yet intense. From Lagos Street, I went through Yaba on Murtala Muhammad Way through Alagomeji and crossed under Ojuelegba Flyover and linked Mushin Market thence to NIPOST Oshodi. By the time I headed to Oshodi, I had had two sets of perspirations. After over an hour, I crossed over Apapa-Oshodi Expressway and branched off on Airport Road for the final lap.

By now I had been walking vigorously for over two hours. The sweating ceased but my upper torso was damp. I got to my destination, but I was only hopeful that my deliverer would be on seat because I arrived without notice. So, I filled-in the visitor's forms at the reception and waited to be ushered in.

I looked emaciated and dishevelled. In my current situation I was not bothered about smart looks but getting a favourable response to my voyage of mendicancy. Graciously, I was called into the presence of this young lady. As I walked in with a gaunt gait, I felt thoroughly diminished deep within.

My host was genuinely elated. She offered me a seat and water in a strongly chilled room. If the icy water was meant to chill my innards, it triggered an opposite reaction as I was drenched in a deluge of sweat. I had a feeling she saw through the scheme but could only seethe in anger and inadequacy as we exchanged pleasantries, as she commended me for my tenacity by completing my training at the Academy. I absorbed her sincerity and felt sour because my mission here although truthful, was based on falsehood.

Eventually, I narrated my windy story and could not tell whether she believed me or not. Afterwards, I remained downcast and silent for a prolonged period and abruptly announced my departure when I came to. She was understanding and gave me a substantial amount of cash. As I left her office, I was both happy and miserable in equal measure.

When I got outside, I ate a meal that distended my belly and caused me severe discomfort. In fact, that I escaped an ulcerous stomach after that prolonged hunger was inexplicable. The next day, I got to open a bank account and had cash remaining at hand with which I paid for transit to Zaria to report to my unit.

Basawa Barracks

My mother unit, NASMP, was stationed at Basawa Barracks, a sprawling military installation that was home to many units. I recall that during my university days, I often came over there to spend holidays. Therefore, it was a place I knew very well because I visited my elder brother who was an instructor at the school.

It was one of the military installations commissioned in the 1970s. The barracks was a massive cluster designed for offices and residential accommodation with integrated and functional utilities. There was a hospital and a set of primary and secondary schools incorporated in the spatial design. The barracks was intended to be a self-contained community. Unfortunately, right from the start, the installation was never ever fully occupied.

When I first visited the barracks in 1983, it was a bustling community segmented into Engineers, Artillery and Military Police zones. However, there were still vacant rooms in the lines and the initial stages of wear and tear were visible and by the time I reported as an officer in the barracks, much of the structures were crumbling and in need of extensive repairs, which was a widespread trend in NA barracks then.

Reception

It was a little disconcerting as I arrived during the weekend, on a Saturday to be precise, without fanfare. There was neither red carpet nor triumphal. I reached the barracks late in the evening, so there was little I could do and asked around for any colleague and stumbled upon an SSC officer. The officer had graduated from the Academy about four months earlier. In fact, he was of the 30SSC, the course my fellows and I, almost maimed during Camp Kurata, in a tyrannical avowal of seniority.

An Oddball Quartermaster

The next morning, I went over to the unit QM to request for a temporary accommodation, pending my official resumption the next day. I thought I had met eccentric people since joining the army but my encounter with this oddball QM, was a lesson in the awkward. It was obvious that he lived by himself. For a start, he made me wait for him for a long time as he kept coming and going, crisscrossing his poorly furnished living room, while he susurrated to himself. When he was done and ready to attend to me, he approached with an insipid face and queried.

"Yes, my friend, who are you and how may I help you?" He was straight-faced, and it was obvious he wanted me out of the way. By now, I was no longer a novice to the irritability of superior-subordinate interaction. I wanted to give him a bruising answer, but I reined myself.

"Sir, I am Second Lieutenant T Gberikon, I was recently posted to the school, and reported late yesterday. I came to you in the hope that you could provide me a temporary accommodation to settle-in pending a permanent allocation of quarters." I put up my best performance to mask my disdain for red tape. The QM unexpectedly became animated. Maybe, it was something I said that triggered his excitement.

"Just like that? You have not even reported officially, and you are in a hurry to be allocated quarters? By whose authority?" He asked rhetorically. He was a captain, and from his age, a Q-commissioned officer who started service as a soldier. This class of officers' trademark was protocol and red tape. I just mopped at him.

"Things are not done like that. I must take orders from the commandant that you have been posted here and taken on strength and should be accommodated. Otherwise, I have no business with you. When you people pass out from that your Academy and you get here, we teach you what is obtainable in the field." He ended on a cynical note. In fact, I was being gradually inducted to the scorn of the army job.

By now, I was fully chastened and asked for permission to disappear from his sight to which he quickly objected. This eccentric persisted in rambling about anything and everything that was not right with the system. I was not listening to him anymore. But at the same time, I found this old man thoroughly entertaining and began to admire his negative ripostes. He was not being malicious but professional in his mannerisms.

"Just give me a couple of minutes, let me put on something" It was an order not a request. It did not take long, when he came out and asked me to accompany him to an adjacent backroom and unlocked the place, and I could see it was filled with junks. It was more of a storehouse. More importantly, there were mattresses lying about. At least, I could get good rest.

"Consider yourself lucky that you can find a place to lay your head. Make yourself comfortable here, until I receive official authorization to provide you quarters." For all his acerbity, there was no tinge of malice in his vituperations. He handed me the key to the room, and I immediately packed in without as much as cleaning the place.

The next morning, I reported to HQ NASMP. When I met the commandant, he lamented about being sent such a young officer despite his repeated requests for officers to be posted to the school. I felt injured the more. Ultimately, I was deployed to the training branch as an instructor. Later, I was marched to the Chief Instructor (CI). After some small talk, he directed me to the QM with instructions to be provided living quarters.

I got back to the QM and by now I knew his kind of character. He did not disappoint as he took off on another flight of proper thing and procedure mantra and allocated me a flat at the Single Officers' Quarters. The QM then instructed the Regimental Quartermaster Sergeant (RQMS), to march me into my official residence.

When he opened the door, all I could see was a one-room affair with a toilet and bathroom without a kitchen. O yes, by army tradition, I was not expected to cook at home as a young officer. In the past, we were told, young officers were fed centrally at a mess or under whatever plan. That afternoon, there was nothing, I mean absolutely nothing, in that house. Both the small living room and bedroom were bereft of any furnishings. It was a football field according to service personnel.

It was stymying that the authorities expected a newly commissioned officer to furnish his house. Even without privileged information, I knew something was fundamentally wrong with this deliberate failure to provide for neophytes. Nobody cared and it was hard for officers but worse for soldiers.

The RQMS got young soldiers to assist with the cleaning and immediately afterwards I packed in. Apart from my personal effects, I commandeered two mattresses, a single sofa and an old rug that was lying fallow in a corner. I cleaned out the rug, dropped the mattresses on the concrete floor and I had a bed. So, by that evening, I had a house to myself, notwithstanding whether it was furnished or not, , there was a place I could come back to as my pad.

Funnily, as I settled in, the first visitor to my new abode was the QM. He arrived uninvited and made himself comfortable on the lone sofa I had appropriated from the storehouse. This visit marked the beginning of a long friendship. I soon discovered he was such a stimulating character and as abstracted as the degree in psychology he studied at the university in his old age. He was better described as a cynic. Subsequently, as we got engrossed in intellectual sparring, he always took extreme positions and often had alarming contrary opinions. In fact, he was the only person without guile in the whole unit, as I came to know later.

Makurdi 2016

Nigerian Army Day Celebration 1995

Chapter Twenty-Two

Disbelief

On 23 October 1993, it was reported that the Nigeria National Guard had been disbanded. Although the news was distant, it marked the beginning of events that eventually nullified the temporary political contraption hastily instituted by the retreating military junta. It was further reported that about a hundred and twenty officers of the force that were poached from the various arms of the services, were returned to their units because the Interim National Government had no provisions for funding the outfit.[1]

The events of the frenzied year poured in torrents, and it was almost impossible to keep track of all. So, I took the news with equanimity, as it was nothing so distinguishing to attract any griping. But two weeks later, one of the former NNG1 cadets reported to NASMP as an instructor. Along the line, the lot had been commissioned as lieutenants. Meanwhile, I was still a second lieutenant. It was really an awkward situation. Tragically, it was not an isolated case, but it became a seriatim policy cartwheel that engendered arguments over seniority between 40RC, 29SSC and NNG1.

On an Empty Stomach

While in training, it was repeatedly drummed into our ears that an army marched on its stomach. In simple terms, regardless of the technological gizmo, formed up troops, still needed daily sustenance. This could be in the form of rations that nourished them to be in a state of readiness to execute missions. However, mechanized, and advanced technology-driven armies demanded more in terms of materiel such as petroleum, oils, and lubricants for the continuous maintenance of cavalcades.

Even so, these considerations did not take away from the central necessity of basic maintenance in the field. Indeed, irrespective of doctrines or equipment states, all armies eventually succumbed to mortal craving for nourishment and the certainty of hunger. So, I was caught in an ironic twist of ideology against reality. While the system paid lip service to the welfare of its troops, it knowingly left its young entrants to fend for themselves.

Renumeration

The NA had a multitude of strange policies on its plate. Of these, the most bizarre was the procedure deployed to document and pay salaries to new personnel. It was evident that the originators of the policy were not charitable.

Due to its ineptness, although we were commissioned by September, we would not draw salaries until December of 1993, a quarter of a year down the line. There was nothing on the statutes books to justify this torment or why it took so long to include young officers and soldiers on the payroll despite the manifest physical deprivation and embarrassment it caused all.

It was apparent that looking prim and well turned-out was only a small portion in the complex algorithm of survival. There was nothing special sleeping in a bare room but contending with hunger at the same time was an existential scuffle. It was not a time to indulge in self-pity but to be creative as it became essential to throw out pride and face the daily tribulations.

At last, three months accrued salary was paid. Nonetheless, the arithmetic was not rosy. For my first paycheck, I drew slightly over the sum of One thousand eight hundred as a second lieutenant as of December 1993. The market value of this sum at that point was grossly inadequate. It was such a miserly amount that being paid felt more like an anti-climax to the excitement that built-up.

From the moment I drew my first salary, I knew it was too derisory to tend to my upkeep in a month. In fact, if for anything at all, I was always near penniless a week after I got paid. It was not a matter of imprudence or wasteful expenditure but squarely because of its insufficiency.

This was the kind of situation that we all went through as young officers. However, the coping mechanism of individuals differed. For instance, some officers got support from their families and in-laws. This could take the form of a car gift, furnishing of lodgings or being financially augmented. I remember my accounts officer at the bank, was like, do you get paid extra elsewhere or what I received in my account was it? I replied in the affirmative, yet she was unconvinced given that the military ruled then.

Try as I could, I was in a fix, because my salary could not cover my expenses, so the question of saving a portion of it was unnecessary. In fact, I emptied my account each time I got paid. For a better part of my years in service, I lived in penury and had to resort to mendicancy and low-level borrowing to scrape through.

An Anorexic Benefactor

I contended with multiple challenges, until an unlikely angel materialized. He was an officer of a unit co-located at Basawa Barracks. Despite his peculiar routine, he was a gentleman who unfailingly stocked foodstuff and invited me to feed out of his kitchen. Although it was gracious enough, I observed his eating habits were extremely poor.

Occasionally, he managed to concoct a broth that was remarkable for its strong garlic flavour. Once, I tried to eat out of a soup he prepared, and my tongue was almost lacerated from too much garlic. In fact, except for himself, absolutely no one could eat the meals he fixed. Although, I rarely saw him eat, he puffed endlessly on cigarettes, as a stick always hung from his pout at any given time.

This was a rare and helpful gesture from a colleague. However, it could not last for long, much less forever. Still, modesty demanded that such benevolence was not abused. Therefore, I took one meal per day from this offer. In which case, it could be lunch or dinner, depending on how famished I was but over time, this progressed to alternate days, and ceased finally when I found a way around the challenge.

While settling in and exploring my immediate environment, as I do at every new location, I discovered a local restaurant at Palladan, a haven of speakeasies opposite the Aviation School at Zaria. It was a granny and daughter run outfit. Although its surroundings were not hygienic, the meals were wholesome, plus along the line, I was able to open a credit facility.

I had gotten myself a lifeline. By this arrangement, I could eat as much as I wished and pay at a future date. Even if it was tarnishing, I was pragmatic enough to understand that I needed to ditch fripperies and face my demons to survive.

NASMP

Having resolved the great matter of daily sustenance, I now redirected my focus to my unit. NASMP was a training school and in service jargon, a non-operational unit. The school, as it was so-called, was dedicated to academic and training activities. I took time to apprise myself with the setup. I could see that the school's operational structure was composed of a HQ and two arms namely Training and Administrative Branches. Of these two, only the training arm had its near full complement of staff. As for the Admin Branch, there was never enough staff, in fact, the only officer operating from there was the egoistical QM we encountered earlier.

It was not long before I discovered some unsettling facts about the unit. It was one of those establishments derisively labelled hardship units. By this classification, the unit in name and spirit, its finances, physical structures, facilities, and personnel were hard done in. So, scheming officers and soldiers ensured they were never posted to such units.

The classrooms and offices at NASMP needed renovation. Worse still, the edifices were deprived of the traditional coatings of many colours. The iron tables and chairs commonly shared by instructors and students in the classes, offices and living quarters were as ancient as they were primitive.

Furthermore, the office equipment then were mostly old noisy typewriters and cyclostyling machines, in an age of computers and digital devices. More worrisome was the state of the office stationeries. It was quite unsettling when I observed clerks flipped used envelopes and papers to be repurposed for new dispatches and correspondences. I understood that things were tough, but the level of degeneracy especially when the military were ruling the country was objectionable. It was obvious that the military were not taking care of its own.

However, the level of infrastructural decay paled compared to the reasons for, and the calibre of officers and soldiers assembled at the school as staff and instructors. It was apparent that neither merit nor extraordinary gifts, recommended individuals for posting and appointment at the school.

Without prejudice, most personnel were posted to the school if they were found disagreeable elsewhere. In fact, a little common mix-up at another unit, could get someone maliciously posted to the school. Meanwhile on many occasions, officers and soldiers brazenly spurned postings to the unit.

On a personal note, the school was my mother unit, and I was not posted here because I was a repulsive person. O yes, so far there was nothing offensive to warrant such a penal deployment. Yet subsequent postings validated these perceptions as individuals were harried to this place under the threats of severe sanctions. It was noticeable because they arrived chastened, dazed, and unrehearsed. The point was that the flotsam assembled were unqualified and even those that made the cut were indifferent, or in the least not motivated.

Even more, I repudiated any such insinuations and said so anytime an opportunity presented itself. The school, I believed was about merit, but willful denigration of the unit and love of preferment, tainted service here, and likened it to penance. So, through no fault of mine, I started service amidst the disagreeable and unmotivated.

Authority at the School

The ultimate authority at the unit lay with the commandant. In absolute terms, nothing happened without his approval. The resources at the school, both financial and otherwise, were lean and necessarily micro-managed as a one-man setup. In my first tour of duty, the incumbent Commandant was a fatherly colonel, who could easily be aroused to anger. Given the difficult circumstances under which he administered the place, his bumpy and explosive countenance were quite understandable.

The second principal officer was the Chief Instructor (CI), who superintended over the Training Branch. The CI could be successful if he was a dynamic personality. This, of course, was dependent of how much of the commandant's powers he could safely appropriate and more importantly his standing with the boss. I served under a couple of them, and found they shared the common ingredients of bombast and love for being addressed in adulatory terms.

The balance of the smorgasbord were instructors and staff officers deployed to complementary sections like Finance, Medical, MT yard, QM, PT and Catering departments. Together, we combinated in a struggle to run training activities at the school, on bare-bone budgets and training support. It was indeed a hardship place.

Given the mishmash of the personnel assembled, it was only natural that the work environment was saturated with animosity. As earlier observed, because the criteria for postings to the school were ill-defined, the citadel literarily became a dumpsite of individuals out of favour. It was therefore a place characterized by brusqueness and irritability. Worse still, a significant section of the staff serving at the school then, especially officers, were unhappy to be there.

Jealous-Wives-Like

My experiences as a cadet gave me an insight into the proximate conduct to expect of personnel in the field. However, I was unprepared for what cropped up. For it was such a toxic community, as officers and soldiers openly competed for the attention of commanders, akin to jealous wives in a polygamous marriage. There was no level of fawning, duplicity, and venom, by which personnel from both spectrums did not deploy, to upend others in pursuit of favours and positions.

I observed the whole shebang and concluded that the process of gaining a commander's trust was too wearisome. Apart from getting close and personal, it involved collating numbers on persons and always being a repository of both positive and negative info on everyone and every subject. Regrettably, a combination of such proximity and a compulsion to be useful, led these villains to blurt out too many details about everybody and everything, which not only terrified but excited distrust instead of endearment to superiors. This was the foundation of eye-service in the Armed Forces of Nigeria.

From my days as a cadet, I was deliberately detached but made friends with selected superiors, peers, and subordinates alike. I smiled back at those that beamed at me and scowled at any person that despised me because I did not have any pressing need to be admired by everybody. So, by choice, I kept aloof but still, I was always involved in altercations with my superiors. I was not markedly rebellious but all around, I identified deceit and resolved to ask questions always. I spent time serving one form of puttee or the other at the Academy, and as an officer, I serially navigated acerbic exchanges.

My resolve was never to be overwhelmed by the manifold detractions abound but to ensure that I was materially present at all official parades. I was not given to malingering, and as a result, despite the physical buffeting and multiple obstacles in my path, I endured and confined myself, first at the Academy and later as an officer.

Grumbling

Grumbling was a four-star general, it had always been there since the first intake into the army. This was repeatedly stated by our seniors at the Academy. For so long, public institutions in Nigeria were run erratically. Although institutional protocols were clearly defined, the Nigerian mind-set loathed traditions or so it appeared. It was a hopeless situation as irregularities became so deep-rooted that a lot of statutory prerogatives were denied, hoarded and or outrightly forfeited. So, out of a force of habit, personnel complained about everything.

However, even grumbling had options. You could grumble all by yourself or join a therapeutic group grumbling sessions. The latter case always an improvised assembly at which a company vented its frustrations about unspecific concerns. There was so much to complain about as officers. We complained about everything but unfortunately when an opportunity cropped up to make our cases, most chickened out.

Classes of Officers and Soldiers

It could be assumed that everyone came to the service on a tabula rasa. Nevertheless, this was quite debatable. However, over time, experiences, perceptions and other underlying individual dispositions combined to give distinctive characters to officers and soldiers. It was therefore not difficult to classify the lot as professionals, enthusiasts, the apathetic and zealots.

The so-called professionals were very fussy about military traditions, bearing and dignity. They hardly interacted nor held normal conversations if its substance was not military related. By extension too, they personalized the service, and spoke of it in possessive first terms. Typically, they paid too much attention to military protocol, that they often forgot the primacy of fighting wars.

A second category of personnel were the enthusiasts. These were the loud types that exhibited self-serving loyalty to the service. They found neither faults nor shortfalls, despite glaring disparities in the system. Such an engrossed group, they advocated blind compliance and professed dubious loyalty bordered on the servile.

Additionally, they were not exceptionally good on the job, but deployed intensity to affect preferment. Similarly, these types were prone to treachery because of their pressing need to belong. The force of their enthusiasm was such that they could betray colleagues to advance their careers.

Another class of officers and soldiers were the apathetic type. This group incorporated minimalists that conformed to the subjective and haphazard way the affairs of the service were ran. Although, the NA was a colonial creation modelled after the British Army, post-independence, changes were wrought on the service. This was not suggestive that the army remained inflexibly faithful to its roots. In fact, pragmatism called for modifications to address the local needs and primacies of Nigeria.

Unfortunately, when the changes came, they were not only in breach but drastic as to be deleterious. There were distortions. For instance, the basic procedures on provisioning, terms and conditions of service and the material comfort in-built in the system were adulterated to such a degree that they were unrecognizable.

Along the line too, traditions were traded away for unexplained cynicism that was co-opted to veil failure. Gradually, lexicons and expressions like "the-way-and-manner" and "wait-for-your-time," "if-you-don't-like-what-is-happening, pack-your-load-and-go" became a prevalent mantra.

Another angle to these antithetical changes was the demonization of personnel. Certain individuals were vilified across board which led to hardening of attitudes and lukewarm approach to the job. If the service did not care about its shared profile and created room for degeneration due to the arbitrary conduct of its leadership, then the attendant outcome was indifference. Thus, initiative and zeal for the job was weakened or lost.

The other group of officers and soldiers were the zealots. This camp was populated by extremists, tribal jingoists, religionists, regionalists, and alarmists all rolled into one. They claimed the ownership of the service for themselves and whatever irredentist interests they embodied. They loved positions and appointments, not because of their productive capacity but to fill-in quotas. In fact, the allure of advancement was so strong that they took to putsches which was a contrivance that allowed them to own not only just the service but the whole country.

This noxious cocktail made for an abrasive and contentious service which complicated what ordinarily should have been defined by traditions, customs, and procedures. As a result, unhealthy competition became rife, traditions were adulterated and policies were quickly made, altered and discarded, overall, the service limped on.

Work Ethics

When I started, I was determined to be a proper thing officer. Always enthusiastic, I developed a positive work attitude and avoided lateness at work, functions, and parades because naturally, I was not the ceremonial nor red-tape type. I was a stickler to time. As much as possible, I paid attention to my turn-out. In fact, before I joined the army, I was a natty dresser. However, when I was finally overwhelmed by the ubiquity of military uniforms, I made sure I acquired all the obligatory dress sets.

In all these, the most important mind-set was a commitment to grasp the core competencies of a provost officer. Providentially, I was at the school and got immersed in training activities which afforded me an opportunity to understand law enforcement at a conceptual as well as being grounded at the operational levels, i.e., police duties and investigation. I grasped MP work and discharged my duties to the best of my ability.

The Job of An Instructor

The job of an instructor was quite regular. At the school, there was always a course schedule for the year. The courses were divided into General Duties and Investigation Courses, Security Management, Military Police Officers' Basic courses for both officers and soldiers.

Typically, courses at the school, on average, lasted for a duration of twelve weeks except Officers' Basic and Security Management Courses that ran for sixteen weeks. Apart from lectures, activities at the school were not any different from those in the units.

The living quarters in the barracks was a little far from the school area but a walkable distance. I had no car then but luckily there was a school shuttle bus that picked and dropped staff and students. However, this facility was only available if the bus was serviceable. Whatever the shortcomings, the service still shuffled on but along the line ceased.

Instructors' Allowance

Being deployed as instructors at most NA training schools was made to look like a grim task. However, to motivate personnel serving at the schools, the staff was paid an instructor's allowance. As of 1993, the allowance paid was twenty Naira monthly or two hundred and forty Naira per annum. The value of the allowance was worth about four bottles of beer per month, to give an idea of the sum of money involved. For effects, it was paid in two tranches at six months interval. Amusingly, when the paltry sum was paid it was welcomed with so much jubilation.

Interpersonal Relationships

The army job was a teamwork which entailed working at close quarters. Instructions were passed vertically top-down the hierarchy. Even so, it was conjectural that superiors were more experienced and knowledgeable than their subordinates on the job, which was quite misleading because it would appear the older officers and soldiers were more obsessed with reinforcing hierarchy, than recognizing the genuine contributions of subordinates.

The main dilemma was resistance to change. The service evolved silently over the years, nonetheless, new entrants had completely different orientation from their older colleagues. More importantly, the younger officers and soldiers were better educated and more open to innovation than their superiors that were obsessed with customs and traditions, even those that were manifestly antiquated. This inclination deepened ignorance over pragmatism.

The truth was that, although the military was always about drills or procedures, contemporary peacetime reality demanded adjustments to reflect the times. Such was the strength of this belief that our older colleagues demanded that we behaved and conducted business like they did, i.e., through drabness, sycophantishly, daftness, rigidity, and all.

There was so much pettifogging by superiors directed at finding faults such that, the way you walked, talked back, approached tasks, socialized down to an individual's personal possessions all constituted factors for subjective assessment. The most unacceptable part of this posturing was an implied desire to be dreaded or nasty or both. Some superiors combined nastiness in language and countenance, deliberate ferocity to intimidate subordinates. Like I earlier stated, these types, I made it a duty to deflate.

Additionally, religion, tribe and region etc., were all thrown into this deadly struggle. So, there were cases of false religious conversions or spiritual duplicity, dubious claims of origins, to conform to sexier or lucrative ethnicity and regions to gain elevation. An aspect of this trend was veneration or deferring to descendants of traditional hegemonies, in reversed roles, with superiors fawning over subordinates for projected gains, materially and in kind.

Amidst all these, I observed that my peers got attached to certain superiors out of the combined factors of fear, positioning, and lechery, to step-up in the job. I could now see that, growing on the job was not necessarily about capacity but networking, influence peddling and engaging in many unnamable activities and obsessions. For such an existential job, with the prospect of instantaneous death or injury, many of those unwritten laws, traditions and unlikely things that went with-it, were simply unacceptable and I could not deal.

Trouble

So far, I enjoyed my days at the school and immersed myself in the dynamics of the service. The first signs of trouble did not even present as a problem initially. However, there was an encounter, and this marked the beginning of a series of clashes I had with my superiors over the years.

In January 1994, even though I was an instructor, the school denied me the opportunity of being part of the basic police officer's course.

Recall I had reported to the school without the requisite training. After much pleading, I was signed-up for the Military Police Officers' Basic Course (MPOB), the first specialized course as a provost officer. The concession was that officers nominated from the school would not draw a course allowance, i.e., a token sum given to offset the cost incurred during the course. Just about the same time too, I was appointed the acting Sports Officer of the school. Therefore, I was triple hatted as an instructor, the sports officer, and a student, and I was obligated to play all roles.

Customarily, two evenings were set-aside for sports during the week. Of course, this was routine, but the next games day was special because it coincided with the graduation of one of the courses. During such events, matches were played, either football or volleyball and the school HQ provided snacks for players, match officials and a handful of officers. It was nothing elaborate but small chops like groundnuts, sweets, and powdered glucose for the players.

Furthermore, it was the duty of the Sports Officer to prepare an estimated cost of these items, and thereafter make requests for funds to procure them. It was that simple but there was a snag because as a participant of MPOB, I was barred from going to the school HQ. However, I still prepared an estimate as demanded and passed it onward to the HQ, which was approved, and I was informed accordingly. However, for the funds to be released, I was required to personally sign the authorizing documents at the Finance Department at the School HQ.

Therefore, I was caught in a sticky catch-22 situation. I could not go to the HQ but at the same time I was required to get refreshments ready for an event scheduled in the next couple of hours. So, towards the close of the day, I went to the Finance Dept and signed for and collected the funds. On my way out, I met a senior colleague, a captain and noticed his face was clouded. It was like I had personally injured him. There was a brief exchange between us or more like a test of wills.

"Lieutenant Gberikon, what are you doing here?" he demanded imperially while wearing a sneering smile. It would appear he had an axe to grind and was looking for an opportunity to nail me. He did not say anything further while the two of us were isolated because he knew his adversary too well and sought the presence of a third party, as a witness. He ordered I came along with him to the staff common room where other officers were at their desks.

"Lieutenant Gberikon, even though you an instructor, you know that there is a standing order by which students are not allowed at the school HQ. But instead of obeying this directive, you spearheaded its disobedience." He spoke while contorting his face, as if he had been directly violated. The first thing that came to my mind was to tell him off. However, I would not do just that for whatever reason, but was thoroughly amused by his antiques. Funnily, there was a history to this altercation.

This officer started service as a soldier of the 63NA stock. In fact, he attained the lofty rank of a Warrant Officer and along the line was commissioned as an officer. Well, being granted a commission was only one aspect, the difficulty lay with the deportment. Despite his commission, his bearing, countenance, and nuances were better suited for a lowly private soldier. This was a common pattern with other ranks granted commission because, they oscillated between being officers and other ranks.

But I did not disparage him. It was just that between us, we were poles apart no matter the parameters applied i.e., generational, situational, or social orientation. The man was handicapped and antiquated in his entire outlook. In chats with him, he was bound to be off-key. Funnily, by his posturing, he attempted to project finesse, but was eternally awkward. My reactions towards him were always mirthful laughter which made him uncomfortable, and he bore a grudge against me.

He ordered me to report to the Offices' Mess, which was technically, a detention order. I left for the stalls, purchased the required items and afterwards reported myself to the Mess. Although, I was absent during the match, I had made arrangements that covered my schedule at the event.

Later that evening, at about 2100hrs, he sneaked into the Mess, in the hope I would be away and thus provide him added munitions to disparage me. Unfortunately for him, I was there ensconced on a couch. Amusingly, he could not even hide his disappointment and released me after a meaningless homily. Perhaps, he had expected me to be grateful but on the contrary, I was upset and let it show.

The next morning, having slept over the affair, I went to his office to explain the reason for my action and apologized if he felt offended. He was all alone as he sat stone-faced and unbelieving. Worst still, he became more agitated because I employed double entendre to make him feel ridiculous. By the time I left, he was angrier than he was at the so-called original offence.

I left him feeling happier that my request for forgiveness had made him feel unqualified. At all times, I made it a point to apologize each time any of my superiors felt offended by my action or omission. Oddly, I discovered later that each time I apologized, they became more enraged by my choice of words.

I was taken aback when I discovered that my vilifier had escalated the matter and reported me to the CI who invited me for an interview. Good enough, the senior officer diligently listened to my version of what transpired. I narrated the events as they unfolded and capped it up with the fact that I had apologized and sought reprieve.

The CI was genuinely surprised that I went to apologize because the captain in his report did not include that part of our exchange. It was the redeeming quality. Subsequently, I frequently had run-ins with my superiors, especially the conceited and arbitrary types, in the line of duty as a provost officer.

NASMP 1999

Chapter Twenty-Three

Obinze 1995

In July 1995, I was posted to 34 Field Artillery Brigade Provost Platoon Obinze-Owerri, as a Platoon Commander. It was my first command of an operational MP unit. Although, I was the most junior by rank in the formation, officially, I was a staff officer to the Commander, with the statutory powers of arrest. These inherent powers became a point of contention with fellow officers of the formation.

It was at my first command too that I began to appreciate the nuances of military service in its varied dimensions. I say this because at my previous unit, the school, a non-operational unit, all of us were tempered by shared misery. Therefore, there was less invasiveness but more nastiness.

My problem lay with inexperience, as I still believed that there was a system in place. Of course, there were institutional procedures and unit traditions, but far from being inviolate, the organization was run in a very subjective manner. There was so much insolence, or more like frivolity among the officers. Even worse, was the jostling for attention to be in the good books of the commander. This unfortunately made officers and soldiers unnecessarily deceitful.

On assumption of command, the first shadowy precursor of things to come were courtesy visits. When I resumed duty, certain individuals, some of whom dressed in exaggerated manner called bearing gifts to welcome me. The storyline was that they heard about my posting and appointment and came to pay homage. Shortly, I discovered that these magi were influencers adept at pre-emptive machinations to keep me in their debt as the turn of events proved.

In Owerri and its environs, the challenges of law enforcement were multiple. The chief concerns were illegal duties, aka kelebe, perpetrated by officers and soldiers. It would appear the populace had lost faith in the ability of the conventional police, to manage and resolve disputes among parties. Hence, it was a widespread practice for civilians to contract soldiers to settle disputes.

Back then, soldiers were respected and obeyed. So, arising from this fact, for any conceivable dispute between citizens, officers and soldiers were contracted to mediate for a fee. Subsequently, my office was inundated by civilians with complaints about fellow civilians. There were varied disputes, but the most prevalent were land disputes, unredeemed indebtedness, and a variety of skirmishes. At the outset, I declined these complaints because their prayers were civil matters and better managed by the conventional police.

Nevertheless, I noticed that this did not sit well with my SNCOs because behind me, they grumbled until one day the Company Sergeant Major (CSM) summoned courage to confront me over this alleged lapse. The CSM was my second in command.

"Oga, I just wan talk sontin with you sir" he started cautiously and paused. "Yes, CSM shoot." I retorted full of authority and contrived disinterestedness. "Oga, na di mata of dis complainant wey you no dey answer, I wan talk" he further explored. "What happened to complainants" I interjected. "Oga sir, no be efry mata you go dey reject. Some taim e dey good to listen. We na your boys, jus lef am for us, we go handle efrytin, sir." He landed and waited for my response.

"I don't understand; are you suggesting that I should authorize illegal duties in my unit as a provost officer?" In all these, I tried to put up a brave face of a no-nonsense proper thing commander. Meanwhile, deep-down, I was eager to learn the ropes of the thingy because it was an informal lifeline fashioned by military men to address the unending indigence within their ranks.

"My friend, I hope you know what you are talking about?" I tried to conceal my eagerness. In short, I conceded to his suggestions and the outcome was unpleasant. The instant, it was known that I would play along, the rest of the soldiers seized the initiative, and technically, I lost control so to say. After I authorized the first set of illegal duties, the rest were undertaken without my knowledge. In fact, even those I had foreknowledge of, were executed beyond my brief.

In the mix, the commanders too, subtly consented to such underhand dealings because they would be pressured by friends and highly placed individuals. I knew most insisted on this kind of intervention despite objections. When it happened though, they cautioned against irrational conduct that could embarrass the command. Even still, fellow staff officers had one favour or two to ask on behalf of friends, or phantom extended families. On occasions, I was almost overwhelmed as I tried to rescue officers and soldiers from poorly executed illegal duties.

Although there were pecuniary benefits from these escapades, in time, as with all sly transactions, my reputation and integrity were shredded. I was buffeted on all sides, as I tried to navigate through tricky and tarnishing situations of granting favours and being held to account for its fallouts.

Overall, I got my fingers burnt for being a do-gooder, and on occasions, I was repeatedly denied especially by superiors that I volunteered to assist. On my part, the moment I authorized an activity, I stood by my decision and bore the consequences of its outcome.

Socializing in Owerri

In the mid-1990s, Owerri metropolis was renowned for its high-octane social life which was driven by a crop of rich young men. For whatever reasons, these young people were labelled 4-1-9. How they came into money remains to be debated but they had enough and spent freely. Moreover, they loved to be accompanied by men in uniform.

It was not a concern and so I neither asked questions nor sermonized. As a young officer, it was a fun-filled place to be. So, I enthusiastically dipped myself in the hedonism on offer. There was night crawling to be done, sit-outs, hard partying and sundry epicurean pursuits that were ever available in abundance. Meanwhile, I traversed the length and breadth of neighbourhoods and got to know every nook and cranny in the state.

Interface with Nosey Colleagues

As earlier stated, by seniority, as a lieutenant, I was the most junior staff officer in the formation that commanded an influential sub-unit. As a provost officer, I had the combined duties of prevention, physical security, law enforcement, the investigation of occurrences with the ultimate powers of arrest. The latter attribute was one which most officers and soldiers wished for and surreptitiously appropriated for themselves.

In the line of duty, I contended with multiple interests. I went fishing for myself, and on occasions for my superiors and colleagues. All these voyages collectively exacted a toll on my integrity. It was a price to pay. However, I never transferred nor denied liability for any infraction, either from myself or on behalf of any party. So, routinely I got involved in damage control on account of my soldiers' misdemeanours and ran concurrent scandals at any given time.

Often too, my problems arose from being snitched upon by colleagues especially intelligence operators. In all these though, I always found ways to pick them apart no matter how complex they presented. I had developed a simple and effective remedy to occurrences as they evolved. Once I got a clue that a commander had authorized an investigation into an incident in which I was involved, no matter how remotely connected, I just went to them and spilled the truth and even more. In this way, I denied my detractors an opportunity of embellishing the evidence. It was that easy to implement, and it always worked.

Intelligence against the Police

The Intelligence and the MP were two branches of the service that collaborated directly with commanders in formations. While the former scoured for actionable info to support operations, the latter was an enforcement outfit, in the conventional sense. Although both branches worked together closely with a commander to ease his task, both never ever agreed on most issues because mutual distrust and branch rivalry impeded the desirable teamwork.

For a start, the operational doctrines of both branches were different. While the intelligence goons were obsessed with secrecy, the police were of necessity open. However, both branches engaged in investigation activities, except that only MP reports were admissible as evidence in the courts. Despite this fact, intelligence operatives frequently encroached on military police turf. For instance, evidence collected during investigations, were preceded by the so-called cautionary statement, which was a key ingredient in the admissibility of evidence which intelligence reports never bothered about.

In addition, the military ruled Nigeria then. At any given opportunity therefore, there was always a possibility of a putsch. Forever on their watch, everybody and everything was suspected of potential disloyalty. This created an avenue for ambitious individuals who exploited such voids to shore up their eternal craving to be dominant and relevant.

This predisposition adversely distracted the intelligence community. For instance, an arm of the branch, the Security Group, increasingly took on unbridled powers. In the name of state security, they hounded their colleagues and severed the cords of camaraderie that bound the service. Consequently, the branch degenerated particularly when it started reporting on individuals instead of incidents.

At the 34 Field Artillery Brigade, we had a situation by which, each time the intelligence officer arrived amid any assemblage, all conversations ceased. Everyone became guarded because he was not only a nosey character, but his mouth dripped endlessly with mischief. So, instead of operational intelligence, the branch was reduced to what was derisively called mammy market intelligence.

Consequently, officers and soldiers distrusted each other intensely and avoided getting involved in routine group activities like mess life or casual socialization. All these were happening on account of the deleterious actions of a sub-set.

Even worse, officers and soldiers snitched on each other. It was unnerving that every now and then discussions were centred on lowly private soldiers. There was no plausible rationale for this kind of behaviour. But tragically, decisions that altered lives were taken based on these idle gossips

Once and even more, I was a victim of these scandalmongers. I recall in December 1996; I made friends with a young man who came on holiday from Germany. He owned a clean Mercedes Benz 200 car and while on an impromptu business trip to Lagos, he left the car in my care. However, everybody knew I owned a rundown 1977 Audi 100.

The next morning, I drove the car to the office. Within the hour, news had spread that I bought a Mercedes Benz car. It was a big deal in those days to own a car especially a Benz because most officers could not even afford a jalopy. How the commander caught the drift remained a mystery. I could sense the presence of the car generated vile resentment, so I left it at home and hitched a ride with a colleague to the office the next day. I knew there were snide remarks and suppressed murmurs that I was living above my means. It was such low-level small-mindedness that became central to the mentality of service personnel. Truth be told, it was high sorcery for a system not to provide sufficiently for its own and expect its operatives to be without desires.

That morning, the Brigade Major (BM), the chief of staff of the formation, sent for me and we enacted a little drama in his office. "Lieutenant Gberikon, congratulations on your new car." he declared furtively. But I could sense that it was an interrogative intended to confirm the information at hand. "Oga sir, I have not bought a car yet." I tried to keep calm. "But I was told you drove a Benz to the office yesterday." By now he was unsure of himself. "Yes sir, I brought a Benz yesterday, but it belongs to a friend." For me, I considered the conversation closed. "I asked because the commander said I should." he blurted finally.

In fact, his brief was more than find out as he had express instructions to impound the car. It was conclusive that, joining the army was an avowal of poverty. Later that day when I met the commander over a different matter, he still spoke about the car and driveled about the usual claims of officers and soldiers about things owned that belonged to friends or parents. What a gloomy lot.

Truth be told, Owerri was a generous but a difficult environment to serve. By extension too, all military locations were demanding on young officers and soldiers. They were, because in the face of enticement and deprivation, personnel perfected a balancing act between being compliant and deviant in the same breadth. No one was insulated from this existential struggle, and all found their way through the maze. Either way, I had exercised my command at 34 Field Artillery Brigade Provost Platoon and soon enough, my time was up, and I was posted to 3 Brigade Provost Platoon, Bukavu Barracks, Kano.

Kano 1998

In 1998, I assumed my second command at 3 Brigade Provost Platoon. Kano, a sprawling and bustling commercial city was quite different from Owerri. So, those things or tendencies that I had come to expect or used to, were quite different. Bukavu Barracks was the old seat of 5

Battalion (Royal Nigeria Regiment). All its structures were run-down colonial style buildings that had seen time. Apart from new barracks recently built in Abuja, military cantonments were in decrepit state.

My encounter at this formation revolved around toxic colleagues and subordinates. However, there were distinct types of officers at the formation. First, there were NDACE commissioned officers, a group that claimed ownership of the service. They were known for their archaic and arbitrary tendencies, and obstinately persisted even when it was apparent that they were doing things wrongly. Absolutely, there was nothing younger officers could do without being faulted.

The second strain were the executive or quartermaster commissioned group drawn from other ranks. As noted earlier, this group was caught between being officers and other ranks at the same time. They laid claim to being the custodians of the system by virtue of their experiences at both ends of the spectrum. However, the drawback was that their bearing and carriage made them awkward.

The last discernible group was the supportive drifters. These were avid followers that had no opinion of theirs but adept at timing to observe the direction the cat jumped to dive. Mostly though, they never understood issues at stake but lent support to demonstrate dubious loyalty. Lastly, serving directly under you and undermining your command were subordinates driven by tribal jingoism, religious bigotry, and pecuniary incentives. Nothing, no event took place in your unit without being snitched upon.

Control Freaks

The MP was a service branch, and its units were low-level, mostly of platoon or company strength, in the brigades and divisions correspondingly. So, it was common to deploy young officers of the rank of lieutenants or captains and majors for divisional groups.

Hence, it became a widespread trend as superiors serially tried to intimidate, bully, or harass provost officers to elicit pre-determined decisions. For instance, when investigations were ordered, they strove to guide its direction and outcome. Unfortunately, a lot of people were under the illusion that the purpose of investigations was to find suspects culpable. It was an area I continually clashed and stood my ground, no matter what any interloper presumed. I was a provost officer trained at what the statutes demanded and knew what was permissible and admissible in extracting evidence. Clearly, enticement, torture and other unethical practices were unacceptable.

It was common for superiors to suggest that I ensured culprits under investigations were found guilty. If there was evidence, why not? But I could not concoct unverifiable allusions to arrive at an outcome. When such superiors persisted, I took on them and demanded they provided such evidence. Otherwise, I threatened to cite them for obstruction and inform the PM accordingly. Once it became known that I would not countenance nosey parkers, I was left alone to exercise my command.

One morning, I was summoned by the BM. So, I went over to his office. "Captain Gberikon, do you know you are under me?" he asserted. I was at a loss at this line of conversation. "Yes sir, I am." I concurred. Just to assuage his ego. However, in truth, I was not, because by establishment I was a direct staff officer to the commander although the BM had a coordinating role. I got to understand, he was piqued that I never allowed anyone to interfere in my little command.

Declining Unlawful Orders

A soldier always obeyed orders first. It was not the place of the individual to choose which order to obey. This was a sore point because often when matters came to a head, especially after an infraction, you got to know that certain orders were unlawful and were not to be obeyed. It was a difficult balancing act for both officers and soldiers alike.

It was on account of this that I hesitated when the Intelligence Officer conceived a raid on locations in Kano city with the approval of the commander. Of the numerous targets, one spot was directly opposite the barracks, a sports ground at Kofar Ruwa, that hosted local boxing matches, aka "dambe." The rationale for this operation was that hard drugs were peddled on the sides and soldiers in uniform openly patronized the dealers.

The fact that I could be deployed at the whim of the commander notwithstanding, I made my position clear. I let it be known that as a community playground, it would be unfair to raid the location because of our failure to rein in our troops. I was ignored.

Eventually, a raid was sprung as planned but not a single soldier nor any drug dealer were apprehended as everyone within the vicinity fled when a convoy of military vehicles was sighted. Instead, the troops harvested abandoned motorbikes and bicycles. Most were unregistered and stayed unclaimed as at when I left Kano.

On another occasion, I was informed that a soldier was in police custody over alleged armed robbery. Incidentally, the report was brought to my notice by the BM. Also, I discovered that the said soldier was his batman, i.e., he was assigned to him as a personal servant. After a preliminary investigation, it became known that the soldier vanished, intermittently, for lengthy intervals and allegedly returned bearing gifts for his principal. I did not act. Not until I got instructed in writing by the brigade commander with an official letter to the state police command.

I followed up and interviewed the Commissioner of Police, during which he was visibly angry. He was bitter that the police were required to handover errant soldiers to the military, all the time, irrespective of their guilt. I still prevailed on him. But before he relented, he called in the investigating police officer (IPO) to brief him on the status of the case.

During the brief, the IPO displayed gruesome pictorial evidence of his late gang members and invited me to accompany him and the suspect to recover stashed arms. We drove along Gumel road and got to an expansive land with a perimeter fence. The handcuffed soldier then led the team along the fence where he indicated a hole from which a double-barreled gun was recovered.

I was flustered by this damning evidence. It was now apparent that a new trend had emerged by which military personnel became actively involved in violent criminal activities, possibly due to their poor emoluments and lack of welfare schemes.

I returned from the state police command without the soldier because the IPO pleaded for more time to wrap-up his investigation. I could not say what transpired but the soldier was brought back later and locked up at the garrison guardroom instead of being handed over into the custody of MP. I was not aware and much less the rationale for this decision.

The next day the provost was authorized to investigate the allegations. It was at this point that I discovered the soldier had been in detention at the garrison guardroom. It was strange but I kept mum. I led the detectives and obtained his statement. We were done and headed back to the office when commotion broke behind us. The suspect had attempted to bolt while being led back into the guardroom.

The team joined in the pursuit, and the fleeing suspect was quickly apprehended. At which point, so many questions came to mind. Why did I suddenly get thrown out of the loop on a case I did a preliminary investigation on? Why was he kept in the custody of the garrison instead of the MP? Most importantly, he had been in custody for days before our team of investigators came, why did he not attempt to bolt before our coming? Things were not looking good.

Portentously, the BM called me the next day and blabbed endlessly about an attempted escape and verbally instructed me to hand over the suspect to the police. It was a wrong procedure because the investigation was not completed yet. Besides, he could not have instructed except the commander directed. It was obvious that he had more than a passing interest in the suspect.

I just ignored him and continued my investigation. Moreover, the soldier was not in my custody but once the investigation was completed, I needed to seek further directives from the appropriate authority. Therefore, I refused to yield to someone attempting to obstruct my inquiry. The next morning, he ordered my detention. As my senior, he could if it were justified. I stayed overnight at the mess because it was authorized to detain an individual for twenty-four hours.

I could see that he thrived on randomness but was not conversant with the extant law. When the permissible time elapsed, I went to his house and opposed him. I acknowledged his powers to detain me but not endlessly and that I was going to report him for obstruction of a provost officer. He was so peeved at the time I left.

Coincidentally, both of us headed for the commander's residence and arrived minutes apart. The substance of the ballyhoo was my insistence on observing the proper procedure to safeguard myself, and by extension, the command, against any untoward development. The commander ordered for my release because as a provost officer, I could not be detained beyond the lawful time without consequences.

It was obvious that the soldier's case had generated so much negative energy and I wanted to get done with it. When the commander instructed finally, I handed over the soldier to the State Police Command. Days later, we got the news that the soldier was extra-judicially murdered. It was his cross to bear.

Animal Letters

In the service, there were provisions to lay complaints and, or seek redress. An individual could verbally ask to interview a superior or write formally to apply for same. However, for unknown reasons, personnel resorted to writing anonymous letters which were known as Animal Letter.

Soldiers originated most animal letters. The matters raised could bear elements of truth but were typically garnished or embellished with falsehoods. Even more, they were appended with false names and addresses. These types wanted to benefit from anonymity. But the cardinal rule in law was that whoever made allegations had the onus of proof. This was what these letters avoided and unfortunately, the authorities took these letters seriously.

In 1999, my season of animal letter came as I was called by the intelligence officer (IO) and handed a letter to read and reply to allegations raised therein. I asked that a copy be made for me to allow for a studied response. He declined and I also refused to comment on the letter. It was only logical that, if someone took time to construct a damning letter, enough time should be given to respondents too.

The IO may have reported my response to whoever authorized the investigation. The next action was a Board of Inquiry (BOI). This was a team composed for formal fact-finding. However, I was not bothered because I knew that a BOI should not be instituted because of an anonymous letter.

The petition was about a litany of alleged infractions I had committed in my unit. The claims were so outrageous as to excite indignation from any normal person or organization, but we were not dealing with regular individuals nor everyday situation. At the point I stood before the board to testify, it had already gotten testimonies from my soldiers, and I was setup to incriminate myself.

My opening statement deflated the work of the board. I told the board directly that I was not obliged to make any statement since an anonymous letter was not a subject of inquiry. I further reiterated that I would only address what I knew about, and not speculations. By the time we got half-way through the session, the board had lost steam and were engaged in fishing for facts and details. I declined response to almost half of their meaningless questions and insisted that the author was in a better position to give details of the allegation he had made, that I would not make it easy for anyone to benefit from their mischief.

At the end of the day, a poorly crafted report was submitted but it never saw the light of the day. I suspected a particular soldier, but let it be. But again, another animal letter came and this time it was directed against the brigade commander. I quickly had the soldier arrested and alerted the command that he could help with investigation. Funnily, it was declined for whatever reason. So much for double standards. Much later, during a PM(A) Annual Conference, I repeatedly asked about the status of animal letters, and nobody paid attention because I wanted to elicit an official position on this edgy matter, at a place that all provost officers were assembled.

A Dreaded Detainee

On 21 October 1998, Major Hamza Al-Mustapha, the former Chief Security Officer (CSO), to the late General Sani Abacha was arrested at Enugu where he was temporarily deployed after the death of his principal. A week later, he was brought to Kano and handed over to me as the OC MP. The team was led by the commanders of 1 Division Provost and Intelligence Groups.[1]

They were in Kano to search the residences of late General Abacha and his former CSO. Both houses were in the same neighbourhood on Gidado Road in the Nasarawa area of Kano metropolis. I took the high value detainee into custody.

However, during the handing and taking over rites, both commanders were full of threats of dire consequences should the detainee escape. They reminded me it was a serious national security matter, and the implications would be inconceivable. The duo further warned that the presence of the subject should not be leaked to anyone, especially the press. All the threats were unnecessary because as a provost officer, a detainee was a detainee irrespective of his status. Even more, I was not so undiscerning as not to classify and escalate the level of security around such a high value prisoner.

My main task was the custody of the prisoner overnight. So, apart from an armed retinue of my MP soldiers, a larger protection party was provided by Garrison troops. The culprit was held at 3 Brigade Officers' Mess at Bukavu Barracks. I also secured the former CSO's house overnight prior to its search.

The next morning, there was a long delay before the team leaders arrived for the search. The intelligence commander did not show up as it was claimed he had a runny stomach. It looked suspiciously sudden. The detainee was of the same service branch with the commander though. My colleague declined to accompany the search party as well for whatever nebulous reasons.

It was known that both commanders were contemporaries of the former CSO at the Academy. But unstated was the fact that they dreaded him. It was evident that self-preservation prevented both from being party to the physical searches. Although, technically a detainee, given his much-vaunted legendary web, he could still be lethal to these senior officers. Hence, the command of the search party devolved to yours truly.

I was considered an insignificant pawn that could be sacrificed. Since there was nothing at stake to induce fear in me, I carried on as there was nothing special nor personal but a routine task. So, I led the team to the houses of the late C-in-C and his former CSO.

The team searched the former CSO's house first because it was the smaller of the two and few items like ammo and documents were picked up there and proceeded to the late C-in-C's house, a vast stone compound, which made it more difficult to even decide where to start. The search itself was short indeed because after only a couple of minutes at the boy's quarter, it was called off.

Afterwards, the team then proceeded to Bompai in a different district of town and combed the house of the younger brother to the former CSO. Here too, nothing incriminating was found, and the search party retired to the barracks. The next planned action was to prepare for a trip out of town to Nguru, to search the former CSO's ancestral home.

Later that evening after the searches, my group commander called me aside. I could see he was agitated and livid that a local hound had picked up the news of the former CSO's detention and published it.

Therefore, he wanted to know if I knew who leaked the information. I answered in the negative, but he was not convinced.

The next morning, we got to Nguru and searched an undeveloped plot of land and came back empty handed. The team slept over in Kano and left for Abuja where I handed over the detainee to Guards Brigade Provost. It was on my way out that my group commander delivered a coup de grace. I was to report to the mess on arrival at Kano, i.e., I was to be detained.

I was infuriated by this directive. To think that such a cowardly senior officer who could not look a detainee in the eye was posturing. First, just like them, I was not comfortable with such a dangerous detainee in my custody. I had kept a sleepless watch over him, to ensure that no funny stories arose. Perhaps, he thought the detention of the former CSO was a secret. So, to which point did he trace the leak? Was it at Enugu, Kaduna, or Kano? His suspicions were unfounded and detention order quite an unnecessary abuse of power. I was released after forty-eight hours.

The above incident was the last seminal event that took place while I was at 3 Brigade Kano. Afterwards, the Brigade commander, averted my eyes when he spoke to me. On another occasion, I could see him whispering to my group commander (his village man), while stealing stares at me. They were not within earshot, but I suspected he gossiped about me, about what things he could not say in front of me.

A Decision to Retire

Meanwhile, every passing day, I contemplated my service in the army and became increasingly irritated and unhappy. I began to question the rationality of remaining within an enclave that was not truthful to its ethos. From all perspectives, I found my continued service as a soldier less and less appealing. In all my dealings, I never contemplated the possibility of being referred to as a model of a bad character. I took a decision; I wanted out and wrote for voluntary retirement.

On receipt of the notification, I was invited to Lagos to interact with the PM. The interview took place in company of staff officers at HQ NACMP. During the session, some were alarmed especially, as they could not muster courage to even contemplate retirement. One of them missed the drift and tended to be intimidatory. Such self-conceit I had never seen before. To sum up, my application was denied. Not long after, I was posted out from 3 Brigade to NASMP for a second spell.

My desire to retire voluntarily from the service was not an isolated case. Coincidentally, a couple of my course mates also applied to leave about the same time. Everyone had their reason for wanting out or remaining in the service. We were not impatient or not enduring, some may have been more elastic, but the fact that so many younger officers were applying to leave attracted the attention of the authorities. I was denied my wish and to stem the tide, an embargo was placed on all retirements, and thereafter, I remained in service for another ten years.

Note

(1). www.thisdaylive.com (4 June 2017).

Being decorated Lieutenant 1994

Chapter Twenty-Four

Warehoused: 1999-2004

I reported to NASMP for a second tour of duty in July 1999. It was a familiar ground as my mother unit. I should have been proud that I came back there but I was not. My first time around was a routine deployment, but the second coming was a slight. It followed a pattern of posting-in folks that were disagreeable elsewhere.

I took time to ponder over the contending issues revolving around me and concluded that I was not an intractable officer, but then in my line of duty which dealt with getting people into or out of trouble, demanded a degree of fairness and independent judgment. I understood what constituted lawful order and was averse to any form of invasiveness and herd mentality. On many occasions, from being an impartial detective, I ended up with ill will towards me owing to the wrong notion that if a superior was mad at an officer or a soldier over some alleged infraction, it indeed became an offence which was not. Or even worse, culprits expected me to vitiate their culpability based on camaraderie.

Unfortunately, people in their vengeful rage forgot that offences were defined by statutes and not by the peevishness of superiors. Even more, for an act or omission to approximate an offence, certain unassailable facts needed to be proved, not mere conjectures. Accordingly, at all the units I served, I made it clear that it was not my responsibility to manufacture guilt by association, just to assuage grumpiness.

Furthermore, my operative principle was that no individual was perfect. Everyone had their rough edges, although others possessed barbs. Hence, I was never condemnatory of anyone just because a certain group was inclined to do so. I observed that officers and soldiers alike suffered indignity and loss of self-esteem because of a conspiracy to make them feel worthless.

Again, I was inclined to say my mind. I never shied away from making known my opinion on any subject matter, whether in the line of duty or mere perception. Just because exchanges in military circles were of a drab call and response pattern, was not enough to validate the frivolity of superiors. From this posture and simple working guide I crafted for myself, I was perceived as impossible and not negotiable. Hence, it was contrived that I should be warehoused at NASMP, the dumping ground for MP refuseniks.

Redundancy

My personal disposition was to be eternally cheerful. More like a survival mechanism, I never allowed anyone or a group, to overwhelm my spirit of happiness. More so, I did not contrive to grouse over any matter, especially if I had no control over its product. Therefore, I resumed at my new unit in high spirit.

However, after two weeks at NASMP, I noticed that I was not assigned any tasks nor featured for lectures. I demanded to know from the Courses Coordinator what it was that I was being kept idle. It was then that he divulged that it was the Commandant's directives.

What an order. What this meant was that long before I reported I had been maligned and a decision was reached that I should not be tasked and left redundant. Ordinarily, I found the idea of being left indolent quite appealing. For as far as it took nothing from me, it could as well persist if the author so wished. But instinctively, I was determined to ensure such a meaningless order was not left unchallenged, otherwise the so-called commandant might as well imagine he possessed limitless powers.

The Commandant I met on my second coming to NASMP was one of my former instructors at the Academy. An adept power monger, he barely escaped being caught into the dragnet of the Orkar coup of 1990 as a mutineer. He was a very haughty individual that managed to hang around the corridors of power for the rest of his career.

The senior officer was an epitome of pretension and eye service in its worst form. A very sly individual, he cultivated a false mien of conviviality and finesse and cast himself in the mould of a supportive commander and went out of his way to court adulation from his superiors and subordinates alike. In truth, he was an ardent slave driver that pushed colleagues to toil laboriously so he could take the glory. Just a little scratch on him and it exposed a malicious social climber and a wannabe. I remembered all these attributes as I entered his office.

On enquiry, he confirmed that he gave the directive and insisted that the reports he got about me were such that he would not allow me to do any material damage to the standard of the school. The sum of his assessment was that I was an unproductive lout. Someone had flagged me as incompetent.

After the exchange, my misgivings about him were reinforced. He had been persuaded to believe my so-called ineptitude without proof. This was the typical way the service operated, i.e., there was abundance of derisiveness, and deliberate slanders to deflect opportunities, favours and appointments from others.

"Sir, all these stories you were told are not true. Even I were to concede everything that may have been said, I do not consider myself incompetent since I approached all tasks assigned to me to the best of my ability. More importantly, I had been an instructor here before now. In fact, the school was my mother unit." I closed my testament. It took supreme restraint to stop myself from making snide remarks that could escalate the interface.

"Oh, really? You have been here previously? Nobody told me about that." He appeared genuinely surprised. It was not a strange revelation because it was a technique deployed by detractors, i.e., to propagate half-truths or embellished details about people behind them. I could see he became pensive.

"So, why did you come to me" he blurted. I could see too from his countenance that he was reviewing the falsehoods about me.

"I came to let you know about my primary competence as an instructor." I said this inoffensively even though I was at liberty to give it an added bite like, his directive was as ill-informed as it was baseless.

"It is ok. I was told so much about you. The things said were quite ridiculous. But all that is in the past. Now that you are here, you have an opportunity to prove yourself." He said closing the interview.

"You will be programmed for a lecture to confirm what you have said about yourself. However, before you deliver the lecture, prepare a lesson note for my perusal." It was an ultimate expression of distrust. I did and he approved and subsequently, I was regularly tasked.

My interaction with the Commandant threw up several issues. To begin with, I was not to freely express my competence at the workplace but attempt to be falsely impressive. Even more, no matter what I did, I was not trusted. Consequently, my tour of duty was aggregated to being monitored for negative authentication.

In any case, I applied myself to assigned tasks without any desire to be validated by anyone because I had a responsibility to be truthful to myself and not to any superfluous snoops that were not any better. Always, the measure of my accomplishments would be validated by myself. Once I adopted this benchmark, I began to experience an inner peace and enhanced productivity.

An Insightful Conference

The school hosted the PM(A) Conference in the year 2000, which provided the Commandant an opportunity to practice his showmanship. As preparations for the event were stepped up, all other routine activities were subdued to ensure a hitch-free conference. To achieve this objective, individual instructors and staff officers were assigned specific roles and I was tasked with signposting and demonstrations.

When the conference eventually began, apart from executing my roles satisfactorily, I persistently asked tough questions that were deflected or ignored. My intention was to purge the branch of its contradictions given the enormous powers it wielded on the service in general. I tried not only to exasperate the assembly, but to coax the branch into recognizing its foibles. In fact, drawing from the feelings of injuries unjustly inflicted on me, I made sure to deploy maximum nuisance during the conference and was eternally happy with my performance.

During an intermission, the PM called me aside. "Gberikon, I thought they said you are not capable of doing anything." He probed obviously impressed with my contributions at the conference. It was an opportunity to market myself and I did.

"PM sir, as you could see, it is not true. I have always tried my best. I do not know where that wrong impression was coming from." I kept it short and straight to the point. He nodded and dismissed me. I felt this short private interrogative, coming from the head of my service branch himself was a redeeming act. If I had presumed that the present dissonance around me was isolated, then I was given a peek into the fact that it was escalated to the highest echelon. In short, it was an affirmation of the slander on my person. Uncharacteristically, military men gossiped to no end.

I felt elated with my triumph. I had commandeered the conference and owned it. It was a great relief that I rubbed the noses of pretenders to excellence in the ground and made it obvious to all. Two years down the line at NASMP, I was nominated to attend the Junior Staff Course.

Junior Staff Course

In January 2001, I reported for Junior Course No. 51/01. This was a low-level staff course. The course marked a gradual climb to the upper echelons of the service. It was a mandatory course that prepared officers in diverse roles as commanders and support staff officers. I navigated my way through the course. Graciously, the course ended. However, I recognized I was a non-performing student. Although, I thought I would be posted out of NASMP, which was a normal practice after such courses, I was retained at the school for another three years.

The Zaki-Biam Massacre 2001

Historically, the Benue valley has been one of the most contested spaces in contemporary Nigeria. Its location in central Nigeria was the meeting point between the arid Sahel of the north and the dense forest to the south. Its lush green and richly endowed landscape supported agriculture, fishing and livestock tending. The region was also an abode to diverse peoples which contributed to conflicts and correlated insecurity in the region.

Even though within its boundaries there was enough resources to cater to all, for a long time, inter-ethnic strife turned the territory into a war zone over borders and land resources. At any given time therefore, diverse groups were locked in violent clashes. This was the backdrop to the instability in the Benue Valley.

Habitually though, communities adjoining Benue State along with Fulani herders have had land claims with demographic designs to uproot or decimate the Tiv people, the single most populous group in the region, especially in Nasarawa, Plateau, Taraba and Cross River states. This was and is the main cause of the prevailing insecurity and the presence of large numbers of internally displaced persons (IDPs) in the general locality.

Furthermore, the situation was compounded by the existence of tribal militias which began life as vigilante groups, armed and supported by communities as their claws. Sadly though, they became unruly and took on a life of their own away from the purpose they were created.

While on a leave pass, I visited my hometown, and everywhere, I saw armed men with diverse types of small firearms. It was strange because these goons open-carried their weapons. It was obviously a prelude to anarchy.

Besides, when I interacted with my armed "brothers", the stories I heard were unsettling. Afterwards, they sent me on an "errand" to NA troops, that they were ready for them. This was on account of soldiers' alleged complicity that escalated the crisis over the years. According to the locals, armed men in military uniforms attacked Tiv communities. So, there were strong suspicions that elements of the military supported their Jukun rivals.

Even more worrying was the fact that soldiers had a Forward Operations Base (FOB) at Wukari (a Jukun town) since 1990, without any corresponding deployment on the Benue side. Unfortunately, reported incidents included Tiv settlements attacked by Jukun militia while accompanied by soldiers. Either way, there were misgivings about the troops' roles in the intractable crisis over the years.

Accordingly, when I returned to the unit, I diligently briefed the commandant on the situation. Unfortunately, on 11 October 2001, less than a week after my return, the local militia struck. From home, someone called with info that a couple of soldiers had been abducted by unknown gunmen at Vaase village along Wukari-Agasha road.[1] Instinctively, I knew that the affair would not end well. By the next morning, nineteen mutilated bodies, presumed to be the abducted soldiers were found at RCM Primary School Zaki Biam, about thirty-five kilometres away from the scene of the abduction. The pictures of the body parts were a gory sight, and at once excited baying for blood in reprisals.[2]

Matters were complicated as military authorities denied the presence of troops in the locality. This uncertainty reinforced the misgivings about their genuineness, given the alleged serial misconduct and complicity of the so-called troops. Within hours, the military retracted their earlier rebuttal and started precipitate actions that culminated in the 2001 Zaki-Biam massacre by NA troops.[3]

The NA deployed blocking forces at Katsina Ala and dominated Logo and Ukum local councils far beyond Zaki Biam where the soldiers were allegedly butchered. On 22 October 2001, the deceased were buried in Abuja, and during the funeral, President Obasanjo's orders and inflammatory remarks incited a reprisal by the military.[4]

Consequently, between 23-25 October 2001, there was a decimation as NA troops executed hundreds of unarmed Tiv civilians. By the time the troops withdrew, they left in their trail scorched hulks of Zaki Biam and other settlements including Gbeji, Vaase, Anyiin, Iorja, Sankera and Kyado. Also, inexplicably, Tse-Adoor, over fifteen kilometres away from Zaki Biam, the home of a former Army Chief, General Victor Malu, was invaded and demolished.[5]

While the troops were stumping innocent and unarmed Tiv villagers, in chorus, other ethnic groups took advantage to implement a grand agenda of displacement and destruction. They set upon their hounded and unprotected Tiv neighbours, killed, burnt homesteads, and looted harvests in four local government areas in Nasarawa state namely Doma, Keana, Awe and Obi. Also, the widespread mayhem was extended to eight councils including Ibi, Bali, Donga, Gassol, Takum, Ussa, Wukari and parts of Gashaka in Taraba state.

When an outcry broke out against the barbaric killings, locally and internationally, the NA and the federal government indulged in a shameful and bizarre posturing. Both claimed such an incident never occurred. It was not until on 6 November 2007, that the then Chief of Army Staff, Lt Gen Luka Yusuf publicly apologized to the people of Benue State for the killings. Graciously too, President Umaru Yar'adua also visited the state and personally apologized on behalf of the federal government of Nigeria.[6] However, my focus was about an exchange that I had with the brigade commander that orchestrated the reprisal at the graduation ceremony of Operation Focus Relief at Serti.

Operation Focus Relief

Operation Focus Relief was a fallout of Nigeria's stellar performance in the ECOMOG meatgrinders in Liberia and Sierra Leone in the 1990s. Apart from being the first regional attempt at a peacekeeping mission, it was the pivotal role of Nigerian troops that intrigued international observers. Despite the apparent glitches, ECOWAS had instituted a new equation in the international system.

So, two years into Nigeria's new democratic dispensation, the United States of America offered to re-train segments of her troops. However, the US facilitators demanded for too many details on the current state of the Nigerian Army that the motives became debatable. These outlandish demands did not sit well with the then army chief, Lt Gen SVL Malu. The chief was not averse to training support but not inclined to accept the excesses and impertinence of the Americans. The argument was that the Americans could not teach Nigerian troops how to be soldiers but could provide logistics support which was the service's main handicap.

The Hype About Focus Relief

Overtly, the boondoggle's primary goal was to equip and train soldiers from Nigeria, Ghana, and Senegal to conduct peace-enforcement operations in Sierra Leone. The training was set to last ten weeks during which participants received uniforms, helmets, web equipment, ponchos, canteens, entrenching tools and new rifles.[7]

Even though, the training took place at 20 Battalion location, the composition of troops was drawn from all arms across different formations. When a firm date was scheduled, nominees for the training assembled. At full mustered strength, it was twenty officers by eight hundred (20 x 800) soldiers.

A Needless Controversy

At first, I was not even nominated as a participant but a substitute candidate since the officer chosen was indisposed. Therefore, I came into camp a little late. Luckily, the tyraining was on hold due to the late arrival of the team of American instructors and kits required for the training at the remote location.

When I left Zaria to marry up with the rest of the trainees, I was penniless. Being flat broke was a staple for me. So, when I arrived the training location and discovered I would be responsible for my upkeep for the next ten weeks, which would be difficult without extra planning, I returned to my unit to shore up my finances. It was while I was away that an unnecessary controversy reared its head.

Typically, units nominated to participate in peace support operations were complementary in nature, i.e., they incorporated all branches of the service and nominees came through the service branches. Although, 20 Battalion was under an armoured brigade, every service branch was trawled to couple a full composite battalion for which I was designated as Officer Commanding the Provost Detachment.

Even so, before I arrived and hurriedly left, soldiers of the proposed detachment were already on the ground. I was later informed that a number were returned to unit because the MP slots had already been filled, or so it was claimed. It was not an idea that should have been thought of in the first place because it was a crude attempt at seizing slots meant for the MP because the unit was projected for a UN mission.

Someone might have reported the attempted heist. But in all honesty, I was not aware of the affair. Nevertheless, it was not even my style. If I had been aware of the attempt, I would have approached the unit command and informed it of the fallout of such an indiscretion. These insinuations were made behind me, so I allowed the gossip to fizzle out.

By now, it was clear that I had a magnetic pull towards tempests. I could not understand why someone failed at their smoke and mirrors, and I still got blamed. Since it was a mere speculation, I did not bother myself any further.

Training Sites

Whilst in Nigeria, the Americans set-up shops at 20 Battalion Serti, 222 Battalion Ilorin and 1 Battalion Birnin Kebbi. At each of these locations, a self-contained camp was setup and run by Pacific Architects and Engineers (PAE), a military contracting company.[8] These camps were effectively inviolate American territories for the duration of the training. Except for a couple of stands outside, most training activities took place within the barracks.

Training Activities

The US Army training system was not markedly different from what we were used to. Apart from enhanced gadgetry, the human nuances were the same. For instance, within a couple of days of arriving Serti, the US soldiers promptly produced satellite enhanced maps of the general area.

A typical training day started as early as 0600hrs. By then, a couple of Dracula trucks were lined up to convey troops to the main training area which was about three kilometres away. Given the number of soldiers to be moved, it took about two hours. However, this logjam was solved in a standard Nigerian Army style. Soldiers were simply ordered to find their way to the training area unfailingly by 0700hrs. How this was accomplished was not anybody's business and all complied.

Apart from uniforms and web equipment, the Op Focus Relief never threw up anything spectacular. The main difference was the military technology available to both armies. For instance, during Map Reading exercises, the Americans fixed their targets within a 1000-metre radius, while we narrowed ours to one hundred metres. The former was primed to be engaged by heavier guns or air assault, while the latter was marked to be neutralized through murderous skirmishing by foot soldiers.

Food and Water Discipline

At the Serti location, the trainees were not catered for throughout the duration of the training. Not even water was provided. In the intense heat, the Americans went everywhere with and intermittently sipped from hydration packs. During intermissions, officers and soldiers, looked for the nearest tree shed and napped while our American instructors choked on burgers and drowned on juices. By lunch breaks, they retired to their camps while their charges were besieged by barrack women turned opportunistic food venders at the training grounds.

The Americans instructors observed and asked questions and were lamely told that the NA practiced food and water discipline. A very watery response indeed. Of course, they took our ridiculous excuses with a pinch of salt but were still concerned and insisted that it was important that troops rehydrated in the intense heat.

Undoubtedly, we could not tell them our top guns were an amoral and parsimonious lot whose avarice could not be satiated. The rationale was that being nominated as participants at the training alone was a special privilege to be grateful for and nothing was to be demanded in return. Otherwise, nothing explained a situation by which a unit fully mustered with troops drawn from far-flung locations, were not catered for.

Poor Safety Practices

As the training progressed, we observed the US troops as much as they did us. First, just like the NA, most of the instructors were NCOs. In fact, we got to know that they were retirees re-engaged as contract staff. So, apart from differences in few key terms, there was communication.

During range classification, we noticed that the targets were close to the firers. While we were used to firing at ranges up to one through two hundred metres with twenty rounds of ammo at any given time, the American instructors gave out boxes of ammo for continuous firing at a range of 50metres only. At the end of the range classification, unlike us, they never bothered to account for nor recover expended shells

More importantly, we were issued new AK47 rifles which we zeroed. This critical procedure was meant to calibrate a new weapon to ensure its optimum performance. Although we were taught about this procedure as trainees, we finally got to do it with new rifles.

It was at the stage of firing heavier calibre weapons that we observed poor safety practices by the American trainers. The weapon at the range was a single-use light anti-tank rocket grenade. It was of a type not found in our inventory.

The target was a rocky bluff of an abandoned quarry, and it was being fired at, from a fifty-metre distance. Apart from the massive blast from the projectiles, the likelihood of a ricochet or broadcast of fragments from the exploded bombs was very real. It was simply unsafe.

During the firing, one of the bombs failed to explode and activities were suspended. By Nigerian Army standard practice, the site would have been barricaded and evacuated immediately. Afterwards, ordnance explosive disposal technicians would have executed elaborate recovery deploying robotic tools or have it detonated in situ.

Yet, we were alarmed as a clutch of instructors advanced towards the unexploded bomb. Perhaps, since ours was a primitive army, its training and procedures took precaution with arms and pyrotechnics. Even still, the way those Americans confidently walked towards that lethal piece, we assumed that they were sure of its safety. Just a few metres away, one of them tripped over rubbles and set off a loud blast.

The bomb exploded and ripped through the American instructors. One of them took a direct hit and others were peppered with fragments. It was a tragic and sad occurrence, but without gloating over the incident, those instructors were simply careless. The haste towards unexploded ordnance arose from entrenched practices or insouciance.

It was so distressing that one of the instructors lost his life and others survived with injuries and were evacuated back to the US. This marked the end of any live firing during the training. Later a team from the US Army came to the scene of the incident to investigate. It was an unfortunate occurrence, and we all wished it had panned out differently.

End of Training

In time, the ten-week training ended. The closing ceremony was scheduled and the Commander, 23 Armoured Brigade Yola, the host formation, was the guest of honour. After the parade and fanfare, officers retired to the Officers' Mess for refreshments. It was at this point that the Commander called me out. But a little background to the altercation would suffice.

An Altercation with a Commander

When I arrived Serti, I just touched down and took off immediately. However, on my way back to 20 Battalion location, I overtook low-load transporters conveying recce and light armoured vehicles from Bauchi towards Jalingo. I knew instinctively where they were headed to.

Shortly after, the Zaki Biam reprisals began. Although Serti was over a hundred-fifty kilometres from the nearest targets being hit, its ripples were felt even in the town as Tiv villages in Gashaka council were concurrently under attack by Fulani and other ethnic militias. As a result, multitudes of Tiv folks were displaced and took refuge at Serti. Even worse for me, my hometown, Kyado, was repeatedly hit and my father's homestead razed to the ground.

It was apparent that the troops were on a mission to inflict death and pains on a vast region instead of fishing out the perpetrators from the innocents. It was futile to sermonize at this point because the spirit of vengeance engendered by a bellicose president had taken hold. Far worse, I seethed as colleagues made jokes out of my Tiv people.

The reprisals were ongoing when an assessment team from the host brigade came visiting the training location. I recall I was accommodated in a shared apartment. One of the visiting team members came to spend time with the younger officers that were my pad mates. The lieutenant was introduced as an Intelligence Officer. While he was regaling his mates with combined untruths and fanciful extrapolations to justify the ongoing reprisals, he dropped the name of my hometown.

I interjected and let him know that is where I was from. Then the young reptilian parvenu delivered a gross fabrication unsurpassed in falsehood. According to him, the locals of Kyado village had locked up Muslims in a mosque during prayers and set fire to it.

I was alarmed that this kind of deliberate fabrication emanated from an officer that should provide actionable intelligence. I did not pander him and told him to his face that he was a liar from the pit of hell. I went further and lectured him that as a young officer, he had started on a wrong trajectory by dissembling. The villain felt bruised and reported our exchange to the brigade commander.

Accordingly, while at the mess, midway into the mess chit-chat, the senior officer cleared his throat and demanded.
"Who is the MP officer?" Perusing the surrounding menacingly with a heavyset face. "Here, sir." I raised my hand expecting a garland of flowers but did not get any. "Where are you from?" He resumed. "Zaria" I told him which was my unit location. "Not your unit. I meant your hometown." He guided. "I am from Kyado in Ukum Council Benue State" Always proud to enunciate my village.

"Then go and tell your people that if they try the government, they will taste its might." He went on and rambled endlessly about my interaction with the young officer days back. I allowed him to finish his sermon as I heard the hall filled with whispers.

I raised my hand to be recognized to respond, and a couple of officers attempted to hush me. I ignored them because I was not endowed with a mouth to complement the symmetry of my face. It was meant for eating and opposing vilifiers. So, I rose to my feet at the same time as I raised my hand.

"First, when I accepted a commission as an officer, I took an oath of attestation of loyalty to Nigeria. I want to affirm that right now." I commanded the attention of all and paused to marshal my thoughts.

"Secondly, If I were killed in such a gruesome manner as those nineteen soldiers, it would be reasonable that colleagues avenged my death. But if there was such action, I expected that it should be directed at the perpetrators of the brutal killing, positively identified and not to target districts indiscriminately." I was warming to my topic. But I had to watch my words too.

"Two wrongs could not make a right. As for the young officer, it was a private conversation I had with him. I did not expect him to drag it to this level. Look at him seated over there, I still stand by what I said to him, that he lied." I closed my response and sat down. There were more murmurs and the commander put a cap on the topic.

When the ceremony ended, a couple of officers attempted to talk me down. However, I declared that I was an NA officer and not a member of any tribal militia. Therefore, any attempt to harass me because of my Tiv origins would be resisted with all my might. It was a trend that was gaining traction service-wide because there were reported cases of officers and soldiers of Tiv origins being bullied on account of the Zaki Biam affair and the accompanying murderous reprisals. In fact, the authorities had to write to warn against such insolence which became widespread.

On Butchery and Reprisals

With the benefit of hindsight, it must be declared unequivocally that the troops had it coming especially every time they lowered their guard in volatile areas. To start with, they were always deployed without considerations of fairness. On occasions, if there was a crisis in an area, soldiers would be deployed on one divide, akin to taking sides.

Often too, they were deployed without sustenance allowances. Although, the stipends trickled in, the sums were too meagre and came too late in the day, as they lived off the host communities. In this way, local factors like council chairpersons, traditional rulers, politicians, and wealthy individuals, threw crumbs at them and easily compromised their neutrality.

Furthermore, it was like an unwritten rule as troops deployed on internal security duties especially at scenes of crises where the Tiv people were involved became parties to the conflict instead of impartial respondents. This was true of other security agencies as well. In fact, the role of the formation and units located at Doma, Takum and new Otukpo barracks followed the same pattern of partisan meddlesomeness.

In a like manner, the NA troops accepted the fallacy that Tiv people occurred only in Benue State of Nigeria which was not true. This people domiciled astride the lower through middle reaches of River Benue and its valley and Northwestern Cameroon. The problems of aboriginals and settlers and land rights against the Tiv in the Benue valley were accentuated by gerrymandering or state creation which started long before 1976.

When new states were created from the above date, they did not follow historical contiguity. For instance, the Wukari Federation was excised from the Lower Benue Province and amalgamated with the old Muri Province in Gongola State, instead of joining their neighbours in Benue State. In its place, the Igala Division of Kabba Province was transferred to Benue State.

Another instance was the creation of Nasarawa States in 1996. At that time, Obi, Awe and Keana councils were ceded to Benue state because of the high population of Tiv people in those localities but inexplicably it was later rescinded. Either way, the Tiv people retained a majority population-wise in Benue, Taraba and Nasarawa states which engendered endless disputations.[10]

Besides, troops deployed to unstable security areas were always distracted as they wrongly assumed that only soldiers bore superior arms. So, instead of being wary and vigilant, they were besotted chasing lasses and blocked roads to extort money from motorists and locals. These acts did not endear them to their hosts. Otherwise, how the soldiers deployed in the general area of Wukari since 1990, missed out on the fact that by 2001, the locals were carrying small arms in profusion, was inexcusable.

Worse still, there was a conspicuous failure of intelligence. If the troops deployed to crises zones mined intelligence, they would not fall prey to surprises. It was evident that those soldiers were oblivious of the magnitude or intensity of the deadly crisis at Wukari then. If there was any semblance of intelligence at all, they would have known that so much small arms were in the hands of the locals.

Finally, how could a ragtag militia ambush and seize an officer and eighteen armed regular soldiers? What transpired said much about the state of readiness of the troops at that point in time and an almost null state of environmental awareness. However, no matter the lapses exhibited by the troops; it was not enough to butcher them in such a grisly manner. So also, was it wrong for the NA, to initiate scorched earth depredations against three councils because of an inexcusable failure on the part of its troops. Soon, the end of training formalities was done with, and the troops dispersed to await mustering and induction into United Nations Mission in Sierra Leone (UNAMSIL), and it would take another eight months before this happened.

Notes
(1-3) www.vanguargngr.com.
(4-9)Wikipedia.com.

Basawa 2000

Chapter Twenty-Five

UNAMSIL

In 1991, the Republic of Sierra Leone was plunged into a civil war, when a former army corporal, Foday Sankoh, and his Revolutionary United Front (RUF), began a campaign against President Joseph Momoh. It was a brutal war characterized by widespread mayhem, limb severing and gross violations of human rights.[1] Unfortunately, all diplomatic efforts to resolve the protracted impasse that led to the war were unsuccessful.

The war escalated and the atrocities increased exponentially, especially after the overthrow of President Tejan Kabbah by Major Johnny Paul Koroma. The dire situation led ECOWAS to review the mandate of its ongoing ECOMOG mission in Liberia to include Sierra Leone in 1997. Yet, the bloodshed persisted until the UN intervened in 1998.

On 13 July 1998, the UN Security Council at its 3902nd meeting adopted Resolution 1181 on the situation with a provision for the deployment of the United Nations Observer Mission in Sierra Leone (UNOMSIL). The mandate was to monitor compliance with the terms of ceasefire stipulated by various peace agreements, but little was achieved.[3]

Again, in May 1999, another ceasefire was negotiated in Freetown, and it was hoped that the civil war would end soon. More negotiations in Lomé by July 1999 led to a peace agreement, under which the RUF received posts in government and assurances of non-prosecution for war crimes.[4] Even more, the Security Council set up another mission, the United Nations Mission in Sierra Leone (UNAMSIL) on 22 October 1999.

Its mandate was to cooperate with the government and the other parties to implement the Lome Peace Agreement and undertake disarmament, demobilization, and reintegration. However, the mission remained ineffectual, which prompted multiple reviews including expanded size, then and only then were UN troops able to deploy peacefully for the first time in rebel-held territory.[5]

Accordingly, 20 Battalion was inducted into the United Nations Mission in Sierra Leone as Nigerian Battalion 14 (NIBATT 14 UNAMSIL), from 14 Aug 2002 through 31 Oct 2003 and I commanded the Provost Detachment. At this point in time, the UN intervention had transitioned from the war-fighting peace-enforcement of ECOMOG days, to peacebuilding and consolidation.

Even then, the intense bitterness was palpable as Sierra Leoneans were unforgiving to themselves. Most citizens, except the women and children, expressed little gratitude to those that interceded to stop the carnage in that country. For instance, Nigerian soldiers were hated, or more like feared but tolerated because of their reciprocal use of extreme violence when it became necessary. It was curious when Sierra Leonean men moaned that Nigerians came to take their womenfolk. It was such a crazy thing to imagine. It was like, who travels thousands of kilometres to take part in a brutal war, just to take women when there were more delectable ladies back home.

Worse still, the Sierra Leoneans erroneously assumed that the funds spent on UN peacekeepers were misapplied, as they were meant for their wellbeing. Where they got such inciting fantasy could not be known. On occasions, they were uncooperative and hostile to the peacekeepers. It was only war-weariness and an aggressive posture that saved the mission.

Furthermore, for all its sacrifices, Nigeria neither demanded immediate benefits, nor guarantees of a future recompense. All the charitable deeds were offered gratis to an ungrateful lot. Instead, Nigeria endured campaigns of calumny by some UN elements and citizens of Sierra Leone, as a lot of attention was focused on the alleged sexual exploitation and abuse by the Nigerian troops.

Also, the UN did not give any special recognition to Nigeria regardless of her long participation and deep knowledge of the dynamics of the civil war in Sierra Leone. Hence, the country was marginally represented in UNAMSIL hierarchy but when it came to deployment of troops at hard-pressed locations, she was called upon.

Deficits

From my experiences in NIBATT 14, the Nigerian contingent had challenges. First, the country opted for wet lease of contingent-owned equipment for the mission. Under this arrangement, a country supplied all its equipment based on the UN table of equipment. The UN system of compensation was tied strictly to the serviceability of the listed equipment.

A second choice was the dry lease agreement. Under this alternative, the UN nominated or contracted a third party, who supplied and supported the equipment. Afterwards, compensations on leased equipment were deducted. In reckoning, the former received a more generous compensation than the latter.

Nonetheless, the Nigerian authorities continually opted for wet leases without a corresponding willingness to adhere to the stipulated standards. Consequently, when UN Inspection and Compliance teams visited, units borrowed equipment to display in the hope the inspection teams would not notice. Overall, Nigeria was barely adequately compensated.

Also, the allowances of Nigerian peacekeepers were always delayed. There was a clumsy arrangement in place by which funds were moved from Nigeria to the mission area and handed in cash to the units. Funnily enough, we got news of the arrival of our allowances from girls in town.

Also, in NIBATT 14, a compulsory saving scheme was set up for the troops. So, apart from Habit Allowance (the so-called Cigarette Allowance), only part of the monthly stipends was paid out to personnel. The scheme later became a sticking point because the accumulated funds got tampered with, and at the end of the mission, the beneficiaries were short paid.

Furthermore, the UN supplied logistic support to the units in terms of food, beverages, tats, and diesel. Funnily, the unit scaled the rations for individual peacekeepers which were reduced by a factor of three quarters and a bucket measure of diesel, was issued to run vehicles per week. The balance was then illegally sold off. Nothing extraordinary took place during the mission. Although, the Nigerian contingent through a combination of dereliction and avarice shuffled along, NIBATT 14's tour of duty ended after fifteen months.

Notes

(1-4). unscr.com

(5). www.digitallibrary.un.org

Chapter Twenty-Six

Ascending A Wobbly Ladder

Any soldier irrespective of background could rise above the ranks so long as he had the potential to lead. As earlier noted, each type of commission in the NA, came with different bolts and nuts vis-à-vis growth in the service. For my kind of commission, which was the regular combatant, there were hands-on upgrading courses which were commanded to advance to the next rank in seniority.

All things being equal, there was a timeline by which folks were elevated to the next rank. During my time in service, the interval was four years on the rank. If the math was summed, it was expected that by the time an individual spent thirty-four years in service, they ought to have gone through the ranks, i.e., from second lieutenant to major general. However, all things were never meant to be equal.

Therefore, as a course, we started on the same baseline from the beginning. Apart from a few colleagues who got commissioned at an earlier date, on account of being trained at Royal Military Academy Sandhurst, we had the same seniority date. Six months into commission, we were jointly and automatically promoted to the next rank, so we all maintained our precedence and progressed. However, this marked the last time we got promoted in one swoop as a group. Afterwards, we took courses and qualifying examinations to step-up to the next higher rank, and from this point too, our seniorities became staggered and cases of trailing to the ranks were recorded.

As a regular officer, it was mandatory that an officer got trained on a specialist course in their service branch along with Young Officers' Course (Infantry). The more courses one participated at, the merrier. The only snag was that, for every course attended, the individual was expected to put up stellar performance, otherwise it counted to nothing. However, there were junior, intermediate, and senior courses, relative to the rank held.

While regular officers exerted themselves and expended extra resources to attend requisite courses, the other types of commissions, especially DRC, did not attend any apart from core courses related to their service branches in conjunction with evaluation reports. However, despite the dichotomy, they held appointments and positions, in direct competition with the regular officers.

Also reckoned for promotion was the annual Performance Evaluation Reports (PER). Commanders were obligated to evaluated officers under their command annually. The format was a pro-forma booklet with sections on personal data, current medical status, physical tests, and a general assessment on performances, during a year under review.

Its main report was a pen-picture on an individual by a reporting officer. Each of the queries were weighted in points and the officers reported upon were expected to counter endorse such reports. It was that simple but equally a very subjective evaluation system I had ever encountered in any organization. It was a gap exploited by machinates, ethnic jingoists, chauvinists, and conceited superiors to shore up acolytes and mar non-friendly individuals and those out of favour.

Promotion and qualifying examinations were a third leg of the tripod. All exams were conducted by HQ Training and Doctrine Command (TRADOC). The first in the series was Lieutenant to Captain Practical Promotion Examinations (LCPPE). I recall mine was held at Dutsin Ma in 1994. I performed so well and ranked in the top ten out of over two hundred candidates. It was during this exam too that one of the honourees during our POP, a Sword of Honour awardee failed. I was seated close to him when the results were called, the officer almost fainted after the pronouncement.

Captain to Major Qualifying Exams

In step, the Captain to Major Staff Course Qualifying Exams came up. It was an exam that qualified candidates to participate at the senior staff course. Just like previous exams, my bosom friend, Rotgak, came and dragged me along for the promotion cadre course. He clearly understood the system better than I since he was an Ex-Jam. Always, he made it a point to apprise me of the latest events. This time too, he came for me at Kano, and we took off to Bauchi.

Cadre Courses

For promotion exams, the service branches were expected to organize cadre courses to prepare their officers. These were usually run like routine courses but tailored specifically to the syllabus of each exam. Seasonally, cadre courses were held at 82 Division Enugu, Infantry Corps Centre and School Jaji, Nigerian Army School of Education Ilorin and Armoured Corps Centre and School Bauchi. Nonetheless, the Bauchi centre was the most proficient in terms of intensity of organization and thus became the most subscribed. So, apart from private studies, those cadre instructions held in formal classroom settings reinforced our knowledge.

A valid unit leave pass was the only requirement to be enrolled on the cadre course. Once an officer got to the Armoured Corps Centre and School at Bauchi, he only needed to append his name to a register and that was it. The school then took over the programming and conduct of the course from there.

Nothing additional was provided in terms of sustenance and individuals had to cater for themselves. It was a standard practice that officers and soldiers paid to get trained for the service. All routine regulations while on a course at a military institution applied.

The Armoured School positioned cadre courses highly to reinforce its status as a top training centre. As a result, all resources were deployed to instruct in the classes and run field exercises. In fact, there was a mock dry-run before the exams itself. The culminating point of the course was an FTX. It was run successfully but Brig Gen Abu Ali, a highly committed Commandant, extended the course for an extra week. The training ended on a high note, and we all returned to our units shortly before the exams proper.

Conduct and Declaration of Results

The exams were held over a four-day period. When the candidates assembled at Rukuba Cantonment, it was discovered that the Armoured Corps Centre and School were the host and lead in the conduct of the exams. The same faces that instructed during the cadre course were the main directing staff at the exams. So it happened that once your face was registered as having participated at the cadre course, it was enough preparation to earn a sizeable mark.

However, I was distressed during the broadcast of the results because apart from the 1994 assessment that I was in the top-ten bracket, it was long and agonizing. For me, it was immaterial or so I thought, having passed the exam was good enough. But I was mistaken because this gradual drift marked a point of my regression into lacklustre performance at exams. I had reached a point that despite my luminescence, I found myself straggling at academic tasks.

It was a tense atmosphere while the announcement was ongoing. Candidates were called in order of merit. When a candidate was called upon, they stood up and the scores for each subject were shouted and the final remark was either failed or passed. I passed this exam too. However, unlike the Lieutenant to Captain version, I was not a top performer. For real?

The roll was almost exhausted before my name was finally called. Meanwhile, officers attached to government houses, pay officers and other influential officers topped the list. These groups of officers had learnt the hard way in the previous test and took no chances. They would not allow themselves to be surprised again. Remotely though, there was a cloud of misgiving that the exams' integrity may have been compromised; it was a suspicion that hung on all courses and exams.

After the Junior Staff Course was Captain to Major Written Examinations. By now, too many things had happened that could not be undone which further reinforced a change in seniority status of each one of us, as I had course mates, but we no longer ran the same seniority.

Pseudo-Intellectualism

Before I joined the army, I thought the service was insulated from intellectual posturing. In fact, during conversations, servicemembers dismissed civilians as being needlessly voluble. This was so clear to see and was further strengthened during my time at the Academy. It was common to be frowned at on account of speaking too much grammar.

Nonetheless, I knew that war fighting required intellectual exertion but most execution lay with brawn. Although no amount of training could truthfully simulate how any engagement played out, whatever the outcome, intensive drilling and war-gaming aided commanders and troops to respond to fluid situations. This to me, was the purpose of training.

More importantly, at each stage, continual training was meant to prepare career officers to assume higher responsibilities. Nevertheless, it was apparent that the driving force behind these training, promotions and career growth were awkwardly directed at pseudo-intellectual excellence. Thus, instead of deepening service knowledge, the design and product of courses tended to be eliminatory.

Field and Clerical Officers

In all standing armies, individuals were endowed differently. Whereas there were effective field commanders, others were gifted as capable staff officers. This truth came to fore over time specifically during operations. Although, it was not known if Nigeria's operations were documented, there were stories of chivalrous officers and soldiers. More intriguing were unlikely candidates, who were unassuming individuals that were universally acknowledged for their tactical wizardry.

The Corps of Directing Staff

The corps of Directing Staff (DS) was the faculty at Armed Forces Colleges. They were a tribe of cynical obscurantists that facilitated three career courses, specifically, the junior, senior staff and lately the defence college courses. Like every faculty, a cross-section of its composition, was an admixture of the brilliant and the exceptionally daft. While a lot of DSs deserved their positions; the presence of others was rather inexplicable.

Much later, I discovered that the process of getting selected as a DS was characterized by preferment, cronyism, tribal jingoism and religious extremism, with a dash of brilliance. To attain the position of a DS therefore was the ultimate path individuals positioned themselves for guaranteed promotion. However, the corps of DS were as vainglorious as they came.

Meanwhile, these pretenders were great armchair warlords that relished renouncing others as middling or below average, knowing this negatively impacted career prospects. It was not that one advocated for mediocrity or collective institutional ignorance. Far from it, my worry was about the rate of attrition, the damage it entrenched and the continual decimation of the ranks of the officers corps.

I personally thought this bent of training counterproductive because even in peacetime, it was important to discriminate between field and clerical officers. More importantly, the combat expeditions during peace-enforcement missions in Liberia and Sierra Leone in the 1990s threw up unlikely but brilliant tacticians. These were a set of hard-core brawlers, and not house officers, who were obsessed with appearances and treachery.

Moreover, each of these tendencies were important and complementary. It was therefore important to leverage on the core competencies of each subset. Without a doubt, the activities that took place during the staff courses had profound impact on individual officers and the services overall.

In the intervening time, it was evident that the high turnover of retired officers countervailed the massive resources, human and material, which were expended in training of personnel ab initio. It was therefore a misplaced and unsound strategy that academism was allowed to swamp the services. I could not understand the fascination, but it engendered unethical and adverse consequences for the services.

The Unethical and Adverse

As earlier identified, the junior and senior staff courses were central to a career officers' growth. While most on-the-job courses were pursued at service branch and individual pace, the junior, senior staff and higher courses were centrally programmed and tri-service in nature. It was during these courses that officers resorted to despicable practices to gain undue advantages.

The career progression of each officer in the NA was programmed. Once a subset was due for the next junior or senior course, they were routinely shortlisted by the Military Secretary (Army). When the time came, it unleashed a flurry of groundwork especially among officers that understood the inner mechanism of the system.

Prisoners of War

During these courses, Prisoners of War (PoW) were aggressively deployed. It was not about enemy combatants captured during wars. No, far from it, it was an affair more sinister. In this instance, PoW or past work, was a collection of past student solutions and official marking schemes of the staff course modules that rarely changed. More so, the military had a peculiar system of instruction, by which assigned tasks, usually preceded the instructional period. It was so baffling to be assessed before being instructed on a theme.

Ever timid, I never knew how or where to procure PoWs. Part of the challenge lay with a self-delusion that I was capable and needed no tarnishing props to scale up my performance. It was a near fatal error of judgement because by official reckoning, I would consistently trail behind individuals that were not as thought through as I was.
These working documents were contraband and closely protected assets. The owners hid and mined the nuggets surreptitiously. It took a long time for me to realize the pivotal role of these gobbets, vis-a-vis the overall performance of the students. I got to see a packet from a close friend, apart from easing the tedium of rigorous original thinking it was nothing out of the ordinary. It was also very disappointing to discover that on occasions, being in possession of past stuff did not necessarily translate to sterling performance.

I had a tell-tale encounter with a colleague during my senior course. Daily we were tasked and required to hand in solutions the next morning. It was usually a two-fold task i.e., two solutions namely a group work and individual presentation. So, each time the syndicate was tasked, we all assembled and deliberated upon the requirement and produced a solution. However, each student was also expected to hand-in an individual presentation and typically, the exertion at both tasks were the same.

I wanted to find out why it was always an aggravation each time I handed-in my individual presentation. Each morning too, I came in exhausted and yet the sum of my efforts did not attract generous marks. On a hunch, I speculated that something was amiss because other students appeared so unchallenged by these endless tasking.

Of course, a sizable number were in possession of electronic copies of past works and solutions. It was a simple act of editing, updating and printing the script. Otherwise, by whatever considerations, I was not a slow learner. I knew I had flashes of brilliance but inexplicably, I found myself trailing at the staff college.

I was miffed by my mediocre performance and reflected over it and began to doubt my aptitude at a point. So, I continued to languish as the course progressed at an agonizingly slow pace. The outlook was not good.

By the third of the five-term course, I was appointed the course senior of a new syndicate. It was a mixed group of my superiors and subordinates. When the term commenced, one of the members, a pseudo-intellectual and an ambitious type, and there were a couple of them in the syndicate, openly challenged my appointment. He derisively demanded to know who made me a syndicate leader over them. It was a slight, but I came to realize that I had breached cardinal exclusivists hold on grouping during the course and even worse I was appointed the leader of a subset. I just smiled at him and allowed the insolence to slide but I plotted my reprisal.

An opportunity to get at him came earlier than expected. Soon enough, the next sets of tasks were assigned. So, after receiving the first requirement, I deployed a simple scheme to enrage. The syndicate agreed on a time to convene for a group discussion but before then I imperially addressed members of the group thus:

"Gentlemen, we have come a long way on the course," I said and paused for effects. Having attracted the kind of concentration I wanted, I continued. "We have a requirement to submit tomorrow morning, and our group meeting is by 2000hrs, and everyone must be there." I purposely sounded audacious amidst hissings and snide remarks.

"Please take note that the deliberations would not last more than two hours. Anything beyond the stipulated time, I shall dismiss the parade." By now I had created a bedlam. My seniors were already chastising and openly challenging my impetuosity, but I was having fun. "Finally, if you know that you have "this thing," please don't waste everybody's time, bring it along so that we can have enough time to attend to our individual tasks." There was more murmuring as the syndicate dispersed for an intermission.

By 2000hrs, we assembled at the appointed rendezvous or trickled in. It was apparent that co-members of the group did not reckon with my resolve to enforce the decision I had earlier declared. In fact, thirty minutes on, deliberations had not commenced and even when it eventually started it was a convoluted rigmarole. I waited and when it was exactly 2200hrs I stood up, packed my bag, and cleared my throat noisily.

"Gentlemen, it is now 2200hrs, as earlier relayed, by the powers conferred on me as the syndicate course senior, I hereby declare this group discussion closed." I did not wait to entertain reactions, I simply walked out of the hall. By this act, I had displayed an uncommon leadership, positively or negatively. Much later, I discovered that my departure collapsed the group meeting. This drastic action offered me time to prepare my personal presentation and for the first time, I got to bed in good time.

The next morning, I arrived the syndicate room, without the paper I was expected to hand-in. It was not for me to grouse because I had already measured and knew my weight, so I left that to the maximalists. Well finally, one of them, arrived with a bound copy of the solution in hand. I could see that his visage was very dim as he thrust the paper at me:

"That useless Gberikon, collect and submit." Most fittingly, he did not forget to remind me that there would be refunds to offset the cost of production. To me, the use of the word "useless" sounded more complimentary than condemnatory. I had finally inflicted a proportionate vexation on pretenders to excellence in my immediate subset.

It was also known that those in possession of contrabands took extra precaution to limit their circle of confidants and even more by moving into hiding while working on assigned tasks. But there was more to it than met the eye because a lot of scheming took place long before resumption at the staff college.

Orchestrated Confusion

Firstly, the senior staff course had a defining impact on the career of all officers. The catch was not just participating but scoring a C+ grade. But unfortunately, it was not possible for every student to make the cut. A higher score like a B grade was attainable but it was a difficult target therefore officers deployed all devices to attain the mentioned grade.

Secondly, the design and conduct of the course was deliberately chaotic with a propensity for subjective assessment and manipulation. While the course unfurled in a state of chaos, it was better described as a systematic dissonance. Thus, as it lasted, it was possible to gain and drop form in one breathe as the turn of events was characterized by uncertainty. So discerning officers left nothing to chance throughout the duration of the course.

For a start, these intellectual charlatans ensured they were posted to the staff college to assume funny sounding and unconvincing portfolios. It was like getting employed at a bank while one actively plotted to breach its vaults. It was evident that these placements ensured clandestine and unimpeded access to controlled documents that were shortly deployed to gain undue advantage.

The next scheme was syndication. The staff college operated a syndicate system. Typically, students were divvied into smaller and more manageable subsets under a DS. The syndication therefore ensured there was low student-directing staff ratio, closer supervision and an assurance that the course modules would be uniformly delivered.

However, the schemers who never left any event to chance, ensured they were not assigned to any directing staff or random group. They went even beyond and determined membership of the syndicates they belonged to. In which case, if any random guy happened in an exclusivist group, it upset carefully calibrated schematics. This was a deep-seated anomy.

The allotment of accommodation was equally critical. It was clear that a swindler would never accept just any lodging for fear of entertaining unwanted visitors, prying eyes and interlopers. A host of them chose to live at the staff quarters unlike the larger body of students in the student lines. It was a necessary arrangement to enhance secrecy. The conjurers among this lot went an extra length and often procured accommodation in Kaduna city, away from the prying eyes of fellow students. In fact, the desperation to post excellent performance drove many officers to crazy schemes.

Circa 1978

Obudu 2012

Chapter Twenty-Seven

Command and Staff Course

In June 2004, a senior colleague casually told me to get ready because I could be nominated to attend the next senior staff course. I dismissed this early warning specifically because my superiors were yet to attend the same course. In fact, there were a couple of potential students before my course. More so, in a ranked system there was little or no room for shunting. So, I went to sleep until I was rudely awakened.

Along the line there was talk of a backlog of potential students, which needed to be cleared. Consequently, what started as a rumour was validated by a publication mid-July 2004 by which I was listed as a student. It may have been spontaneous, but there was little time before resumption. All considered, at that point in time, I was not materially ready for the course. I had ignored a head start and was now forced to make hasty preparations.

The course usually lasted a year and was demanding in terms of funds and material resources. First, I needed to couple basic supplies like papers and specified writing materials, sundry expenses, as well as personal administration to sort out my expanding family. It was a hefty sum, which I always never had during my time in service for whatever reasons.

First and foremost, shame would not allow me to trawl in my unit. So, I went to a co-located unit. It was a very chastening experience as the accompanying level of obsequiousness was debasing. Either way, the embarrassment was not any different. Almost, on my knees, cheque-in-hand, asking for cash in exchange, redeemable at month end. It was such a humbling experience that no self-respecting gentleman should go through. After presenting my prayers, I was deeply distraught.

However, my younger benefactor sensed a change in my countenance and tried to distract me by small talk. He insisted unconvincingly that he expected me to perform well on the course. Although flattered, I was not persuaded. He granted my wish, but graciously it was a cash gift and not a loan. I was thankful but mortified because it was an act that should not have taken place at all.

Finally, I resumed for Senior Course 27 on 4 August 2004. It was a large course with a strength of about four hundred and fifty students. This was unwieldy, and it stretched the resources of the college, directing staff and students to a snapping point. It was a first time because at no time in its history, had the college accepted such large number of students on a single course.

Accommodation

On arrival, I was given a room. However, because I was too far down the perking order, I could not attract a more desirable accommodation at the September 26 Suites. These were purpose-built self-contained apartments. Instead, I was lodged at the rat-infested Junior Division Quarters. In fact, during my Junior Course in 2001, I could not make the cut and was accommodated at the Warrant Officer' Academy dormitory.

Divisions and Syndicates

Customarily, students were distributed to divisions and syndicates for ease of administration and assessment. While the attachment to a division lasted for the duration of the course, each student went through five different syndicates that corresponded with the number of terms spent on the course.

However, I had a chance encounter with a DS, my village man, as we called it. Our conversation drifted to the subject of my preference for a DS as he was able to determine that choice. Ever timid in such matters, I was non-committal to such underhand dealing. My resolve was to rely on my aptitude to see me through the course.

Auditoria

The first challenge the course grappled with was auditoria or halls for presentations. The largest venue at the college was Danjuma Hall. Unfortunately, the space could not seat the posted strength of the course. While it could conveniently accommodate the Land Warfare Component, during joint presentations, i.e., combining Maritime and Air components, its capacity was grossly inadequate. Sensibly though, a way was found around the challenge by converting Ogundana Hall at the Officers' Mess into a lecture venue.

Ogundana Hall

Ogundana Hall was an illustration of how the services benefitted from the sagacity of an individual. In this case, it was Air Vice Marshall AO Ogundana, a former commandant of the college. No one could tell how he managed it but somehow, he got funding with which he constructed a massive edifice that the mess was. It was not only well built, but lavishly furnished. Providentially, the messing hall of the building served as a venue for joint presentations throughout the course.

On the obverse side, the hall was not designed as a lecture theatre as there were no fixed seats and its floor was not stepped, and so, everyone sat at the same level. However, the college improvised by procuring old-fashioned school chairs, the types that were combined with foldable tables. These were arranged row after row, although not too comfortable, they still served. Nonetheless, the venue was always stuffy, and the conveniences were easily overwhelmed within minutes of settling in place due to the enormous number of students staying for extended period. More tellingly, the hall's sleep-inducing capacity was unrivalled.

Starting on a Morbid Note

On Monday, 7 August 2004, the Senior Course 27 started on a morbid note. After the inauguration of the course earlier that morning, a joint presentation was scheduled at Ogundana Hall. Unfortunately, just as the students were converging, one of us, slumped at his desk and ominously drenched himself in urine. He was speedily evacuated to the Cantonment Medical Centre where he was certified brought-in-dead.

In fact, the officer arrived late on the course and even missed the inauguration ceremony. Subsequent revelations established that the deceased officer was lately involved in a car crash and just discharged from a hospital. It was even rumoured that his doctor recommended he stayed away from the course. Head or tail, he still found his way to the college, and it ended on a sorrowful note.

The deceased officer's case was not unprecedented. Often, officers were lost on courses. I recall losing my closest friend during the Junior

Staff Course. I had observed his health deteriorated each passing day and advised him to withdraw from the course, but he was adamant.

One morning, he was absent from the syndicate room, and I was sent for to find out his situation. I felt guilty because I had skipped checking on him that morning. I hurried to his room and found him on bed almost lifeless. Also, I observed that his stomach had begun to distend. His condition was serious, and I needed to act fast. So, I told him I was going to withdraw him from the course to which he resisted feebly.

He was more worried about the consequences of leaving the course halfway. But I persuaded him to recognize that he needed to stay alive to continue the army job. More importantly, he could resume on another course if his health improved. He mumbled inaudibly and I went back to the syndicate blocks.

"Sir, James is my closest friend as you have been told. I am aware he has been sick lately." I told his DS calmly. I watched him digest my opening remarks and continued. "Between us, we have deliberated on his wellbeing, and he agreed that it would be best for him to withdraw from the course." I stopped and awaited his response since I was not sure what he would decide. "Are you sure of what you just said? I answered in the affirmative.

He stood up and motioned me to come along with him and entered the office of the Divisional Chief Instructor while I waited at the door. I was called in shortly and asked to confirm my prayer which I did. I returned to my desk. Later in the day, I was informed that the college had approved my request to withdraw my friend from the course.

Unfortunately, we lost him. Worse still, on a day he was supposed to graduate from the course, he was being interred. James, like many of his colleagues, had literally died on his feet not only for the love of the job, but more out of fear of repercussions from contemptuous custodians and interpreters of the system.

In the Syndicate Room

Most tutorial at the college took place in the syndicate rooms. The average size of each group varied between ten to twelve students, superintended by a DS. As mentioned earlier, a good number of those instructors were quite brilliant while others had no business populating their ranks. It was apparent that there was a cartelization of this corps.

One of my DSs seemed incapable of stringing a complete sentence in standard English without resorting to pidgin English. Outside the green paper or workable solutions, he held unto, he was clearly incapable of expressing original thoughts which cast a pall of doubts about his suitability because if he were, he could not prove it throughout the term.

Modus Operandi

The system of instruction at the college was strange and deliberately chaotic. In the modules, students were assigned tasks, assessed, scored, and then afterwards given a run-through. It was a bizarre system. I had misgivings about this methodology but through some magical agencies, my fellows were not only coping but doing well at it. It was clear that, either the system was stood on its head, or I was at the wrong party.

To a degree, there may have been justification for this deliberate state of confusion that pervaded at the college since the kernel of training was upgrading of command and staff capability. It was presumed that in the heat of a battle, there would be no luxury of time and space to leisurely decide issues. However, this mindset became too obsessive as to distort the essence of the course.

Change of Operational Doctrine

During my time on the staff course, a new war-fighting doctrine was instituted. Before now, the NA's operational doctrine was attrition warfare, i.e., to wear out the enemy by non-stop skirmishing and overwhelming the adversary to attain victory. It was the oldest known system of warfare. Although, grinding, it assuredly produced the desired results. It was the established doctrine on which all NA cadets and recruits were trained. But like a bolt from the blue, a new system of warfare was instituted.

Manoeuvrist Approach to Warfare

The new-fangled doctrine was the Manoeuvrist Approach to Warfare. More sensibly, the new obsession should have been introduced from the ground up. In any case, a decision was made, and it began midlife.

This shibboleth was appropriated from the British military, the colonial founders of the NA.

The doctrine was about indirect approach based on attacking enemy's cohesion and will to fight rather than focusing purely on the destruction of his physical component. It was based on hypothetical assumptions that relied less on set of tactics or techniques and concentrated on defeating the enemy's will to fight rather than his ability.[1]

So, what factors necessitated this precipitate change in doctrine? Above all, what was the order of battle of the British Army? Specifically, its operational scale and table of equipment? Perhaps the British Army may have committed enough time to the proof of concept before adopting the doctrine. Comparatively, one army was technologically driven, while the other was composed of scrappy primitive foot soldiers. In which case, the former could indulge in mind games while the latter had to necessarily wear out an adversary by attrition. So, conclusively, there was no nexus in the character nor the operational capabilities between both armies to warrant such an across-the-board change of doctrine.

This new policy came with encumbrances due to its novelty. The Senior Course 27 was the second in the series to run the new doctrine. Thus, the DSs were still struggling to come to terms with its brass tacks. For such a proud corps, they were subjected to the indignity of open disputations and contradictions, due majorly to the attrition mindset with which they approached the canon.

Therefore, instructional sessions were characterized by loud arguments between staff and students and among the staff themselves. Many contentious issues required further clarifications from the higher kahunas that were equally unhelpful. Suffice to say that these disagreements were often noisily unresolved in condemnatory terms for the complications wrought by the new mantra.

Hence, when the course eventually started, there was a marked weakness in the faculty. It was a case of the unacquainted leading the miseducation of the confounded. So much that at every stage on the course, there was impediment as the directing staff fumbled through the syllabus in attempts to master the task at hand. It was even worse on the part of the students that were doubly flustered.

However, both staff and students were obligated to play their roles and put up a semblance of teaching and learning. Overall, this contraption inflicted unforeseen damage to the system because the new training was not tied to field operations that staff training was meant to improve on, in the first place. On the one hand, the staff had to instruct, assess, and score the students. On the other, the students were expected to not only perform, but perform well.

The downside was that there was scarcely enough time to absorb the lessons, even less been measured and scored. This equally proved to be a lacuna that was exploited through the instrumentality of dubious syndication, use of past works with active connivance of pliant staff. Hence confusion became the keyword.

Additionally, habits die hard especially as the mindset of the instructors and students was attuned to attrition warfare than the new manoeuvrist doctrine the course underscored. The fact remained that the entirety of our primary orientation and subsequent on-the-job training remained unchanged until the senior course. The epiphany was all too superficial to reflect any marginal changes in the grand strategy or low-level tactics of the Nigerian military.

A Litany of Allegations

There were unconfirmed and partially substantiated allegations over the manner the senior staff course was conducted. These misgivings bordered on the consuming influence of staff and students in determining the critical final grading of individual students. The allegations were legion but the most infamous included projection of students, poor DS fostered by students and stacking of performance, among others.

Projection of Students

Like all normal people, there was a propensity to network in the military too. People had cause to group as course mates, friends, and business partners, with bonds of common interest in ribaldry, epicurean tastes, debauchery, and more that led to interactions and reinforcement of subsets for mutual benefits and pleasures. In this manner, superiors shared intimacy and private dealings with subordinates. These relations were perfectly normal but equally unsettling as they were unfairly projected onto official dealings.

During the senior staff course, these combinating liaisons came to fore. DS and students clustered to determine syndicate membership, tour groups and even lowly events as who went to the foyer for small chops after guest presentations and or, who gave the vote of thanks. In the latter instance, it was bizarre when students were put through rehearsals to deliver a vote of thanks. It was such an ordinary act that only needed pointing to a random guy to do it, unfortunately, it was appropriated and shared among schemers.

Even more, underperforming students could be propped through unscrupulous means like being handed leaked question papers before examinations, or withdrawing already handed-in solutions to be rewritten and enabling countless unethical malpractices to gain undue advantages.

I recall an instance during my final exercise on the senior course, during which I was deployed as MP officer, which, was my core service branch. At the initial stages of the exercise, I setup an Information Centre at which I briefed visiting dignitaries satisfactorily. However, midway through the exercise, I was appointed the Info Officer of Blue Land, one of the parties to the conflict that the exercise simulated.

The latter appointment did not come as a surprise to me as I had quite a reputation as an aspiring DJ and music buff. During group work at Ogundana Hall, I played melodious music, and it took persuasion and threats to stop me. Somehow, it was noticed hence my subsequent appointment.

It was an appointment at which I further acquitted myself well. I made up a tag-team with a public relations officer and converted the intercom system of the college into a radio station for intense Blue Land propaganda. It was such a remarkable and effective innovation that staff and students came visiting to watch us in action. I was so proud of our resourcefulness.

Worryingly though, three days after the exercise, the dampener came. My supervising DS called me over to his residence and slyly asked me what roles I had played during the exercise and that he was finding it difficult to grade my performance. I was dumbfounded. Was this bloke baiting me? My first instinct was to tell off this pretender, but I held my horses and calmly explained my dual roles to the elf. He persisted that he had no proof of my claims. So, I requested for time to get the physical evidence of my participation.

As a proof, I showed him an Information Centre Board which I had painstakingly designed and preserved after the exercise. But even at that, he was still skeptical and wanted to know my commanders for each phase of the exercise. I was not sure to what purpose this line of nit-picking was directed. It was only fair to pay no further attention to him since I had never negotiated for grades before, and would not be doing it any time soon, so I snubbed him. He could as well award any scores that he wished because I was not confused if he were.

When I contemplated this interaction, I could not make any sense of it. In any case, I was his contemporary at the Academy and even more, we were in the same cadet training battalion. I did not recall him for any special abilities, as he was unremarkable. During our time at the Academy, this goon was neither a cadet appointment nor an athlete, marksman nor an academy horse (good at running), he was a rifleman and truly belonged to the class of officers that advanced their career by questionable methods. I refused to indulge him and left him to his mind games. I could discern that he was treading a worn path i.e., to cast aspersions on others while in the same breath shoring up non-performing students.

Directing Staff and Indigence

Lack was a byword and companion of servicemembers because most personnel lived from hand to mouth, outside a handful of descendants of the aristocratic and other accumulator classes. Perchance, individuals could be poor owing to their lifestyle choices or profligacy. But what was available in the first place was a pittance and licentiousness was even out of the equation.

For instructors and DSs in training schools, the situation was dire. These institutions, in military parlance, were non-operational units and were officially designated hardship areas by the authorities. However, instructors were the more impoverished subset within a group buffeted by privation.

Every so often, wealthier students became benefactors to their instructors. It was a simple working symbiosis in which superior and affiliate subordinates granted themselves mutual positions, favours, and privileges. This fraternity was perfectly lawful except it engendered misgivings about stacking the performances of acolytes.

There were exchanges in cash and kind and other utilitarian freebies which included tv sets, car tyres, freezers, and all manner of materially beneficial articles deployed to oil the machinery of preferment. It was clear that the piper's beaming performance was dictated by an underhand recompense. At most, these claims remained speculatory and unsubstantiated. Nonetheless, its latency made it no less potent and determinative as no quarter was given in this existentialist pursuit of elevation.

To be guarded, it must be stated unequivocally that, even with the pervasiveness of adverse manipulation to gain undeserved advantages, it would be disingenuous to dismiss all the students as non-performers. The students at the staff college reflected all shades of the spectrum that regressed from the brilliant to the extremely daft. However, the point to note was that through elaborate intrigues of charlatans and their collaborators, what ordinarily should have been an exciting and pleasurable year-long immersive course was grossly undermined.

The Angry Kahuna

The senior staff course was the single most definitive of all the career courses military officers were required to attend. As expected, every officer worth their commission was conscious of this sacrament. The course was held in high esteem especially as it was then the apex career course before the advent of National War College (renamed Defence College) in 1992, as the highest military institution in Nigeria.[3]

Therefore, qualified officers eagerly awaited the course, as it conferred the prestigious status of a staff trained officer. It was designed to crown all the training and field experiences, both as a staff and field officer. The technique on the course was to simulate decision-making and candour under adverse situations, with little or no quarter for triteness. This was perfectly in order, except for the stories coming out of the college. The students took to calling the course as "Come and See Confusion.

The expression did not faithfully convey the frenzied state students grappled with the course especially during the first days at the college. However, a drawback to this approach was that it was overdone as it became an impediment to the overall purpose of the course. The British Army under whose guidance the staff college was established and modelled, did not intend to thwart students. Unfortunately, the college became a ground for haunting, hounding, and instituting primordial jingoisms.

During the first couple of weeks at the college, the citadel was inundated by visits of important military dignitaries from the Chief of Defence Staff (CDS) to service chiefs. The CDS visited during a Joint Studies presentation at Ogundana Hall during which the big chief was noticeably uncomfortable and agitated and it was apparent something did not add up.

"It is nice to be around again after ages. My visit this morning has brought back nostalgia of my days as a student in the early 1980s" the CDS mused. But there was no punch in his remarks. He looked unhappy. "We all have been through this great college" he continued hesitantly. He looked around to confirm the mien of the students. Afterwards he mumbled inaudibly and ended his remarks on a melancholic note.

"I am very sorry; I did not know it was this bad." He said apologetically and terminated his remarks. Since none of us was privy to what he knew, we could not tell what it was. The CDS left abruptly and did not wait to exchange banters with staff and students at the mess foyer as was customary with each visiting dignitary. All we could do was to speculate and wished he were really enraged to the extent that many heads got severed from their torsos.

Each of the service chiefs visited on the appointed date and finally the Chief of the Army Staff (COAS) arrived. I had personally met the chief and thought highly of him. He was a cosmopolitan and polished public figure due to a distinguished international career before his appointment to the exalted office. Strangely, the kahuna who came to address the students that morning was quite different. The chief was visibly nervous as his remarks were incoherent and full of bile. His speech was dismissive of the students as an unserious bunch. In fact, once I established that it was going to be a sanctimonious diatribe, I shut my mind off and waited him out. He closed his address aggressively.

"The directing staff should take the pressure off me. You should reduce my job for me. I do not have enough vacancy to promote everyone here. Please go to work and eliminate the undeserving." If everybody was not horrified, I personally was perturbed by such a brazen indiscretion. It was an unfortunate and inane gaffe that a chief could be so unhinged in expressing his sentiments and frustrations. The consequences of his inciting remarks went far afield by unwisely offering spin doctors free reins to exploit an ill-advised public outburst.

A Leg and an Arm for the Career

The senior course lasted a year and involved ample expenditure, both incidental and unanticipated. Apart from personal daily sustenance, students expended massive resources to run the course. in fact, an abundant quantity of stationery was utilized for work production.

Also, there were lots of activities and assigned tasks, both individual and group, which were monetarily demanding. For instance, every group task assigned; the first action of the new syndicate was to create a pool of funds to offset the cost of production. I was always broken but still coped well.

However, these incessant financial contributions always left me distressed. It was unsettling to be compelled to cough out money just when I had none but the whole thing persisted. One day, a tragicomical drama played out in front of the students after the United Nations Peace Support Package of the course.

In terms of funding, huge and elaborate shows were put up by all syndicates with customary extortion. During the after-action review, the Director of Joint Studies stood up and said:

"How did you guys manage it; because I recall only the sum of five hundred thousand Naira was approved for this package." His remarks sounded ridiculous. So, like other countless speeches earlier made to the students, I could barely restrain myself from telling him to go sing his lullabies to infants.

When he left, the next officer in line took to the podium and ruefully confessed he had been given only a hundred thousand. Finally, the Term Coordinator, the most junior of the lot, came forward to exorcise himself and revealed that he was given ten reams of A4 sized paper. This bizarre scene was akin to an enforced confessional. The show of shame was that monies appropriated to offset the cost of the exercise were embezzled and the cost transferred to the students in the name of career.

Course Allowance

It would be dishonest not to mention that the students were paid a course allowance. The previous staff courses were paid the sum of fifty thousand Naira only, with which students were expected to sustain themselves over a twelve-month period. The paltry sum was intended to cover feeding, transportation, computer-based work production and all the thingamajigs that went into the course. This was inadequate, but the chaunt of careerism justified the transfer of costs by the authorities to the students.

On the other hand, Senior Course 27 had a better deal. The course allowance was enhanced to one hundred and fifty thousand Naira. However, a simple math showed that the sum divvied by 365-days amounted to Four Hundred and Eleven Naira per day in a declining Nigerian economy of 2005. In short, the cost of papers and computer-based work production alone on the course consumed more than doubled the so-called course allowance.

Feeding

For the first time too, funds were allocated for students to be centrally fed. Unfortunately, this was seized upon by a depraved primitive accumulator that behaved like a wicked foster mother that grudgingly fed hungry kids. Apart from serving orphanage-size helping, the menu was not guaranteed and there were shortages as not everyone who went to the lounge got served.

There were a thousand excuses for the shoddy service that was paid for upfront. While nobody had the balls to complain, there was so much grumbling. We got to know that the wife of an "authority person" was the caterer which made it even more unlikely for any student to voice out against it. It was a grand failure, clearly a matter of profiteering and or outright larceny. This development led to a board of inquiry.

One day, I was working at a task at Ogundana Mess, when I was accosted by the board which was then seating to give evidence. I protested vehemently but the members were unrelenting. I was compelled to testify. Deep inside me, I knew nothing I said would be important since the alleged caterer was a spouse of the responsible authority. Why couldn't the big man just confront his wife and caution her against such ruinous indiscretion? Was it necessary to waste everyone's time to give evidence over a brazen robbery?

Well, not being the type to shy away from speaking my mind, I told the board my observations in the strongest and most disparaging terms possible. When I was asked why I never complained, I let it be known that I was not doing very well on the course I came for, so I needed not bother myself complaining about the feeding which threw the team into a prolonged laughter.

It was a sad development that the military authorities had graciously made funds available to feed about four hundred and fifty students on a materially demanding course, yet avarice and callousness, had reduced it to spousal manipulations, without considerations of providing a wholesome meal to fill an adult. In short, it must be asked how the feeding of students migrated from the official College Catering Officer to a bedroom scheming of a husband-and-wife duo.

I strongly believed that the findings of the board were trashed. Otherwise, the services at the kitchen remained epileptic and even got poorer until the end of the course. The inquiry was possibly designed to feign ignorance and provide an alibi of official response, in case of unpleasant retributive recriminations in the future.

An Aborted Tour

Incorporated into the senior course module was a study tour to African countries. The number of countries visited varied but on the average about fifteen could be designated. Typically, students were then split into syndicates and assigned to a particular country.

When the time for our study tour came, I was assigned to a syndicate destined for Malawi. However, just a day before departure, the trip was postponed. The trip was aborted a second time and the country declined to accept visitors. To salvage the situation my syndicate was projected for a trip to Central African Republic. Nevertheless, this too was cancelled because of the untenable security situation in that country. Finally, the other syndicates travelled, and our lone syndicate was left behind. We had missed out on the African Study tour. Why me always, I kept muttering.

End of Course

Whether good or bad, either way, the Senior Course 27 came to an end. Whether learning had taken place or not, was a matter of conjecture. In retrospect, even with the chaotic manner it was conducted, I discovered that I learnt more than I had previously thought. I collected my average grade as determined by showy pseudo-intellectuals and moved on.

The final act on the course was an ultimate national embarrassment by the catering contractor. Despite a board of inquiry and ceaseless grumbling, the feeding never improved but one last act of infamy by the caterer stood out. A day before graduation was by tradition programmed as Dinner Night.

A Dinner Night was a formal ceremonial event outstanding for its dress code and etiquette to match. It was meant to be a festive treat but unfortunately, the catering service provider ruined the night. The main dish for the night was fried rice served with chicken. It was not the usual drab meals served to students. The presentation looked good but when dinner started and diners attacked the chicken parts served, the whole dining hall was enveloped in putrid smell.

The caterer knew ab initio that the chicken served was rotten. Cleverly though, they thought it could be managed by deep frying. Indeed, the stale stuff was camouflaged but only superficially. Unfortunately, without consideration to the health implications of the diners, and the national embarrassment it would cause in the presence of allied students, an unwholesome meal was served. Consequently, all of us were collectively shamed because of the blind pursuit of lucre by a barefaced husband-wife duet.

Chapter Twenty-Eight

Posted At Last

At long last, the course came to an end and I scored an average grade. However, knowing what I knew, and more so, since nothing could be changed about the fact, I took it in its stride and life never ceased. It was no mean accomplishment in recession, to go from astute self-assuredness to an overtly timid personality. I had been thoroughly miseducated.

I had to be cleared at the QM, Library, Arms store, and other sections of the college, just to ensure that I did not retain any consumable items I may have loaned while on the course. Afterwards, I collected my diploma.

The next step was to identify my new unit. Customarily, following graduation, officers got posted. The responsible authority got things tied up just in time before passing out. As I eagerly checked through the voluminous publication, I pondered my previous postings. I was posted to 81 Division Provost Company as Officer Commanding (OC).

At last, I was posted to a new unit. It was a command. The last time I was posted was July 1999. By August 2005, I had been warehoused for six years at NASMP. It was not normal. In fact, in May 2004, I was posted out to 2 Brigade Provost Company but the Commandant for whatever reasons refused to release me to report to my new station. But then commanders were so powerful and capriciously abused their positions. I did not drag the matter especially as the senior staff course came up.

Nevertheless, what I did not countenance was the nepotic conduct of the same senior officer that refused to release me. I recall that on the same bulletin a colleague was posted to the school and when he got a wind of it, he became hysterical and went into a long harangue and rambunctiously announced that he would not serve in the school.

I found the scenario hilarious. No personnel willingly served at a hardship unit if it could be avoided. So expectedly his posting was officially cancelled. Even more sullying, within the same period, when the former Commandant was appointed a HQ branch chief, he chose the same officer as his Military Assistant because of ethnic affiliations.

To restate the obvious, postings at face value, were routine administrative events not necessarily subject to manipulations. It was important to affirm that a greater proportion of officers by dint of merit deserved their appointments and positions but regrettably underhand dealings by influence peddlers and their minions, frequently undermined those exercises. It was not normal, but still, influence merchants, determined when and where their next units would be.

Whereas a greater majority of personnel served diligently wherever they found themselves, others spent time scheming. In this way, favours and positions were inequitably bestowed to the unworthy. Thus, a dichotomy between oily appointments and hardship units was entrenched and it engendered a detestable contest to avoid the latter.

It was a negative trend that persisted throughout the service. If every individual questioned their deployment and units were disparaged, would that not have adversely impacted the system? Why were the schools, supposedly the centres of excellence, turned into dumping grounds for individuals deemed out of favour, wayward or incompetent? Why was it that certain individuals were repeatedly posted to these derided locations while others were grafted onto units at which they had no merit or practical utility?

Much of these intrigues took place because it was peace-time service. On occasions, when actual fighting was involved, like the war with Cameroon over the Bakassi peninsula and peace-enforcement operations in Liberia and Sierra Leone, many of these schemers declined to show and were even shielded by their benefactors. At the end of it all, I was posted as OC 81 Division Provost Company deployed to enforce law at the sprawling Ojo Military Cantonment.

Ojo Military Cantonment

Ojo Military Cantonment was a large military installation in Lagos, situated along the busy Mile Two-Badagry-Seme transnational commercial corridor. From a law enforcement perspective, its location within this axis was a nightmare as it portended challenges given the range of lucrative opportunities, both legal and illegal, that were abound.

As earlier observed, there was widespread indigence among personnel occasioned by poor remunerations and derisory financial incentives native to the services. All these malevolent neediness pushed officers and soldiers into acts of desperation and self-help to alleviate the ever-present penury. This situation was not only limited to military personnel but incorporated all national security agencies in their numbers as they came. There were police officers, correctional services, civil defence and just about all uniformed services were involved in fireworks pronounced "fayawo".

Fayawo was an inoffensive appellation for smuggling rings. Although, there were lots of illegal trafficking across the Nigeria-Benin border, there was a distinction between the heavy importer class cartels as against low-level artisanal border vermin. The latter were countless and cumulatively accounted for large scale crossing of contrabands like textiles, rice, vegetable oil, turkey, poultry products, used clothes, shoes and cars into Nigeria through thousands of bush footpaths and creeks.

Over time, it was possible to identify two categories of fayawo that paramilitary and military personnel were involved in. Most of these hands were engaged in small scale running while others were employed as escorts for a fee. Cumulatively, both groups instituted reciprocal systems of graft and collaboration with the Nigeria Customs Service. This unwritten pact guaranteed dereliction of duties, as the enforcers turned the other way provided palms were copiously greased. Nonetheless, things easily got bloody which excited violent skirmishing when agreed upon obligations were overlooked.

The activities of these errant personnel from all the services over time got out of hand and became a source of embarrassment to the authorities. This open display of improper conduct, by these alleged soldiers became a malignant tumour on the body of a disciplined organization. Worse still, the identities of these servicemembers could not be easily ascertained because irrespective of the arm of service, they were universally decked in NA camouflage fatigue.

It was known that most soldiers involved in fayawo staged their nefarious activities from Ojo Cantonment. These sundry unauthorized activities and needless visibility of soldiers, in open display of impunity, led to the institution of Operation Checkmate. In fact, between 1999 and 2008, Op Checkmate was vigorously pursued and many service personnel caught in the act were summarily dealt with.

The cantonment was also home to a massive mammy market. Apart from being a hub of entertainment with countless shebeens, it was renowned for its large abattoir, manufacturing concerns and general services. In short, everything imaginable, both permitted and illicit took place within the market.

Similarly, illegal residents populated the cantonment. At one point, it was not an exaggeration to say that there were more civilians or so-called dependents than soldiers in the cantonment. All these factors combined to make the regulating job in the barracks very demanding indeed.

Swimming to Work

When I reported to 81 Division Provost Company, there was a dilapidated complex of two buildings housing the unit. There was a duty room and an OC's office. The office was an enclave in a forest of offices adjacent to a Medical Reception Station. I felt it was not pathologically safe to be collocated with a health facility. So, I decided to get out of that location as fast as possible.

Later, I scoured the cantonment and identified some structures abandoned by 25 Field Engineer Regiment relocated to Badagry. The place was waterlogged but it could be made useful with minor engineering. So, I sought authorization to take over the location and it was approved.

About the same time too, the then PM was on tour of formations and visited. While briefing him, I intimated him of my plan to find a more suitable office space. The visiting senior officer cynically remarked that everything would be done to ensure I got a befitting office. The jerk was one of those who enjoyed and wielded enormous powers in the system, yet he was blind to a simple initiative to add value to a unit.

Afterwards, it took me about three months to get the new office set up. I neither asked for nor got money from anyone but still I was able to accomplish the task. When a new PM was appointed, he commended me. In fact, he asked for the cost of the works and gave back a token reimbursement.

Military Spouses

A component of military service, i.e., military spouses, needed to be spoken of. After commission as officers, it was difficult to understand the posturing of spouses of servicemembers. The wives of superior officers, despite not being in service, routinely assumed they were higher-ups too.

Ordinarily, there was supposed to be a clear dichotomy between matrimony and the service proper. However, these womenfolk contrived to become significantly intrusive with the active support of their husbands. One could hear such expressions like the "Home Front" and other encomiums. It was confounding. But over time, it was entrenched when obsequious officers begun to give military salute to superior officers' wives.

Even worse, this eccentricity was consolidated into a powerful cartel that sought to propagate overarching ascendancy over spouses in a negative manner. I recall my wife joined an officer wives' association in my absence. I was away on a course and when I returned, I was transfixed and watched in amazement as she spoke expansively about issues that were discussed during their meetings. However, not too long after, she withdrew from the body citing the overbearing power of the leadership of the group, more so, she felt those wives, often not working were given to much idle chatter.

An Encounter

At a duty post in the cantonment, I encountered a recalcitrant officer's wife. As part of the build-up to the 2007 General Elections, an Internal Security (IS) exercise, EX-IDAPADA, was scheduled by HQ 81 Division at Ojo Military Cantonment. It was an event that ran for five days, and every resident of the cantonment was aware due to the massive publicity. There was also unusual marking especially along the main routes in the barracks. As the OC, 81 Provost Company domiciled in the cantonment, I was tasked with traffic control and set up an Information Centre.

That morning, a riot was being enacted by soldiers with mock checkpoints mounted along the main entrance to the cantonment. So, vehicular traffic was a little sluggish and windy. Suddenly, a vehicle was seen driving against the traffic, at a speed and in a manner dangerous. The provost intercepted the vehicle and took it to the duty-room.

The culprit was a lady, an officer's wife she claimed. Later, she came to my duty post full of arrogance and contempt. Her flimsy excuse for endangering everyone was that she had forgotten to give out money to her maid to prepare food for her children, but I told her it was not enough justification to risk the lives of others. Then she started whining that, she had explained herself, but I was not being negotiable in a distasteful manner. At which point, I ordered the car be impounded until she sobered up.

I watched as she initiated calls and handed me her phone that I should talk to a general. It was one of those generals, a provost like me, who enjoyed a deity-like status in the service. He was an individual that never suffered altercations and had benefitted from all forms of arbitrariness of the system, and here he was aiding and abetting an intractable woman to undermine my authority at a duty post. It was such unmitigated impudence that I could not countenance.

I refused to take the cell phone from her, and the general asked that she handed it to any officer around and she did. After many shouts from the other end, the officer stretched out the phone to me pleading that I spoke to the general. I felt betrayed but took the handset. All I heard from his end was a torrent of invectives and expletives. My reaction to his outpour, was to tell him that I did not believe I was talking to a general, because he didn't sound like one and dropped the call. I released the car to the woman later that day, when I felt she was chastened enough.

A Spiteful Deployment

After the exchange with the officer's sassy spouse and the imperious general, rumours started flying about. The doohickie was that the senior officer had promised that not only would I be posted out but equally dealt with. Over time, I was hardened against individuals dedicated to making my service unpleasant.

I was not bothered because I was not one individual that could be easily unsettled on account of the pre-eminence of rank. I knew I was subject to hierarchy but stood my ground when it became binding to oppose the profusion of bullies that populated the system. Moreover, as far as the service was concerned, we were all co-equal employees.

Soon after the elections, the same senior officer was appointed the head of my branch of service. True to form, I was in the office one day when another officer came along with a signal posting, a paper token, with instructions to hand over my position to him instantaneously and move to 81 Division Group as the Deputy Commander. Although it was a higher appointment, it was not done in good taste. This particular action only reinforced the general's extraordinary capacity for frivolity and a great appetite for malice and vindictiveness. Although, I had a right to demand for an official notification, I chose to acquiesce and quietly handed over.

With the parents of my Bosom Friend James Rotgak Danyil on POP Day 1993

Makurdi 2018

Chapter Twenty-Nine

Victoria Island 2006

When I reported at 81 Division Provost Group, my new commander had been a fellow instructor. A long time ago, we met during my years of service at the school. I knew him as a shifty reptilian that exuded false charm typical of those trying to conceal their true asinine character. In sum, he was a crude gambler of the cards variety, mediocre bigot, and an ethnic jingoist to the hilt, that inundated the system. The senior officer was a talebearer per excellence and his only distinction was that he had joined the service before others.

As OC 81 Provost Company, I was his subordinate in the group. Just like with all my commanders, I kept personal interaction at a distance, and stuck exclusively to official business. I observed that repeatedly, he tried to undermine my command by planting moles in the unit, the motive of which I never understood, but I uncovered the treachery. To sum his persona, he belonged to the class of superiors that tried to ascribe their criminal proclivities to others.

In addition, he brazenly embezzled my running cost, duty tour allowances and other entitlements. When I first resumed duty as a subordinate commander in the group, he paid half of the running cost to the unit. Subsequently, he kept it and advanced flimsy excuses for his inability to release the statutory unit funds.

No explanation was offered for being relieved of my appointment suddenly. On the contrary, I was not owed any because the military hated clarifications. Besides, I put the whole doodad behind me due to my previous experiences and a personal resolve not to fawn over superiors. Nothing changed except that from being an independent commander, I was now an underling. By now, I was used to being cast around, not on account of incompetence but aggravation because I never got tired of being true to myself.

Meanwhile, commuting daily from Ojo Military Cantonment to my new place of work on Victoria Island was a nightmare. This distance was cluttered by traffic. Although, Lagos was notorious for its traffic snarls, the years between 2006 through 2008, the prevalent congestion was on a scale unprecedented. It was at that time that the Lagos State government was constructing its Bus Rapid Transit (BRT) lanes and to do this, alternate lanes of the narrow roads were always closed at a time. So, everywhere the roads were clogged especially on Lagos and Victoria Islands.

On my first day in the office, I was up early, and road bound by 0500hrs It was still dark and I got to office by 0745hrs after about two and a quarter hour commute. I observed that apart from young soldiers and junior NCOs, no officer was in sight until around 0930hrs. It was the last time I would start my day that early. Subsequently, I waited and only ventured out when it was visibly dawn.

I could not recall any remarkable events under this commander at the group. But it would appear he took joy in tasking me as a bait. The idea was to validate the wrongly held notion that I was incompetent at my job. I could not tell how such a misleading flag gained traction. Nonetheless, I understood it was deployed as a psychological tool by doubters to take the shine off individuals, to cause them to work under duress and make silly errors to validate preconceived inanities.

It was a burden working in a place where there was mutual suspicion and unease between the commander and myself. Even if it was not the friendliest of workplaces, the positive side was that everyone was guarded as a reluctant unwritten covenant of decorum prevailed.

I found myself working under circumstances that amounted to inquisition. At any given time, I completed whatever tasks that were assigned to me quickly and capably. In fact, it took me little time to get chores done with, especially where it involved composing lengthy papers. I observed my commander's ostensive disbelief at my fecundity, and then a deliberate refusal to shed specious beliefs. I had demonstrated forceful capability that left him dumbfounded. Finally, it was time to draw the curtain on this commander. Later that year, he was retired from the service due to age on rank.

A Commander and His Controversies

A new commander was posted to take over from the retired senior officer. He was an old hand in the provost. In fact, he just came off from the then National War College. Obviously, he performed impressively and got nominated for a higher degree in Defence and Strategic Studies jointly facilitated by the College and the University of Ibadan. Unfortunately, despite his seniority and brilliance, he was not cautious about scandalous conduct especially when money was involved. The new commander split his time between Ibadan and Lagos during which time I deputized.

One day, a sensitive case came up while he was away. A female soldier reported her younger brother of suspected involvement in armed robberies. It was not the first time, because she had previously reported him to the MP at Ojo Military Cantonment, but the boy was cautioned and left off the hook because of lack of evidence.

On this occasion though, she reported that her brother brought home a sack stuffed with cash and could not satisfactorily explain the source of the money. She seized the loot and went ahead to report to the MP again. The

OC in turn referred the case to the Group Headquarters and I ordered an investigation.

A preliminary investigation of the case revealed that the boy was part of a motorcycle gang of four armed robbers that targeted and raided a fuel station and snatched the proceeds of the day's sales. While trying to get away from the scene of the crime, two of the muggers were shot dead but the boy and his riding partner barely escaped, and he took the money home in the hope that the trail would get cold before they split their loot. The case was kept in view, awaiting the decision of the commander, and the OC was directed to keep the exhibit.

When the commander came around, I briefed him on the case and ordered the OC to come over with the suspect and exhibit. When he did, it would appear I was kept out of the loop, as I was unaware of any decisions taken. As it turned out, it was a development that ended well for me.

As usual with things like that, it did not take long before sordid stories filtered in. The commander had simply collected the exhibit money and embezzled it wholesale. I could not tell if the complainant, the OC, and lead investigator were offered part of the loot. Whatever transpired the complainant was not satisfied and sought for a redress from the GOC. One morning, the GOC sent for me and asked after my commander. In fact, since the commander was still at the university, he had not officially presented himself to the GOC, so the kahuna asked who the group commander was, and I mentioned his name. Immediately, I observed the very senior officer's face contorted. He queried if was I aware of a case involving a female soldier and I responded in the affirmative. Of course, I was not aware that the exhibit money had evaporated.

After I left the GOC's office, I called the commander and informed him of my interview and what other snippets I had picked up. Additionally, I told him that the countenance of the GOC was not good and that he needed to act fast if he was involved with the disappeared money. At least, I had done my duty by him.

I later discovered that there was a history of animosity between the two senior officers. Both had served in the same formation in the past. The story was that, at the height of the labour-induced fuel scarcity of 1994, the one was a brigade commander and lead of a petroleum task force, while the other was the OC MP, and member of the same task force and they had a major dispute.

The task force had intercepted a 33000-litre fuel tanker diverting its consignment and it was kept in the custody of the MP pending further directives. This consignment was duly reported to higher authorities and a directive was issued for its distribution to the units.

By the time the team got to the MP, the fuel had mysteriously disappeared which was both awkward and tarnishing. Then this happened again in a different form thirteen years later. The GOC then ordered that the group commander be posted out of the formation at once and it also marked the end of his command.

The Omniscient One

Another commander was posted-in shortly afterwards. We were contemporaries at the Academy and served at the school in the past.

Much as he tried to exude intellectual prowess, the senior officer was a mediocre exasperator. His worst attribute, universally shared by all senior officers, was omniscience, a fatuous claim to be all-knowing.

As a chief instructor at the NASMP, he was averse to delegating responsibilities and coalesced the functions of the training branch to his desk. He was an amalgam of senior instructor, exams officer, sports officer, and all. It would appear he did not trust anyone, and suspected instructors were manipulating students' grades. He was so secretive even with official matters.

The senior officer's tendency to overcentralize functions led to disruption and confusion of activities that were ordinarily routine. For instance, a graduation was scheduled but because he kept the master scoresheet to himself, even on the morning of the event, nobody could figure out the order of merit to allow for award of plaques to deserving students. It was either he forgot, or he was not aware that, there was a requirement to list participants in order of performance.

So, there was confusion during the ceremony. We knew the source of the mix-up, but nobody dared point a finger because in the military, superiors were always right even when their actions depicted otherwise. His work ethic was simply tiresome especially with a tinge of pseudo-sagacity.

When he resumed command, I found out nothing much had changed about him but over the years he became more galling. He came to office, always before 0800hrs and insisted all his staff officers did the same. Not persuaded, I held on to my prior resolve not to venture out in the dark until daylight. It was admirable that he came to office on time, but the only snag was that nobody was sure of the closing time.

By 1700hrs, he would still be hunched at his desk. The official closing time was 1400hrs, give or take an hour. Always, by the time I got to my residence, it would be 2200hrs and sometimes much later. It was unnecessary and unsafe. Moreover, official matters could be treated within the specified hours working smartly, as it was pointless to close late day after day.

I waited to see how long this would continue, but obviously, it was his style keeping late at office. In time, officers and soldiers began to insinuate that he was afraid of returning home to his garrulous spouse.

On my part, once it was 1600hrs, I packed my bag quietly and headed home because I was not obliged to accept unnecessary risks.

Also, I learnt to be patient and follow his style. It was important to do this for every commander you met. If he tasked you to write a piece for him, you could be sure that he would mutilate the write-up sentence by sentence and line by line to reflect his penchant for gobbledygook. However, it was defensible because staff training stressed that officers aligned to the preferred writing styles of their superiors. At the end, he wrote most correspondences himself.

Just as we adapted to his peculiar approach to headship he was posted out. The senior officer was nominated for a United Nations Observer Mission. So, it came to be that within a span of six months, I had worked with and outlasted three different commanders.

Acting Commander

The outgoing commander was to be inducted into the mission in about a week. In the interim, he cleared his table while awaiting his successor. But a couple of days to his departure there was still no new appointment made. It was about then that I eavesdropped on his phone call to the PM.

"Good morning, sir." He hesitated while peering downwards in his cheap medicated spectacles. There was a faint voice from the other end which was obviously the PM given his fawning genuflections.

"Sir, I just wanted to remind the PM that I am due to be inducted in the mission area, in the next five days. But a new commander is yet to be posted in my place. Only Major Gberikon is here." He paused while awaiting the response of the PM.

Really? So, what if I were the only one around? What was this senior officer implying? That he did not find me worthy of command? How mistaken he was, because apart from being an instructor, I had commanded two platoons, one detachment and a company. In fact, I had held all junior level appointments command-wise.

Afterwards, he told me that I would be the acting commander pending new postings and appointments. He was clearly defeated. Funnily, he belonged to a class of officers that rated themselves far above their capability. It was clear that he was not comfortable with the fact of yours truly succeeding him. But he was left with little choice as I took over command.

Unbelieving Folks

Being a commander was not a new vocation for me. However, certain individuals felt it was too much to deploy a major to hold an appointment statutorily meant for a colonel. They neither reckoned with the judgement of the PM nor my competence.

So, for the next eleven months, I was at the helm of 81 Division Provost Group. First, I discovered the finances of the formation. All these times, I was deployed in the platoons, not a dime was given to administer the subunits. The group consisted of four companies at Ojo Military Cantonment, Ikeja Cantonment, the Admin Company at Dodan Barracks and a projected Company at Bonny Camp which was approved but never operationalized.

Alongside the Group, each sub-unit in the formation was allotted Running Cost, Duty Tour Allowance (DTA), and Ration Cash Allowance (RCA) monthly. Although these may not have been huge, collectively the funds were quite large and handy. These were perks due to low-level commanders that were for long denied.

Even though these were statutory overheads, it took ages to access them and when eventually released, the funds were embezzled. This was made the easier because scheduled quarterly administrative and training activities were either skipped or implemented notionally. For instance, events were planned and scheduled in advance, but when funds were not released as at when due, they were all but brushed aside. However, since it was not possible to turn back the hand of the clock, and because the formations would have been already administered without funds, when the funds were released at all, they were either misappropriated or misapplied.

The fallout of this omissions was systemic rot, which was reflected in the dilapidated barracks, furniture, vehicles, and in the poor turn-out and low morale of personnel. It was obvious that the service was run in a manner suggestive its managers were bent on its liquidation.

My second window into the finances of the group was through acrow or whatever it was so-called. For all its high-decibel chime, it was simply a spreadsheet that contained a list of personnel that drew their salary in the command. The Finance Clerk made two copies of the document. One copy which captured the near true parade state was usually pasted on a notice board at the end of each month and a second copy was meant for the clerk's eyes only. When I had occasion to peruse the list, I was astonished by what I saw because it was a bloated list populated with late, retired, or fictitious personnel.

After the discovery, I was furious and demanded an explanation. From his countenance, the clerk was non-committal and did not betray any anxiety nor was he alarmed.

"Oga sir, there is no cause for alarm. Na so e be since time immemorial." It was clear that the graft had been in place for years and he understood what was at stake.

"My friend, I have no problem with how long this thing has been ongoing. What I am horrified about is the name of a female SNCO we lost about six months ago that is still captured on the spreadsheet. How do you justify that?"

"Oga, it takes a long time to clean-up these records. This list is from the Army Personnel Pay Office (APPO). They have a way of doing it, but I believe they would soon adjust it." He rounded his explanation. I thought about the situation deeply but concluded that although the clerk may have been complicit in this manifestly illegal act, it was clear that he was conspiring with a larger syndicate. So, I chose not to rock the boat.

Standing My Ground

As a sound provost officer, I knew my job too well. However, since the MP was a minor service, its order of battle (ORBATT), always meant younger officers were deployed in the field. As earlier told, in a twist of irony, one of the most powerful officers in any formation, was always the most junior in rank.

For this, I endured all kinds of opposition from individuals that tried to interfere in cases at hand. Routinely, officers tried own their own or tried to commission me onto an illegal or unauthorized tasks while standing at a distance. They all knew that, as the enforcement guy, I bore full responsibility for any fallout arising from taking part in such tasks. Let me illustrate.

One day, the GOC directed that there was a lady living at a defence quarter with generals that needed to be ejected. Information on the subject was scanty but the lady in question was not a service personnel nor a spouse. However, she gained the privilege of living there by giving libidinous services to a former defence kahuna. It was alleged that she was uncouth. Perhaps, knowing the character of soldiers, the very senior officers might have made passes at her which she may have spurned. It was not my cup of tea to grouse as my instruction was to eject.

In the army, the task of ejection lay with army engineers leading a duly constituted team. Therefore, I constituted a proper team including engineers, intelligence and MP and informed the GOC accordingly. I quickly swung into action and found the residence in question, but the tenant was not present. So, I got her cell phone number and called that she needed to see me at Div HQ, but she claimed she was away on a trip.

It was possible that she had gotten a clue of her imminent removal and may have tried to circumvent her fate. I waited for two days, but she never showed up. In any case, I had a task to accomplish and would not allow myself to be detracted. Accordingly, I ordered the team to break-in and compile an inventory of her personal effects and remove them.

Subsequently, the whole exercise became a subject of contention not because it was improperly conducted but because the big kahuna felt slighted. The GOC called me offensive names, but I absorbed the whole uproar without retort. When he dismissed me, I went back and wrote him a report and included the details of what happened which he never reverted.

The lesson of this incident was that the managers of the system that discriminated against their own kind, especially in housing, granted their concubines and pimps such privileges. Worse still, the very senior officer tried to throw me under the bus as they were inclined to do. However, I was saved by the meticulous records and legal approach. It was not my duty to fail at a task, nor to indulge a perfidious superior.

But then, I had learnt the ropes from my days as a platoon commander and found ways to manage nosey and uppity colleagues. People were at liberty to insinuate whatever they wished but you could not fault my grip on the job. More importantly, I enjoyed myself absolutely.

Promotion

As the year got to a close, it was another season of promotions. Graciously, I got promoted to the rank of a Lieutenant Colonel. It would be my last. It was possible to miss a second time as no reason could be adduced for the last failure. In fact, occasionally, promotions were not only questionable but ridiculous. During the decoration ceremony, the GOC showered encomiums on me and appreciated my loyalty, confidence, and competence.

Not long after, a new commander was appointed. The senior officer was one of those influential officers connected to high-wired politics and had just finished a tour of duty at one of Nigeria's foreign missions. Weeks later, he was at the AHQ to debrief and got appointed as a branch chief. Yet again, I was in the driving seat. It took another two months before a substantive commander was appointed. I knew the senior provost officer too. Apart from being contemporaries at the Academy, we were in the same training battalion as cadets and at a time instructors at NASMP.

For whatever reasons, my new commander was visibly angry when he arrived to take over the command. He and others could not understand the rationale behind my extended stay as an acting commander. Even more, his intake formed a sizeable bloc within the corps. As a result, they felt entitled to all the higher appointments. Worse still, my acting appointment broke their ranks, and they seethed in agony as my stay became long-drawn-out.

Whatever his misgivings, we began the process of handing and taking over of the command. It was a very antagonistic exercise to say the least. The senior officer neighed endlessly. He complained that the floor of the office was laid with rug carpet instead of being tiled, that there was no satellite television installed nor a standby power generator. What a jerk.

I took over a command provisionally. So, why would I dissipate time and resources in pursuit of vain embellishment. It took days to craft the handing and taking over notes which he faulted at every turn.

However, he ensured that he displayed his greed much quicker as he skipped all stages of the process and demanded for a change of signatories to the formation's bank accounts. It was an unwritten rule that the successor allowed the predecessor to disburse the funds that came in his last month of command. But he denied me my rights and I handed over the unit and walked away.

The Crew 2012

Chapter Thirty

The Nomadic Years

I was posted to Special Investigation Bureau (SIB), as the second-in-command. This was a specialist investigative branch of the MP. As a unit, it was not attached to any formation, so the unit took orders directly from the PM or COAS. It was a clear attestation of my growing competence as a field officer.

So, I reported to SIB after leave. When I got to the unit, I met the commander who was equally new. This senior officer was a power monger. The worst kind of officers that thrived on the subjective nature of the system. In fact, so many things about him were indeterminate. For instance, his real identity was unknown. Although he claimed origins from the core north of Nigeria, he spoke the Hausa language with an inflection of a non-native speaker and deployed so much effort to conceal his identity.

Furthermore, he had a thing for women. On a peace mission in the early 2000s, he got amorous and grabbed a Sierra Leonean's spouse. It was the subject of a petition to the Force HQ and litigation at a court by the husband. The Nigerian Contingent hurriedly repatriated him from the mission area to avoid the escalation of bad publicity.

When he returned to Nigeria, his next shameless enterprise was to engage a young female soldier as his batman. Typically, a batman or an orderly was a soldier assigned to a commissioned officer as a personal servant. It was not only unethical but alarming, given his antecedence and suspicious health status. It was obvious; that he was actively involved in carnal liaison with the young female soldier.

Somehow, granting we never had any personal encounters, it was clear from our interactions that both of us mutually detested each other. Despite this, it was still not an obstacle because I never had any compelling need to be loved by colleagues, senior or junior alike. It was against this background that I reported for duty at SIB.

When the commander got to the office, I formally reported resumption for duty. But the senior officer was agitated and started whining about being new at the unit and that the second-in-command too had been posted out. He droned on and on about needing the second-in-command to be around and that he had spoken to the PM about it.

How the scenario he painted became a challenge I could not understand. I thought there was a handing and taking over notes, such that all pending cases were outlined, and every other thing would be new. He lied about his true intentions. It was because he had personalized the unit. More so, he exerted so much influence on the PM and could extract any favours he wanted. Sure enough, two days later, I was redeployed to MP Directorate.

I thought over the situation and concluded that it was not right that I should have my appointments repeatedly undermined by colleagues. It was a case of abuse of power. Even worse, was the bendiness of very senior officers, rolling stones so to say. It was not fair to any individual to have their positions diminished at the whim of another.

HQ NACMP Directorate

My new place of work, the MP Directorate, was not a unit to all intents and purposes. It was not a command but more of a rear administrative facility. It was originally HQ NACMP, until HQs of all corps and services were moved from Lagos to Abuja, the new federal capital. What remained of the hulk of the former HQ was run by a clutch of skeletal staff.

It was here that I was dumped along with a senior colonel on his way out of the service due to age on rank. I sat at this practically abandoned complex and chipped away at time. Apart from routine paperwork, nothing really happened. Everything was leisurely done as no specific action was expected of the staff here.

An Interloper

The MP Directorate was a restful place of work. We were two officers and a couple of soldiers. All we did was regularly get to work by 0800hrs, hang in there and take off by 1400hrs. It was drab and unexacting as it could get as there were no hecklers nor busybodies around here.

All was quite peaceful until sometime in December 2008, when an interloper from HQ NACMP Main came snooping around the Directorate. The intruder, a senior officer may have come to Lagos on pass. Whatever took him to the place, I could not tell because I was not on seat.

All told, he was not there in any official role nor on assignment but just drifted there. Incidentally, none of us officers were on seat. So, he contrived to write me a query and demanded an explanation for my absence. However, the irritant was sound enough not to extend the same to the other colleague because he was his superior.

I could defend myself well, especially where no offence was committed. In fact, the meddler had no mandate to issue any query, he was just being presumptuous. Worse still, he was one of those who loved control for the sake of being influential.

HQ NACMP Abuja

After the encounter with the nosey parker, I started year 2009 with yet another posting. He thought I was idling away at the Directorate and needed to be posted where I would be pestered. Hence, I reported to HQ NACMP as G1/G3 Training and Operations. The schedule of a G1/G3 included authoring papers, compiling reports, and analyzing data of reported and settled cases from formations as they were funneled in.

This new workplace was not without its challenges. First, the meddler that came posturing at my former workplace two months earlier, was the chief of staff (CoS) at the HQ. Unfortunately, he was very unorganized. At any given time, his table was cluttered with files which he struggled with. He was a classic red-tape type and perpetually worked under pressure or in an oppressively time-consuming sequence. I could not tell whether it was from lack of capacity or ineptitude or both.

For instance, since he had come to expect me to be non-performing, he was doubly flustered by my work rate. When he tasked me, within ten to fifteen minutes, I got the job meticulously done. Like all other jerks, we had never worked together before but latched on stories of my incompetence to judge me.

As time passed, I saw that he was not comfortable with my presence and aptitude, but his problem was self-induced. He could not harness his self-importance to any extraordinary gifts or ability. Too bad for him, I did not care about being obsequious. Later he became a PM but was ignominiously removed due to avarice and gross incompetence only to be replaced by his subordinate.

Worse still, he belonged to an odd detachment of officers. For example, he would task you and derisively declare that the way and manner you did it was your business. Well, this was a common dismissive statement favoured by senior officers to cover their idiocy or shirk responsibility. For my part, it was not a problem. You tasked me and gave me the resources and you got results, otherwise things hung.

His frustration showed as he came to me one morning and mournfully confessed. "Lt Col Gberikon, I think it was an error to have you posted to the HQ." He stuttered. What an imp. That you manipulated, unsettled, and moved me to a new city, only to turn around to own up to the failure of your judgement was the highest level of inanity.

"You are better off as a field officer not a staff officer." He announced. It was a funny summation coming from an individual without distinction nor special abilities, questioning my staff training. Besides, where were officers supposed to work at, if not in the field. It was a grudging acknowledgement of my practical ability as against fawning drudgery of a desk officer. Sadly, the next day the PM was parroting the same apocryphal submission.

A Reluctant Branch Chief

The chief of police was a character I remembered for his insensitive role in the withdrawal of passing out cadets arising from the so-called battalion parties. We had also worked at the school where he was a chief instructor. All these years, I figured out that he was an alarmist. He never listened to any story without groaning as if he had been hit or purring like a cat. He was so malleable, such that if ten people spoke to him, he would generate ten opinions and impulsively adopt the position of the last person that spoke to him.

As the chief of police, he came to his position without the requisite rank. It would appear his mind was already pitched outside the service.

By his attitude, he practically ran the corps aground. During his time, HQ NACMP was always short on stationery, office equipment and he did nothing to improve the lot of the MP.

Eternally, his table was beset with a mountain of unattended correspondences. Typically, he spent his mornings reading newspapers, then dutifully filled-in the cross puzzles at the back of the papers. Afterwards, he received a stream of visitors and rounded the day grumbling loudly over his non-promotion to the rank of a major general. Outside this obsession, there was nothing about him to inspire nor to be emulated.

A New Chief of Staff

It was plain that the combination of a reluctant PM and a chaotic CoS could not make for a productive team. Soon enough, we could see that all was not well between the two. Every passing day, the CoS would emerge from the PM's office agitated and whinnying. There was always an argument between the pair. Unfortunately, he could not attract sympathy, least from yours sincerely. Finally, the vain CoS was posted out for gross incompetence and replaced by my traducer at SIB.

The first act of the new CoS was tour of offices to meet other staff officers. When he saw me, he hailed me in a very duplicitous manner. We were not friends, so when he smiled at me, it was as good as baring his fangs. Later he called and tasked me to write him a paper on the roles of the MP.

As a senior provost officer, it was not necessary for me to author an elementary paper outlining the statutory roles of the MP. I could sense that there was a sinister motive for this innocuous task. On occasions, if seniors wanted to exasperate or waste the time of their subordinates, they put them to the task of writing papers which were destined for the trash bins. I dutifully wrote him a paper.

The next morning, he came to my office with a paper which according to him was written by one of my subordinates on the same topic. He adjudged the younger officer's paper better written than mine. What if he composed a better essay? So be it. Moreso, coming from an individual that could not have written a better piece, I ignored him. It was apparent he was not yet done with trampling my career path.

81 Division Provost Group Redux

From all indications, I sensed it would not be long before another posting out of NACMP HQ. but just before then I had a conversation with the PM.

"Lt Col Gberikon, have you held a command before." He asked me without looking in my direction, he was evading my stare as he was unto no good. So, I needed to stare him down. "Yes sir, apart from being a platoon and company commander in a couple of units, I was an acting commander in 81 Division Provost Group. In fact, I handed over to the present commander."

"No, you never held a command before, but I feel you could be better off as a field officer, so I am appointing you as second-in-command in 81 Division Provost Group." He concluded. There was no need to stretch the conversation since he was at liberty to exercise his discretion no matter how ridiculous or insensate.

The posting did come and like he said, I was sent back to 81 Division Provost Group as the deputy commander. The same unit and appointment all within a brief period? The whole thing did not make any sense to me again. Why was I being pushed around in circles? All because someone or a group hated my guts and were envious of my carriage?

Retirement

Ultimately, by now I had made up my mind that I would voluntarily retire and stop being a soldier. It was a personal sacrifice, as I had bent backwards to fit in and endured psychological and physical abuse and denigration to serve my country. The more years I served, the less I became unsure whether the exertion was even necessary at all. Apart from walking around with a false hunchback and swagger, I had nothing in my name.

Whatsoever resources I was able to muster during my years of service came from sources that were on occasion not only undignified but plainly unacceptable. The Nigerian Army as an institution needed rescuing and even more so for its personnel. So finally, in July 2009, I applied for voluntary retirement from the army after twenty-one years and a couple of months.

With my wife Professor Grace Gberikon

Chapter Thirty-One

Gratuity and Pension

Following the approval of my application for retirement, I began my leave on 1 September with a terminal date of 31 December 2009. The Nigerian Army paid me a gratuity of One Million Two Hundred Thousand Naira only. Subsequently, I drew a pension of Eighteen Thousand Naira monthly for the next three years. I was contented with what was paid as a compensation for over two decades of service and could not take umbrage, since I retired voluntarily.

However, it must be categorically stated that the leadership of Nigeria's military forces did not show enough compassion for its troops when the pernicious Contributory Pension Scheme was instituted. What happened was a gross betrayal of personnel when service chiefs out of self-centeredness, could not argue for fair severance packages for retirees. It would appear they were collectively overawed by the bullish former military pretender turned politician.

When civil rule returned in 1999 after sixteen years of military rule, the new chant was "subordination of military to civil authority." Although it was a great philosophy not questioned, it was unfortunate that the military high command was easily browbeaten by a president who took care to primitively accumulate enough for his generations unborn while engaged in dubious parsimony against others. It was a known fact that politicians granted themselves jumbo allowances while proclaiming paucity of funds for the rest of the populace.

Again, it was an orchestrated fallacy to equate entrenchment of penury to subservience to nebulous authority. Of course, the military leaders could not be bothered because they had their greasy hands deep in the tills of the services.

Latent Injuries

It was evident that Nigeria's military forces did not appreciate the dynamics of ergonomics or the science of being comfortable in training. Too much emphasis was placed on being all too physical. Thus, most activities from routine running (called endurance to accent its punitive bent), cross-country, dash back, obstacle crossing and sundry engagements, inflicted latent injuries on recruits, soldiers, cadets and officers.

All training activities, especially those conducted by cadets at the Academy were overstretched. On an average day, a first termer could do five hundred repetitions of squats, leaping on one leg, push-ups and more. It was at the Academy too, that I first saw foot-drop syndrome, stress fractures and dementia. All the cadets were affected as they ran in the hot sun, rain and cold harmattan winds of Northern Nigeria.

Additionally, the military boots issued to cadets were too hard and not soft-lined. In fact, all the trainees, young and seniors, came off with blisters during the first weeks of wearing those contraptions. Everyone assumed that it was normal to have scalded feet from running or sustained off-track walking.

The situation got worse in those years when Nigeria was under economic sanctions by Western powers. Yet, we persisted in doing hard running and rhythmically stamping our feet, which directly impacted the skeleton, especially the spinal cord. Our young bodies were strained beyond the ordinary.

During those tough times, it was common to be issued oil company type hard toes. So, cadets became ingenious and padded boots with layers of thick used wool stockings, inoffensively named "Socks for All by the Year 2000", a parody of UN benchmarks for development schemes. Despite these measures, all ended up with blistered and infected feet.

Hence, in retirement, I had to contend with unexplained soreness all over my body. I had designed a rigorous regime of exercises to keep fit but the aches persisted. My knees buckled, my waist creaked, and I had spasm all over, muscle pulls, persistent lower back pains, later diagnosed as slipped discs, and all kinds of seizures. Also, I was rusty and cranky. All these were indicators of the latent injuries that were concealed but as aging set in, they presented.

An Introspection

Like I stated from the onset, when I joined the service, I thought of myself as a participant-observer. In the most traditional manner, the

NA was setup by statutes and all. But then, there were manifold challenges confronting the service some of which I have tried to highlight.

Accoutrements

Soldiers always wore uniforms. However, apart from the first issue during the first days at the Academy or Depot NA; recruits, cadets, soldiers, and officers were compelled to buy boots and uniforms from fellow soldiers and a motley of other sources. It was not important if those items met the specifications of the service.

Although, from time to time, the authorities gave new kits, it was far between. During my five years at the Academy, we got new kits thrice. Meanwhile, the average life span of boots on a trainee was six months at most. So, if an individual chose to wait for those erratic replenishments, they would go about barefooted and in rags.

Administration of Justice

The Nigerian Army, like all regular military forces, was a monocratic institution built on the canons of law and order. The key element was that instructions, directives or orders were to be obeyed always, i.e., at the level of the service, cascading down every rung of the ladder. This was codified in the Nigerian Army Act 1960 (NA Act 1960).

While the NA Act 1960 (replaced by The Armed Forces Act CAP A20 1999 As Amended), not only outlined the general principles on its purpose and functions, it also equally defined the basic law and prescribed penalties against infractions. By its provisions, the administration of justice lay with commanders down the hierarchy.

Therefore, the dispensation of justice customarily begun after an act of commission or omission and a complaint. This was followed by an investigation, by an authorized individual or team. If an allegation were substantiated, it was officially reported on Form B252 aka Charge Sheet. The charge sheet specified the statement of offence and the second part outlined particulars or ingredients of the offence allegedly committed. Filling the form led to an orderly room procedure or summary trial and or a court martial.

Even though regulations were condensed on the statute books, there were still gaps in the laws. Since, it was not possible to capture all offences and so whatever was not provided for in the law was devolved to acdministrative instructions, directives and most subjectively, at the discretion of individual commanders and it was into the latter that manipulations were built. The shades of penalties against offenders could be condonation by which infractions were ignored or pardoned. Also, it could be a reprimand, but in extreme cases, whatever penalties specified in the books were enforced.

However, it was noticed that on countless occasions, once a commander formed an opinion about a matter in issue, it was translated to guilt irrespective of its substantiation. So, it was common that offences jointly committed and tried imposed disparate penalties.

Even more, there were situations by which the outcomes of investigations were manipulated to absolve or connect individuals to allegations just to appease the expectations of a commander. In time, there was manipulation and injustice which prematurely terminated careers along with denial of positions and favours.

The NA as a Fighting Force

The operational doctrine of the Nigerian Army was attrition warfare. It was about wearing out an enemy through non-stop skirmishing, fire, and manoeuvre. Although grinding, assuredly, it produced the desired results. The army has never fought a manoeuvrist war in its entire history. Its first test of combat came during the 30-month Nigerian civil war (6 July 1967-15 January 1970). It was a long hard-fought conflict. Without depreciating the exertion of both belligerents, it was as primitive as wars came.

The war was fought with a mix of trench warfare, short and sharp skirmishes, road bound advances, by-passing manoeuvres, encirclements, ambushes, withdrawals (often in disarray) and attacks in human waves. When both sides were necessarily fatigued due to a combination of poor logistics support and starvation, one party gained a slim advantage and it led to a quick termination of a war that should not have been fought in the first place.

After the civil war, all went quiet except the military top brass moonlighted political governance. There were neither wars nor major conflicts confronting Nigeria for an extended period. Apart from a spat with Chad republic in 1983, there were no serious threats against Nigeria from her neighbours.

In fact, analysts assessed that Nigeria faced more threats from within than without. These were insightful forecasts that happened with uncanny accuracy. The prolonged hiatus was accompanied by a decline of the institution as the physical state of the barracks, equipment and personnel all showed want of care. For the next twenty years, the Nigerian Army was in continuous decline.

The Bakassi Peninsula War

On the wings of ECOMOG operations, Nigeria Army also conducted a hesitant war against Cameroun over the Bakassi peninsula, from 1994 through 2006. The Bakassi conflict was characterized by a checkerboard domination of creeks and occupation of islands. The war was static and of low intensity. Overall, it was no true test of ability.

ECOMOG

The extended period of inactivity ended in 1990. That year, Nigerian Army, supported by other West African forces intervened in the insurrections in Liberia and Sierra Leone (1990-1999). The ECOWAS Peace Monitoring Group (ECOMOG) intervened to stem the insurgency in Liberia and later in Sierra Leone. Although sister services were marginally involved in the operations; the NA bore the main effort.

While the ECOMOG operations lasted, the Nigerian Army deployed aging troops and equipment against forces composed of younger irregular insurgents in an asymmetrical war. Even still, lots of equipment were unserviceable and in the build-up to deployment, troops were coupled from disparate units and sent into action without pre-deployment training. For a mission that was envisioned as an impartial force, to monitor ceasefire agreed upon by parties to the Liberian conflict, it degenerated into a full-blown war.

So many things were wrongly done with the ECOMOG mission in Liberia ab initio. Although modelled after the UN peacekeeping template, it was not a faithful copy and was replete with complications. First, the cardinal principle of consent of parties to the conflict was not reached. While the government of Liberia accepted the deployment of ECOMOG, the other major parties, especially the National Patriotic Front of Liberia (NPFL) did not accede to the deployment of the monitoring group.[2]

Additionally, it was clear that there were divisions within ECOWAS itself. It was palpable that different member states had dissimilar perspective vis-à-vis the growing insurgency in Liberia. There were also proofs of clandestine support for parties to the conflict thus violating the principle of neutrality.[3]

Another consideration was the use of force. Peace missions were usually implemented without resort to use of force, although in extreme cases lethal force could be applied, especially in self-defence. This was necessary to avoid situations by which peacekeepers got embroiled in conflicts.

Again, the hesitant ECOWAS coalition that spawned ECOMOG was uncoordinated. The agreement that led to the mission did not clearly articulate the finer points of its purpose. Consequently, ECOWAS deployed a peace mission with an indeterminate mandate. The result was a further degeneration of the conflict.[4]

Henceforth, it was left to Nigeria to lead the quest for peace in Liberia at a huge cost. The country was saddled with the burden of not only sustaining the mission but also providing the bulk of its troops and military leadership. The NA was therefore sucked into the vortex of a prolonged and grinding war in terms of cost of resources and high casualty.[5]

Likewise, the situation got worse when the insurgency in Liberia migrated to neighboring Sierra Leone and led to an enlarged scope of the ECOMOG mission. The initial design of the mission had not anticipated such an expansion, and therefore became extended and unwieldy.

Eventually, the mission prevailed before the UN intervened for which the ECOWAS community, specifically Nigeria won accolades. However, this achievement was not really a factor of strategic or tactical brilliance. In fact, the so-called peace mission was a full-blown war fought by ill-equipped and poorly provisioned troops.

It must be acknowledged that the Nigerian contingent fought ferociously with their backs against the wall. This was partially because the troops knew they were far from home with little prospect of close support and therefore had no choice but to fight or die. It was survival and adaptation that won the day. At the end, despite poor material support and dearth of equipment, the NA, played a pivotal role in restoring normalcy in Liberia and Sierra Leone.

The ECOMOG operations in Liberia and Sierra Leone, exacted a great toll on the service as there were countless cases of Missing in Action (MIA), Wounded, and Killed in Action (KIA). Moreso, these grisly wars lasted over a decade and the true numbers of casualties of both wars could not be ascertained using listed parameters.

Thus far, no official records of the human cost of the operations existed because no systematic data was compiled throughout its duration. Nonetheless, it was known that waves and waves of troops cobbled from different units were thrown into the meatgrinder and casualties were recorded at the point of disembarkations at Freeport in Monrovia and Lungi Airport in Freetown.[6]

Lives were lost, the number of combatants MIA were unknown, and a sizable number of soldiers were maimed for life. Initially, KIA were brought back to Nigeria for burial but as casualty figures began to climb, attempts were made to inter the remains of the fallen at the fronts in Liberia and Sierra Leone. The latter decision was resisted by the troops when they got a whiff of it.[7]

As the war lasted, so did the casualty continue to mount. There was an undercurrent of discontent among service personnel and Nigeria's involvement was queried especially by the families of the deceased soldiers. Eventually, the military authorities evacuated body bags at night and surreptitiously buried the remains in unmarked graves at cemeteries across the country. This unheralded disposal continued for the duration of the war.[8]

Furthermore, the fate of wounded soldiers seethed unattended, some with severed limbs that needed prosthetics. More were maimed and required further medical attention and surgery. For years, the wounded soldiers complained of their plight to the authorities without official response.

The troops were not oblivious of the apathy to the plight of their colleagues. It was clear that an injustice was being perpetrated. The wounded soldiers took their cases to newspaper houses and journalists took to hounding the military authorities with scathing write-ups.

The authorities were thoroughly embarrassed by these tarnishing articles and responded angrily. As a result, the soldiers were mustered and a medical evacuation to Egypt was scheduled. Even at this point, someone did not forget to short-change them of their up-keep allowances for the trip. So, in 2008 on board an Egyptian airliner a group of soldiers mutinied and demanded for their full allowances.[9]

The soldiers were deboarded, arrested and detained at MP HQ Admin Company, Lagos, on the directives of the COAS. What I witnessed was a bedlam, as the provost tried alternately to pacify and subdue the furious soldiers. It was an ugly sight. The soldiers were eventually hauled before a court-martial.

Of course, the whole fiasco only generated more bad publicity for the army. The incident was negatively reviewed within the service and beyond. In fact, the presidency had to intervene to restore the clipped allowances, and ensure a medical evacuation took place as well as halted the trial. In this way, the growing discontent arising from the unpleasant incident was abated.

Finally, the Armed Forces of Nigeria bore unnecessary casualty for both missions. There was massive casualty in material and human terms. Yet, at the end of it, it served no purpose to the ex-combatants, dead or living, especially as neither their living conditions nor welfare were changed to reflect the magnitude of the sacrifices made to the glory of the Fatherland.

Weapons And Equipment State

Generally, between 1958 and 1960, apart from scrap war WWII leftover or excess arms and ammo bought from Russia, Great Britain, Yugoslavia and black-market vendors, no new arms were acquired in the inventory across all services until the presidency of Alhaji Shehu Shagari in 1980. It was these assortments of weapons and ammo types that were used to prosecute the Nigerian civil war. This was largely because Nigeria had no serious external threats despite the shenanigans and irredentism of neighbouring Chad and Cameroon.

All went quiet until General Ibrahim Babangida chose to distract the troops in Liberia towards an agenda to keep himself and prop a murderous dictator in power. The incredible feat in Liberia and Sierra Leone led to renewed interest in the Armed Forces of Nigeria in the name of training teams and relief. These snoopers found nothing except hard-core old-fashioned combatants with little or no motivation and poor field support mechanism.

The lengthy period of the military in political governance in Nigeria i.e., from 1966-1979 and 1983-1999, was another factor that affected the acquisition of weapons. Despite an external image of hardiness, the military rulers were vulnerable and haunted by the spectre of overthrow. To stem this likelihood, the regimes began to systemically weaken its forces.

The degeneration of the army became very noticeable during the military regime of General Ibrahim Babangida. Under the guise of restructuring the service, the era witnessed a near dismemberment of the services. The predisposition was that certain sections of the service were reinforced while others were deliberately weakened. Along the line, units and formations were disbanded, and installations abandoned all over the country.

Unfortunately, weapons and equipment suffered deliberate neglect. In fact, even the little that was available, were abandoned to rot in storage and lack of proper maintenance. A sordid instance was the insensate abandonment of fighter aircrafts to the elements at the Nigerian Air Force Base Makurdi when sheds could have been constructed to store such expensive platforms. This was a fallout of the alleged participation of air personnel in the botched coup of 1986.

Additionally, ammo for small arms and heavy guns were scarce and supplies erratic. Armoured vehicles, bridging equipment and heavy guns were not run regularly to ensure their integrity. Diesel was not supplied to run the engines nor lubricants for working parts nor transmission fluids for hydraulic systems. Regrettably, a lot of high value stuff was abandoned and fell into disuse. It was always at the point of deployment that such equipment was found to be unserviceable.

It was the same story down to the level of personal weapons. The NA still had in its inventory FN and G3 Self Loading Rifles which were the relics of WWII. Of course, in modern times, most armies preferred the more reliable Kalashnikovs. It was such a dire situation that units could not muster weapons for its posted strength.

To illustrate this pathetic shortfall, it was reported that units arrived the mission area in Liberia and Sierra Leone without personal weapons. To stretch the matter further, it became a standard practice that units on rotation left without their weapons holding. In this kind of situation, it was difficult to fathom out how such locations were secured without the requisite arms.

Moreover, a substantial part of the weapons and ammo that had been acquired by the service came from the Soviet bloc. Apart from being obsolete, spares were not readily available in the open markets nor was there a possibility of retrofitting them because the factories that fabricated those weapons and ammo were long disbanded. Thus, the Nigerian Army, was burdened with mountains of weapons systems and ammo which could not be safely and effectively deployed.

Worryingly too, the ECOMOG missions in Liberia and Sierra Leone became a giant graveyard for Nigeria's boarded military weapons and equipment. When the missions wound down, tonnes and tonnes of those equipment were not backloaded but abandoned. It was a contentious dereliction that later became a subject of inquiry because someone or a group had scrapped the carcasses without authorization. This was the state of Nigerian Army weapons and equipment before the outbreak of the Boko Haram terrorist insurgency in 2009, the same year I voluntarily retired from the army.

Officers and Men

Like all armies, the NA was composed of officers and men. Partially, due to its origins as colonial occupation army, there was a huge divide between commissioned officers and the troops they led. Like earlier noted, the first set of officers holding senior and medium appointments, WOs and SNCOs in WAFF were British and white, while the main body of troops were Black Africans.

All through the early years of WAFF, a subdivision which evolved into the NA in 1963, there were deliberate policies in place to reinforce apartness and pre-eminence. British officers, while deputized to colonial armies were more obsessed with, and asserted dominance that in turn fostered a disconnect between officers and men.

After 1963, the NA that evolved further reinforced these inequalities. It was clear that the liaison between officers and men was fraught with mutual distrust. As a result, there was grumbling all over the place as ORs and junior officers felt disenchanted with their senior colleagues for not showing enough concern for their welfare.

Meanwhile, it could be observed that certain senior officers developed cozy ties with soldiers. However, a closer scrutiny revealed that such associations were driven by cronyism, tribalism, cultism, religionism, regionalism, pursuit of lucre and mercantilist interests that serviced both ends. Often, these combines were devised to undermine their colleagues and exert unfair influences on the system.

Even more, officers lived apart from their charges and sometimes there was a dismal lack of contact with reality. Further down the rung, SNCOs were also separated from NCOs. Despite all these defects, the troops performed their duty as best as they could and readily acquiesced to military leadership.

Another dimension was the discrepancy of educational qualifications between officers and men. Whereas majority of officers had edification in the range of high school or college education, the men especially the early recruits were primary school leavers or illiterates. It was reasoned that, as far as potential recruits were able to understand the mechanism of weaponry and elementary tactics, it sufficed without unnecessary sophistication.

More importantly, entrenched ignorance served the cynical purpose of continually subjugating the troops. This was the bottom line because a little schooling could lead to searching questions and demands on the system. Thus, it was important to keep the segment tasked with the hard fighting not learned intentionally. In fact, during recruitment exercises, potential recruits with exceptional qualifications were denied in favour of non-performers.

This mindset became a battle ground for young soldiers in the latter years. The bulk of troops classified as NA, 63NA and later 79NA were the trusty army-job type. The first two were ex-combatants of WWII and the Nigerian civil war, while the latter, recruited into the army from 1979, replaced both. With the former, no questions were asked, orders were obeyed without fail and denials were endured as part of service and sacrifice.

Again, it was in the recruitment and training of troops that the shortfall was evident. An average NA soldier spent about six months in training at Depot NA. In contrast, officers' training lasted at least between nine months and five years at the Academy. Hence, it was obvious that the duration spent at training between the two classes of personnel reflected in their countenance, professional bearing, and productivity because hasty training did not turnout high quality officers or soldiers.

Yet again, officers and soldiers also had to attend programmed on-the-job career courses and cadres. However, to all intents and purposes, more emphasis was placed on officers' training than the men. In the end, officers were overtrained while their charges received just enough.

Another challenge was that officers, especially the very senior elements, were not at peace with themselves as they strove to outdo one another. There was mutual wariness as they scrambled dirty and destroyed themselves. Thus, incessant skirmishes for relevance, influence, affluence, promotion, and preferment, generated bad blood.

Therefore, the motley of venomous struggles was driven not by wholesome intentions but crude avarice. A fallout of these narcissistic scuffles was entrenchment of treachery, weakened camaraderie and crumbling social cohesion among colleagues. As a result, officers became suspicious of each other for fear of being snitched upon over the most innocuous remarks as an atmosphere of anxiety pervaded.

The impact of these was a decline in the quality of social functionality and routine interactions among service personnel. Individuals refused to speak out on issues even if they could do so. Even worse, to make a comment and be overheard by a passer-by, could lead to issues one never wished for. Overall, personnel were enveloped in a cloud of fear and as expected, the outcome was indifference and decline in the quality of conversations and contributions, as all decisions were acceded to without a cackle.

Ultimately, this duplicitousness produced toxic consequences by which smart capable people prostrated to imbeciles while brilliant field officers were thrown out by unctuous armchair gurus. Worse for it, the NA began to experience a high rate of wasteful attrition among personnel, especially officers. Too many highly trained and capable officers and soldiers, still useful to the service were thrown out on flimsy excuses as the service bled from self-inflicted wounds. Regrettably, events within the service were indicative of a country that did not need its troops.

Finally, the NA stifled initiative. In the mid-nineties, an eccentric infantry officer had uncannily predicted and named the nature of future conflict the army would oppose. Cut and dried, it would be counterterrorism. From a correct reading of the situation, the challenge was that Nigeria was far more threatened from within than without.

No matter how unsettling his observations were, partly due to his eccentricity, its logic was undoubted. This genius had proposed bilateral cooperation with countries, with similar experiences to train own troops. Although, the forcefulness of his postulations was valid, the authorities preferred half measures.

In time, the Nigerian Army School of Infantry (NASI) hurriedly instituted a Counterterrorist Course. So, in a mixture of humour and ridicule, the originator was made the Chief Instructor and given a freehand to design a module for the course. Hell was let loose because being a body builder, the concept he threw up was extremely intense. The trainees that assembled for the first course about 1994, were nearly maimed from a combination of bruising training and near starvation.

The training involved crawling, breaching obstacles and long treks and endurances. All these took place without the necessary body padding and trainees suffered bruises that festered. Despite the rigours, the feeding was extremely poor. The trainees suffered but endured. Unfortunately, within fifteen years of his write-up, Nigeria was swamped in a war against terror. The first responses were ineffectual, because the service was unacquainted with asymmetrical war. It was a case of a stitch in time could have saved nine.

Conclusion

In conclusion, the NA as an organization is an indispensable national institution. The sovereignty and survival of the country as one indivisible entity is safeguarded not by the political structures, but the NA supported by other sister services. Even more, the service which was statutorily established about a hundred and sixty-one years ago, has through combat experiences and traditions, become one of the foremost organs of the Nigerian state.

However, the NA mirrors the country's convoluted search for society. Although, the statute books elaborated its rules and regulations, lamentably, the human factor ensured glitches planted on purpose impeded smooth running of an otherwise uncomplicated system. No organization rises above the environment that fostered it especially an entrenched mediocrity like Nigeria.

Overall, Service in the Eye of the Nigerian Army could be aggregated to a sacrifice I made to the fatherland, a personal pursuit of lucre or, one of the thousand ways to die. Even still, whatever nomenclature you labelled the service was a factor of your perspective akin to a group of the blind describing an elephant.

On a final note, I recognize the sacrifices of colleagues gone, either dead, unfulfilled, or unceremoniously thrown out of the service over the years of fumbling and wobbling. The NA could be better despite the legions of difficulties. Most importantly, stay alive and tell your story.

Notes

(1). For an insight on Bakassi see: Umoh, Ubong Essien Cameroon, Nigeria and the Bakassi conflict: building blocks for a Non-Democratic Peace Theory: Journal of International Relations and Development: London. Vol. 18, Issue 2, April 2015): 227-247.

(2). For an account on ECOMOG see: Lima, Felix Major, Benin Air Force, Air Command and Staff College: Air University: Exploring the Prospect for Peace in West Africa: Is ECOMOG the Solution? AU/ACSC/070/2002-03: Mar 2002.

(3-5). Lima, Felix Major: Air University. Mar 2002.

(6). For insight on ECOMOG casualty see: Howe Herbert: Lessons of Liberia: ECOMOG and Regional Peacekeeping: International Security, pp. 145-176.

Bibliography

Books

- **Clinton, Edward.** (1986). *The AK47 Story: Evolution of the Kalashnikov Weapons*. Stackpole Books.
- **Haywood, Austin H. W., and Frederick A. S. Clarke.** (1964). *The History of the Royal West African Frontier Force*. Gale and Polden.
- **Ikime, Obaro.** (1968). *Merchant Prince of the Niger Delta: The Rise and Fall of Nana Olomu, Last Governor of the Benin River*. Heinemann.
- **Last, Murray.** (1967). *The Sokoto Caliphate*. Longman.
- **Makar, Tesemchi.** (1994). *The History of Political Change among the Tiv in the 19th and 20th Centuries*. Fourth Dimension Publishing Co Ltd.
- **Mazrui, Ali A.** (2008). *European Exploration and Africa's Self-Discovery*. Cambridge University Press.
- **Omotosho, Kole.** (1988). *Just Before Dawn*. Spectrum Books.
- **Udoji, Jerome.** (1995). *Under Three Masters: Memoirs of an African Administrator*. Spectrum Books.

Journal Articles

- **Csapo, Marg.** (1983). Universal Primary Education in Nigeria: Its Problems and Implications. *African Studies Review*, 26(1), 91–106.
- **Kyaagba, Adom Joseph, Moses Iorakaa Ayoosu, Thomas Terna Aule, et al.** (2024). Mapping Environmental Design Strategies for Preventing Crime and Terrorism for Crowded Urban Places in Nigeria. *Path of Science*, 10(1).
- **Mang, Henry Gyang.** (2017). The Nigerian Army as a Product of Its Colonial History: Problems of Re-building Cohesion for an Army in Transition. *International Affairs and Global Strategy*, 53, 1–15.
- **Mordi, Emmanuel Nwafor.** (2020). Recruitment of Nigerians for Military Service during the Second World War, 1939–45. *Journal of the Society for Army Historical Research*, 98(394), 276–303.
- **Olutola, A.** (1979). Education and Nation Building: The Case of the National Youth Service Corps in Nigeria. *CSD Report 05-18*, Global Service Institute.

- **Philosophy and Social Action.** (1990). *Philosophy and Social Action*, 16(3).
- **Rogers, Roy Anthony, and Pervaiz Ali Mahesar.** (2019). Nexuses between Knowledge and Policy: China Studies in Pakistani Think Tanks. *Malaysian Journal of History, Politics & Strategic Studies*, 46(1).
- **Segal, David R., and Peter Nordlie.** (2000). Racial Inequality in Army Promotions. *Journal of Political & Military Sociology*, 28(1).

Reports, Institutional Publications & Media
- **Air University.** (2002). *Exploring the Prospect for Peace in West Africa: Is ECOMOG the Solution?* (Research Report by Felix Lima). Air Command and Staff College.
- **Radio Nigeria.** (1993, April 22). News Broadcast.
- **ThisDay Live.** (2017, June 4). "NJC Recalls Justices Okoro, Abba Aji, Ademola, 3 Other Suspended Judges."
- **WASSCE History.** *WASSCE History Textbook*. [Online]. Available: https://wasscehistorytextbook.com/

Online Resources & Databases
- **Encyclopaedia Britannica Inc.** https://www.britannica.com
- **Federation of American Scientists (FAS).** https://www.fas.org
- **Gilder Lehrman Institute of American History.** https://www.gilderlehrman.org
- **National Defence Academy (NDA), Nigeria.** https://www.nda.edu.ng
- **Refworld (UNHCR).** https://www.refworld.org
- **Sabinet African Journals.** https://www.journals.co.za
- **United Nations Digital Library.** https://digitallibrary.un.org
- **United Nations Security Council Resolutions.** https://www.unscr.com
- **U.S. Department of Veterans Affairs (PTSD).** https://www.ptsd.va.gov
- **Vanguard Nigeria.** https://www.vanguardngr.com

Index

A